AF000333

RIDING THE WIND

THE LIFE OF GROUP CAPTAIN A. O. LEWIS-ROBERTS DFC, 1896-1966

A pilot's career through two world wars

ROBERT LAWTON

Mereo Books

1A The Wool Market Dyer Street Cirencester Gloucestershire GL7 2PR
An imprint of Memoirs Publishing www.mereobooks.com

First published in Great Britain in 2015
by Mereo Books, an imprint of Memoirs Publishing

ISBN: 978-1-86151-382-3

Copyright ©2015

Robert Lawton has asserted his right under the Copyright Designs and Patents Act 1988 to be identified as the author of this work.

A CIP catalogue record for this book is available from the British Library.

This book is sold subject to the condition that it shall not by way of trade or otherwise be lent, resold, hired out or otherwise circulated without the publisher's prior consent in any form of binding or cover, other than that in which it is published and without a similar condition, including this condition being imposed on the subsequent purchaser.

The address for Memoirs Publishing Group Limited can be found at www.memoirspublishing.com

The Memoirs Publishing Group Ltd Reg. No. 7834348

The Memoirs Publishing Group supports both The Forest Stewardship Council® (FSC®) and the PEFC® leading international forest-certification organisations. Our books carrying both the FSC label and the PEFC® and are printed on FSC®-certified paper. FSC® is the only forest-certification scheme supported by the leading environmental organisations including Greenpeace. Our paper procurement policy can be found at www.memoirspublishing.com/environment

Typeset in 9/14pt Bembo
by Wiltshire Associates Publisher Services Ltd. Printed and bound in Great Britain by Printondemand-Worldwide, Peterborough PE2 6XD

CONTENTS

Preface
Dedication
Acknowledgements

Chapter 1	Kimberley, 1896	P.1
Chapter 2	Post Boer War, 1900-1914	P.19
Chapter 3	The Boer Rebellion and German SW Africa, 1914-15	P.22
Chapter 4	East African campaign, 1916-1917	P.31
Chapter 5	The Royal Flying Corps in France, 1917-1918	P.35
Chapter 6	Egypt and Cambridge, 1919-1924	P.68
Chapter 7	Test pilot, Staff College and marriage, 1924-1931	P.92
Chapter 8	Flying across Africa, 1932	P.113
Chapter 9	World War II 1939-45: A V Roe and the Lancaster Bomber	P.136
Chapter 10	Retirement	P.145
	Appendix A	P.150
	Appendix B	P.151
	Appendix C	P.152
	Appendix D	P.158
	Index	P.165

PREFACE

Thomas Aran Lewis-Roberts was born in Portland, Victoria, Australia in 1862. He qualified as a dentist in America and came to Manchester, England, to improve his skills as a dental surgeon. The atmosphere at that time was so smoggy that doctors advised him to go to South Africa for his health. He arrived in Cape Town and travelled to the diamond boom town of Kimberley, where he set up his dentist practice in Du Toits Pan Road.

Alice Elizabeth Gyngell, with her brother Albert Edmund Gyngell (AEG), who was also under his doctor's orders to improve his health, arrived in SA amazingly within two weeks of Thomas. They met at the Victoria Hotel in the spa town of Cradock, Cape Province and Alice soon fell in love with Thomas and they became engaged. However, she had taken a post as music mistress in a girl's school in Pretoria and had to wait six months before they could be married, on Feb 4th 1895 at St Peter's Church, Cradock.

Meanwhile AEG, an artist, wanting adventure and seeking a job, travelled 1,066 miles on to Rhodesia by ox wagon while the newly-married couple travelled back to Kimberley via Graaff-Reinet to resume his dentist practice. Their first son, Albert Oliver Lewis-Roberts (Bert), was born in Kimberley on 1st February 1896. This is my attempt, as Bert's son-in-law, to put on record his extraordinary life.

DEDICATION

In tribute to the memory of Group Captain A. O. Lewis-Roberts D.F.C. who, with many others, fought for us all in two World Wars. From cavalry in Africa, a hundred years ago, he willingly moved to the primitive R.F.C. fighting machines over the battlefields of France. Attacked on all sides and mostly at night, he had not the comfort of a parachute nor the friendly radio to call on when unable to get home; in open cockpits cold and wet, with frayed nerves, he cheerfully did his duty. It is to his generation, who developed and honed the modern Royal Air Force which helped us to prevail in the Second World War, that I dedicate this story of one of their number.

I have written this book especially for my grandchildren and that generation, who know little of their great-grandfather's exploits, of which they may be justly proud. He would have been pleased to know they had heard of him.

ACKNOWLEDGEMENTS

Group-Captain A. O. Lewis-Roberts DFC, my father-in-law, accumulated quantities of archives and knowing his background in the RAF and South Africa, curiosity led me to research his life in more depth. Family stories about him had intrigued me. With my wife and sister-in-law's support and using many sources, including family records, photographs and letters I began to uncover an absorbing and unusual life story.

It has been a huge privilege to undertake this task, but I could not have achieved anything without the help and encouragement of my wife Mary and her sister Margaret. I am very grateful to Ingrid Preston for leading my research into the military records in Pretoria. I thank the Price, Gyngell and Paterson families in South Africa for always being kind, supportive and generous with information. I am very pleased to recognise the help given by the McGregor Museum and Africana Library in Kimberly, the RAF Museum at Hendon, the Museum of Army Flying and the Lincolnshire Aviation Heritage Centre.

Thanks are due to many people and sources in our travels in South Africa - to Kimberly, Okiep, Upington, Paarl, Oudtshorn, Ficksburg and Dundee, Natal; in Namibia, to Windhoek, Gibeon and Aus.

Grateful thanks to my son Ben, who has given generously of his time and skill to design, beautifully, the many maps and the book covers. Also to Daryl Legg for the wonderful oil painting of Bert's FE2b in action.

While most of the pictures and documents have come from family records I would like to recognise with thanks two pictures of aeroplanes in the public domain from Wikipedia and Wikimedia. While I have tried not to infringe any copyright, it is my earnest wish to apologise if I have inadvertently done so.

My grateful appreciation goes to my publisher, Memoirs Publishing and particularly to their Editor-in-Chief, Chris Newton, for his expert help and advice.

Lastly I should be very sad to have not thanked someone who has helped with writing this book; please accept my apologies and thanks now.

Chapter One

KIMBERLEY, 1896

The lives of many people born at this time were touched by war in the 19th and 20th centuries, particularly in South Africa. The country had been forged by an extraordinary number of conflicts, for instance, nine Xhosa wars around the Great Fish River on the Eastern Cape frontier. Several Zulu wars culminated in the great British defeat at Ishandlewana and the heroic defence of Rorke's Drift in 1879. The first Boer War (1880-1881) had been fought in defence of the two Boer republics of the Orange Free State and the Transvaal, against the British in the Cape. They had again been defeated at the battle of Majuba, and the Boer republics won limited independence.

Into this maelstrom came the discovery of gold in the 1860s on the Reef around Johannesburg and diamonds at Kimberley. The gold mines had attracted many outsiders (*uitlanders*) who, it was rumoured, were arming themselves for a conflict to gain control of the gold industry from the Transvaal Government headed by Paul Kruger. In 1895 Dr Jameson and a contingent of Chartered Company's Police, with the support of Cecil Rhodes, invaded the Transvaal, hoping to spark off the revolt that would wrestle control of the gold fields. The rising failed and Jameson and his men were captured by Boer commandos. Britain was determined to defend the 'rights' of its citizens in the Transvaal. While the Boers amassed weapons, British troop ships began to arrive at the Cape, so war became inevitable. Thus began the second Anglo Boer War, which was declared on 11th October 1899.

Kimberley was in the front line in the Northern Cape; just three miles over the border with the Orange Free State and near Bloemfontein, but isolated, being 500 miles by rail from the nearest port. A Boer attack was expected, and the defences of Kimberley were in an advanced state under Lieutenant-Colonel Robert George Kekewich with the active 'support' of the controversial Cecil Rhodes.

Albert's father (nickname 'Lou') joined the 2500-strong Town Guard and was trained and armed to man the defences of the town. On the 15th October 1899 the telegraph wires and the rail track to Cape Town were cut. Alarm spread through the town as martial law was declared, and Kimberley was under siege.

Albert Oliver had been born three years earlier, on 1st February 1896, at the Homestead just outside Kimberley and delivered by Dr Ashe. While infant mortality rose as high as one in two of those born during the siege, the gallant Dr Ashe fought for extra rations for children (Fig 5) and it was thought, at the time, that he saved young Albert's and baby Arthur's lives.

There are many books written about the siege, most looking at how a few well-entrenched townspeople, the Town Guard, backed by half a battalion of the 1st Loyal Lancashire Regiment, a company of Royal Garrison Artillery and a detachment of Army Service and Medical Corps held off a vastly superior Boer force surrounding them. However, we have a wonderful detailed and personal account of the 123 days of the siege written by

The Gyngell Family at Bath Road, Worcester England, about 1893. L to R: Arthur William, Albert Edmund (AEG), Alice Elizabeth (later Mrs Lewis-Roberts), Elizabeth (seated, née Phillips), Albert, Mabel (Peggy). Arthur died at the age of 33 in 1907 in Mafeking SA. Albert died aged 51 in 1894 in Worcester. (Family archive)

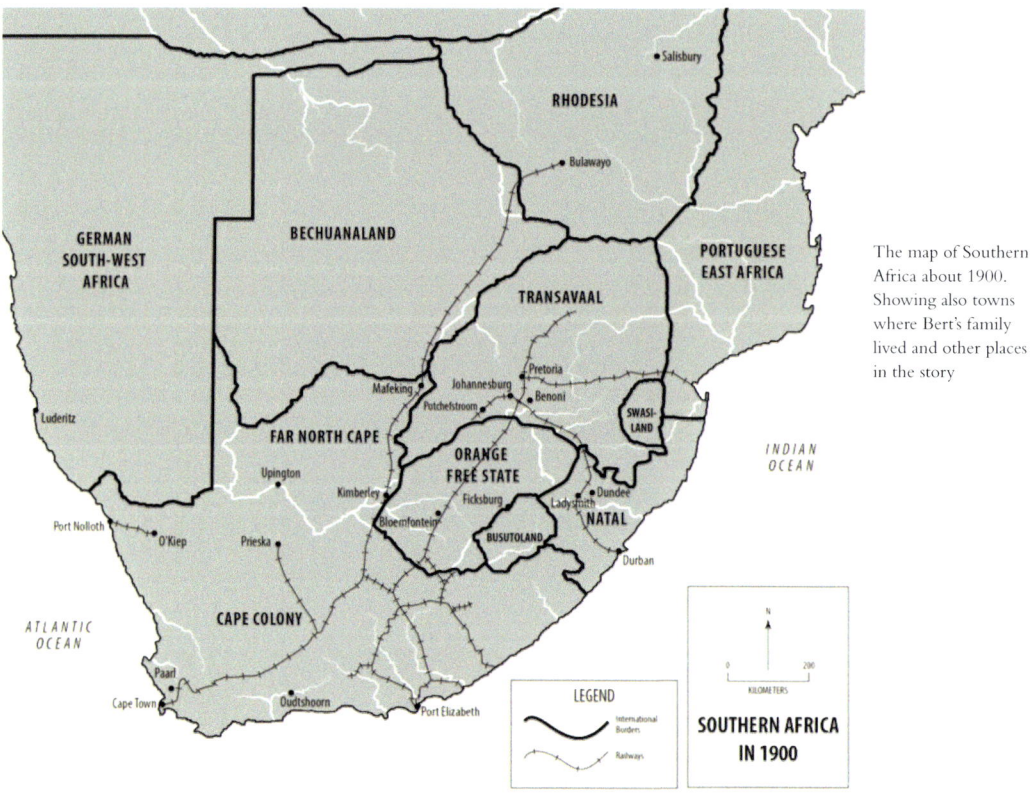

The map of Southern Africa about 1900. Showing also towns where Bert's family lived and other places in the story

3 Baby Albert Oliver (Bert). The Homestead, Kimberly, 1896.

Aunt Mable Gyngell (Peggy) in a letter to record the event. I think it is so charming and interesting that I will quote it in full.

The young married couple's household had been joined at the Homestead near Kimberley by his mother-in-law Elizabeth and her daughter Mabel Gyngell, the surgery being a couple of miles away in the centre of town. They came to South Africa because Elizabeth's husband Albert had died at Wordsley near Worcester, England in 1894. She was devoted to her son, AEG., who had promised his father that he would always care for his mother; this undertaking he dutifully carried out for the rest of her life. After his trip to Rhodesia, AEG. became a copper mine manager in O'okiep, but as we shall see, events stopped his mother and sister joining him there until after the siege of Kimberley.

Siege lasted 123 days
"Refugee Quarters"
The Beleaguered City
Saturday Nov 11th 1899

My Dearest Foster-Mother,
It has occurred to me that we may possibly be able to send a letter to you, to reach you by Christmas or the New Year, and also that you may like to hear of the Siege from my point of view. So here beginneth a true and authentic account, of things pleasant and unpleasant which have happened and are happening in this beleaguered city of Kimberley. Today is the 28th day of the Siege – October the 15th being the first. On that Sunday, we were just finishing breakfast, when the groom came in to say, that the Boers had cut off the water supply at the Intermediate Station and that all Kamfers Dam people were tearing into Kimberley. We knew what that meant – that the Boers were pretty close.

We were not frightened, but we were perfectly breathless with excitement. Loo tore into town to try and get a wagon to bring in our luggage, but no wagon would venture as far as the Homestead. As you know both the babies★ were only just recovering from their illness, but as it was very hot they ran the risk of catching cold. As soon as possible the carts were inspanned, and Mother and the two children with sundry cardboard boxes and bedding came in and were deposited at the

Surgery. In the mean time we were all rushing about - packing up, and wondering what we should do with this, that, and the other. ★ Albert and his brother Arthur

Lal and I had our horses saddled so that if the enemy came suddenly upon us, we should have a chance of bolting. It was about 2 o'clock when we got in with the next load – Adam, Fraser and myself, and just fancy Mother had not been able to get into the Surgery, and she and the children had had to stand in a narrow passage in the sun for two hours.

The dental surgery in Du Toits Pan Road in which the family sheltered during the siege of Kimberley. The sign reads 'Roberts Dentist'. By courtesy of Macgregor Museum.

The key of the Surgery was kept over at the League Club, which owing to the excitement and the men being at the redoubts, was closed; so of course there was no help for it. But you cannot imagine the pitiable sight they presented.

Just before I came up a gentleman had taken them something to drink – thereby refreshing them a little. The Surgery is only two doors above the Queen's, & when I arrived, this same man came out with some 'drinks' (excuse the expression) & insisted on me going with him to see sample rooms of his which we could put our luggage in. He didn't show a very brave front through the shelling, but he was very kind to us & 'Handsome is who Handsome does', he even enquired whether I had remembered to have my breakfast.

In the meantime another gentleman had ridden all over Kimberley to get the League Club key, & this done, we were able with the assistance of his boy to get things inside; and by this time the girls had arrived & we were able to get things a bit in order. I was getting anxious that Lal and Loo hadn't turned up, when I heard, about 5 o'clock, the clattering of horse's hoofs, & they appeared in site. They had been stopped just outside the town by Captain Mallet & two men with pointed rifles – rather startling wasn't it? But the morning proclamations had been issued, and martial law proclaimed nobody could pass or enter the barriers without giving an account of themselves.

I shall never forget seeing them ride up Stockdale Street; they had come at a sharp canter the whole of the way; Lal had her revolver strapped round her waist & Loo had a dagger in one of his top boots (I don't think this latter was meant as a safeguard against the Boers, but rather because he did not wish to lose it, as it was his father's). He had his dinner sent in from Queen's, & although we had our knees as tables, we were awfully glad to get it and go to bed.

The last news we heard on that memorable Sunday was that the telegraph wires were cut, and the rails from Orange River were torn up, so communication with Kimberley was stopped from North and South. As may be expected Mother was ill next day, so I took her down to Ward's to rest, & since then she has slept there. We found Ward's in a state of anxiety. Mrs W. & Mabel were expected from Cape Town on Sunday, but of course the train couldn't proceed, & they haven't been able to hear from them from that day to this. Then the youngest son was in Mafeking under Baden-Powell, & they did not know if he was safe or otherwise. But there was and is trouble everywhere & ruin staring many, many people in the face. Refugees from all-round came in to Kimberley, many with just the things they stood up in & nothing more. I believe the Beaconsfield people were lodged in the Town Hall & were fainting away with the heat.

We were in a fearful muddle on the Monday following our flight, & were feeling very blue and tired, when Mr. Fraser, who

had just sent us in a bottle of champagne, came in to see that we had it & to cheer us up, & we made him stay and have lunch with us. He's been awfully good to us all through bringing us in any little luxuries he could get hold of and sending us sweet smelling gardenias as long as they lasted.

We felt it was awfully hard lines having to leave our pretty home with the lovely garden just at its best. The trees are simply laden with fruit – oranges & lemons coming on well – the flowers were glorious; besides which, we were expecting lots of little chickens & ducks, & who would see after them? Then the Boers looted our two cows & two calves; & our white man was tipsy all day, & let the little pig tumble out of the cart, & it died. Poor little piggy – it was so fat!

Of course the grocers saw a chance of making their fortunes, & at once raised their prices. Paraffin, which we use for cooking purposes, went up from 17/6 a case to £4.10 & condensed milk was a shilling a tin. Now the military have taken things over & they can only charge a certain price. There is no more oil to be obtained, so our cooking has to be done out of doors. There is a water tank up high in a recess in the wall & this affords shelter on three sides for the fire, but it was very wretched cooking on the floor. When it rains you are drenched & when it's hot, as it always is, it is almost worse. Annie has been away ill for a week & the other girl can't cook so we know what it is.

Milk – fresh milk - we couldn't get until about a week ago, & we were in a frightful state. Fancy sick children getting no milk for two days – baby (Arthur) had to have water – arrowroot, & Bert tea; it was too pitiful to hear them begging for 'dense milk', as Sonnie says; it threw them both back considerably. Then Lal got an order from Dr. Ashe, & they let us have one tin which must last five days (Fig5). Now, through a friend we are getting cow's milk. We get a bottle, containing about a pint & a half, per day, & it costs 6/3 a week.

On Tuesday there was a fight at Dronfield, & the Boers had the best of it. As per usual, they were situated on the Kopjes,

Dr A.O. Ashe MD

well protected by boulders, while our men were in the open veldt below them. We lost four men, but the Boers lost more. Since then they have been harassing our lines, killing natives, looting cattle, & doing any little child's play they can think of; until today we are completely surrounded by them. Our men cannot go out to fight them, because if they were cut off, there could not be sufficient left to guard the town.

Lewis & some of the men from Fort Rhodes were escorting the armoured train the other morning when a shell fell just over them & burst, the segments flying all over the place. One of them just caught the side of Loo's cheek & one hit Lady, Lal's mare, which he was riding, causing quite a wound. Colonel Kekewich – of whom we are all very proud, & for whom no praise is too high, says that the Town Guard has saved the

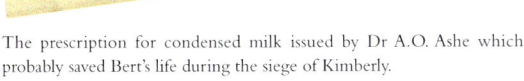

The prescription for condensed milk issued by Dr A.O. Ashe which probably saved Bert's life during the siege of Kimberly.

Town, as the Imperial Troops could not possibly have held out alone. It is difficult to understand the whys and wherefores of these things, but everybody here seems greatly indignant with Schreiner, & they seem to think him mainly responsible for the unprotected state of Kimberley at the present time.

There is great excitement when the "Hooters" go, men rushing from business to the redoubts, shops hastily closing, enormous cash boxes being conveyed to the Banks, children let loose from school & all is hurry, bustle, & tumult for a little while. This morning we were awakened at about 5 o'clock by the noise of the shells. The weird music of the 'Hooter' is terrible enough, I know nothing to compare it with; but you cannot imagine the awful thrill that goes through you when you hear the 'boom – boom', (when it is sent off) & then the cold feeling down your spine, when the shells come whirring through the air, & you don't know where they will fall. As Lal says, it reminds me of rockets being let off & of thunder as you hear it in a theatre. This surgery is a pretty strong building, but we are beginning to feel a bit nervous, as we seem to be in the direct line of fire.

<u>November 15th</u> The enemy woke us up with their shells this morning, but no lives were lost. You know how the Boers boast so tremendously about Providence directing their bullets; well, it seems to me that Providence is directing them, but in a different way to which they thought, for it is simply miraculous how we have escaped. They fired 46 shells into Kimberley this morning, & each day from the 11th, we have had more or less. They have no business to shell the town, with women and children here, but should vent their ire on the redoubts, where the men are simply hungering for a sight of them.

Several times the Boer commandant, Wessels, has sent in demanding Cecil Rhodes & Gardner Williams or they will shell us; & once they gave us women 24 hours to 'scoot'. They say the Colonel sent back word inviting them to do their best, & that there were more dogs here than being true, but such awful tales do get abroad that one hardly knows who or what to believe. It was comical to read in the papers the heading – "Bombardment of Kimberley, British Losses, one Cooking Pot" – (an ode was written to the said pot), but since then there have been several deaths among the Dutch and Coloured here, & as I said before, most marvellous escapes.

We heard of a dear little baby this morning that was killed by the shock, the mortality among children is shocking. You see, the water is not very good, we get very little meat, & the grocers have only stale tinned stuff, & the scarcity of milk all make it hard for the babies & invalids. Lal & Mother are very thin, especially Lal; she says we shall not see her if she stands sideways. She worries so; Loo is in a most dangerous spot – he has to go out on Patrol, & sleep on the veldt every night; & the children are only fairly well, Sonnie so thin & baby so pale.

Sonnie [Bert] gets perfectly wild with excitement when the "hooters" go. He rushes in with "Mummy, put on my 'shoulder' suit (his soldier Khaki suit) & Adam saddle my horse & we'll take my gun and shoot the Dutchmen; those Boers are <u>no</u> good Mummy." He's talking of them morning, noon and night & he knows a lot about them and the war, for such a little chap.

Yesterday. A shell burst in a storeroom of the Queen's, (which is next to our kitchen); it killed two cats and set fire to some coffee. Quite a lot of shells have fallen round about us – into the Kimberley mine & the English Church, but they were all in close proximity to us, & we do not feel too safe. We went to a garden party yesterday given at the Belgravia Redoubt. It was most enjoyable. All the oldest and riches men of the Town Guard are stationed here. Besides the members, there were the Imperial Officers, & the officers of the Mounted and other camps. The Bands of the Kimberley & 1st Loyal North Lancashire Regiments, played lively and inspiring music. All the ladies were in their best and prettiest frocks, & all the brave men wore their uniforms. Some of the Town Guard look so smart you can hardly tell them from regulars, but I think the Cape Police look the finest body of men.

Well, to refer to the garden party – they gave us every dainty in the way of cakes and ices, & tea and iced drinks; it's astonishing what a lot you can take of the latter in this country. The Enemy had been shelling us to within an hour of the party, but we are so used to the shells & hooters & Boer alarms that as soon as they are over there is a lull, we go out just the same.

We often go to the Mounted Camp, as we know most of the officers & we always enjoy ourselves. The band has played there for the last three Fridays & we thoroughly appreciate their entertainment. Last time we couldn't help thinking how mad the Boers would feel if they only knew what we were doing, & how little they frightened us. Major Snow pointed out to us a ridge of trees in the near distance, & he said the enemy were about half a mile beyond the trees. Our men are simply aching to have a chance of potting a few of them. But until more troops come we are helpless. Our guns are not powerful enough to answer theirs at so great a distance, & we haven't sufficient men to go out & fight them on their own ground. They won't come any nearer to Kimberley; there are no kopjes for them to hide in, & they are afraid of the hidden mines of dynamite which are laid in certain directions.

We have been waiting & longing & praying for the troops & for relief; but we have had our hopes raised so often to be dashed to the ground, that we will not believe the column is on the way until we see evidence of it with our own eyes. Why, a week ago, four messages were down from Rhodes & the Mayor & two other important personages; telling the authorities that we were in serious danger, that our water supply was getting exhausted, that provisions were getting scarce, & that they would hold the Government responsible for whatever happened. Still there is no sign of the troops. We all thought that relief would come, as soon as Sir Redvers Buller arrived; we cannot see very well, what a mere dot Kimberley is, in this big campaign; to us it seems everything. It is really pitiable the way some of us believe rumours; the coming of the troops – how they will be welcome when they _do_ come. One man stated that he could see the pennons of the Lancers floating in the breeze; & news went round the town that they would be in next morning, & that they were intercepting the Boers, etc. That was a week ago, & still they come not.

Of course you know better than I about the plucky way the Boers have been fighting in Natal. But up here and at Mafeking, they have been guilty of such despicable, cowardly tricks, that they are held in the greatest contempt possible for a human being, & that we feel nothing is too bad for them. Black-hearted "Black Cronje" is the creature men thirst to lay hands on, people cannot forget his cruelty & barbarity during the war of /81 & notably the siege of Potchefstroom. We have had several skirmishes round Kimberley & have lost more men than we like to think of. Major Macgregor, who spends each evening with us, has been in all the important engagements. He generally lets us know when they are going out, & we have a pretty anxious time till they are back again for we know a good number of them. If they don't come in too early in the morning we usually go and see them; it's an awful sight to see some of them bandaged up & some covered with blood, but the worst sight for me is to see the ambulance wagons going slowly along, containing dead or wounded, you don't know which. There were some fire balloons sent over the other night, & we thought they might belong to the approaching column; but as we have heard nothing further they were apparently not their signals.

<u>Nov. 20th</u>. We are still encompassed by the enemy but they did not shell us yesterday or today. Yesterday was terrifically hot and we had a big thunderstorm. The hailstones were as big as marbles & it sounded like pebbles being showered on the roof; we couldn't hear each other speaking. I cannot believe we are so near Christmas, 'twill be a sorry Christmas for some of us. As for plum-pudding, I'm afraid many of us won't be able to get the plums.

I haven't described the 'Refugee Quarters' yet. Well, we have Loos waiting room as dining and sitting room; the surgery as bedroom; the work room as servant's room & another room next to it as kitchen. There is a narrow passage at the back, & the pavement & street in front; so no wonder the kiddies look pale, being so cooped up after the fresh air of the Homestead. We have another room a hundred yards away to keep our boxes in. Nero the big retriever we have with us, he's just like a dog you read about always walks most sedately by your side & won't let you stir out of his sight if he can help it. The other three dogs, being young and frolicsome, have lodgings elsewhere, though they often break loose & come tearing in helter skelter over everybody & everything.

Loo has sold two horses, & is riding Lady, while Colonel and Whisky are out on the veldt taking their chance with De Beers horses, so now we have no cart to go about in, though several Sundays we have driven down to see Loo, at the Fort beyond Kenilworth. Loo often wishes he could take snap shots of us in our picnic life. We cannot move Loo's dental chair so Lal & I have a mattress on one side of it, and the babies have theirs on the other – it will seem strange to sleep in a bed again. In the morning these beds are rolled up & the room is converted into a Surgery once more & ready for patients & Loo when he comes in at 10 o'clock. The first two or three weeks the patients would come at the most inconvenient hours. As sure as ever the girls were late in doing out the room, somebody would come. Then if we ventured to change our attire after lunch, somebody else would be sure to want a tooth out, & whichever of us was presentable would receive them while the others fled to the outer regions. But now they have to come just when Loo will be home. We have been out a good bit, paying off old calls & going to the different redoubts. (Sonnie says he is writing a letter to Auntie Millie & the ship is a 'wery' good ship to take my letter to Auntie Millie).

November 21st. I got up in reasonable time & took Bert to the gardens to see the regulars drill before breakfast. Poor little chap, he gets so tired & says his legs are "very broke".

It was a great nuisance having to be in by 9 o'clock every night, but now Loo, the good fellow he is, has obtained passes [Fig 7] for us, permitting us to be out till 11 o'clock. We consider ourselves very lucky I can tell you. Last night 'Curley Legs,' a Whitechapel cabman, took us a drive to get a breath of fresh air. He is one of the 'characters' of Kimberley & very amusing. We couldn't go far because of the barriers, & we were halted five times en route. Each time we heard, in the sternest of tones, "Halt, who goes there"? & Curley replied "Friend". Then the soldier came up and examined our passes & Curley said "Dr. Roberts, wife & friend out for a blow". To a Lancashire sentry he said the same, only at the end he added, "the medical adviser has ordered the ladies a moonlight drive". We nearly choked, - his voice & his Cockney twang are really too funny! Loo won't be able to get another night off I expect.

Nov. 22nd. The enemy are quiet today, yesterday they did some "sniping" but no harm was done. If those troops would only come! We shall have no meal with which to make bread soon, we have had no white bread for a long time. The cafe people are not allowed to make cakes now, so good-bye to the dainty little teas down at the Camps. Curley was saying he couldn't get forage for his horses, so he bought two straw mattresses and ground up the straw for them. Many people will be ruined when this is over; some of the Cape Police had come here with just the things they stood up in. It has been frightfully hot the last two or three days, we hardly know how to exist; & at night the mosquitoes are horrible – they almost drive you frantic. I wouldn't be away from Lal for anything, for though I cannot relieve her anxiety, I can, & do, do heaps of little things for her. Poor girl, she says she should feel better if she could see some green fields, or get right away from here & she has a fancy for bread & butter & fresh shrimps. We haven't seen any butter for many weeks, but I heard today of someone who got some from a friend at 6/- a lb. Eggs are 2/- each & jam is a "Medical Comfort", & lard too is not.

Nov. 28th. We have the news that the troops are really fighting their way up, though when they will arrive is hard to say.

Nov. 30th. You will have seen by the papers the loss we have sustained in the death of Lieutenant-Colonel Scott-Turner, who was killed in the fight at Carter's Farm on Tuesday evening. The funeral took place yesterday; we saw it leave the hospital, but it was too sad a sight to wish to see it further – there were 22 who were killed in the fight, buried at the same time. Scott-Turner was an awfully fine looking fellow; we used to call him

The military pass issued by the Kimberly Town Commandant under martial law

"Bonny Prince Charlie". Major Mac and Captain Fisher spent last evening with us. The nights are so lovely we always take our chairs and sit on the stoop outside. They of course were in the engagement & told us all about it. The Major had a very narrow escape a bullet went right through his hat & the time before one grazed his leg. He said men were shot all around him, & that "Carter's Farm" will be written on his heart when he dies, because they had to crawl on their faces for "a deuce of a way", & had a terrible saddening time.

<u>Dec 11th</u>. Nothing has happened lately. Loo is still at Fort Rhodes; the last time we went to see him we could plainly distinguish the Boer tents through the telescope.

At last we have the certainty that the coming troops are somewhere about, as their guns have been firing incessantly all day. (We heard about ten days later that it was the battle of Magersfontein, so we don't expect relief yet.)

<u>Jan. 20th 1900</u>. Have just made the remark that I haven't added a line since Decr. 11th, to which Lal replied "what a blessing for your friends". We passed Christmas & New Year very quietly. Loo got off for the two days but had to return at 5 o'clock. The Major came round as usual & we sat on the stoop and talked. We have the piano in now, & all the furniture - the latter is stored in the next street, but the piano we have in our "dining" room. We had to fetch our things in because the last time there was a skirmish just about by our house & the soldiers came & looted our place. They took all the best books & music & comic operas & oratorios & broke five of the windows. We have recovered 36 of the books – principally Ted's prizes; but the music, which was principally mine, some Ostrich feathers, toys of baby's & most regrettable of all, those half dozen sketches of father's I had chosen in preference to pictures; all are missing. I may be able to replace the music but the latter I never can.

We had quite a concert the first night we had the piano in. First of all Mr Fraser came, then the Major, then Loo came in with Captain Fisher, & to finish up, in dropped Major May. We are getting quite celebrated for our sandwiches composed of bread & anchovy essence, & most evenings Mr Pritchard from the bank & one or two more drop in. Things are getting awfully short now. We are only allowed 1/4lb. of horseflesh or a pint of soup each day, & as you get it in a lump for the family and its often half bone, we don't get much nourishment from it.

Personally I prefer mule to horse – it's not so coarse. Each person can get by permit a loaf of brown bread weighing 10.5 oz. 2 oz. Sugar, 0.5 oz tea, 0.25 oz of coffee, 6 oz boer meal & a little mealie meal or samp. Samp, which we use as a vegetable is like the Indian corn you give to fowls, only stamped rather flat. Can't say I like it. Nobody has any tinned stuff or biscuits, or such luxuries. About a fortnight ago, I went to the only store that had not sold out of these things, & after waiting for an hour and a half, I got two small tins of black treacle, that we could hardly eat, one tiny tin of marmalade & 1 lb of half mouldy biscuits. We have been using salad dressing, chutney, all sorts of sauces, & anchovy essence on our bread; but we have to be careful of it as there is no more at the shops.

We went round to all the poky little Coolie places buying what salad oil & lard oil we could, to use as fat for cooking purposes. The horseflesh is not so bad if it is properly prepared. You have to soak it well in salt & vinegar & water & saltpetre, then stew it next day with plenty of sauce & garlic & so on to give it a taste. Now that the Siege soup has been started, we are faring better because it gets a few vegetables in it, & those you cannot get for love or money, as a rule. A friend of ours who is seriously ill was able to get some tiny new potatoes for 3/6d a lb.

I must tell you that we did get a plum pudding for Xmas after all. Annie went hunting round on Xmas Eve found a little Coolie shop & in it a bit of lard, & we had some raisins, & Loo set it on fire & we tried to imagine it was the proper sort of pudding. We really fared splendidly having saved a couple of our own ducks, which we had in addition to our allowance of meat.

Last Wednesday, the enemy commenced shelling us before it was light & didn't cease till midnight; then they gave us an hour or two's rest & began the same thing again, injuring people and property & also killing some of the former. I wish they wouldn't begin so early; one cannot sleep when you have shells dropping all around you. Loo has been transferred to the Commissariat department at the Town Hall, so we have him at home again, & Lal's anxiety as to his safety is over. A new order was issued with the New Year, forbidding any lights after 9.30. The first night made us feel rather blue because you don't get cool till about 11 o'clock, and as there was no moon, it was decidedly dreary. But one of the Town Guard who patrols this street told Loo that as he was Dr. Roberts, he was a privileged person, so now we have it when we really need it.

We have all been seedy lately so Dr. Ashe gave us permits for 1lb bacon, 1 tin butter, and 1 tin jam. I took the permits to Major Garle, who signed them, then to another man to countersign them & then to the shop where these 'Medical Comforts' are bought. I couldn't stick tinned butter up at Palapye, where they seldom get any other, but now that we have almost forgotten what butter tastes like, it seems perfectly delicious. The Major takes Lal out sometimes; he lends her his horse Khaki. Loo managed to borrow a mount last Sunday, & they all went to see Long Cecil. You will be sure to have heard of it & of the shells conveying "Compliments. C.J.R." on them. The man who made them must be simply wonderful; he's an American, employed by De Beers, & his name is Labram. So now we can reply with "Lady Cecil", to the big Dutch gun that showers her cordite shells on us & which our men have named "Cordita". We have been to sports at the Mounted Camp at Fort Rhodes, & at the Artillery Camp; to several concerts at the latter and to a Cricket Match at the Civil Service Camp. They were mostly like one another, all hot & sunny – same people at each, plenty of fruit and iced drinks. (C.J.R. sees that the camps are well supplied with fruit from Kenilworth). The Artillery Sports and Concert were the best in every respect. Here we saw them unlimber the guns in so many seconds, & saw splendid tugs of war between mounted R.E.'s, & R.A's. Of course the band played at all these places.

We enjoyed the R.A. sports immensely. It was a perfect day, & everybody was smartly dressed – they do dress well here – they don't trouble to think if they can afford it. Colonel Chamier is in command here, & we know several of the officers under him including Major Mac, who always invites us if there is anything on, & who also takes us to other places. I felt a bit nervous the first time we went to see the Major (by special invitation- so we expected no one else) when he made me pour out the tea for Colonel Chamier & afterwards Major May & Lieut. Falconer. It is funny how people shy at my name. You see I hardly knew anybody until the Fancy Dress Ball, & there & from then, I've been called the "Puritan Maid". Sometimes I am called Mrs Roberts because I'm supposed to be like her; but the Major always calls me "Baby" or "Peg". I guess I'm getting spoilt here, but it's nice to be made a fuss of.

Jan 30th. Lal had a hankering after sweets & sent Dodo up for some, but there were none to be had. I wonder if you would be pleased to see us if we came home, but I'm not the least afraid. Just before Christmas there was some talk of compelling all but the fighting men to leave Kimberley for Cape Town. Some were in a dreadful state about it, & even now it is not certain- it all depends how long the troops are.

Feb. 8th. We have had to perform our toilets in the Chemist's dark room, which he has kindly lent us. It has a room above it & our kitchen in front & is about as safe as most places. It's very dark – having no windows, but fairly cool. Yesterday morning they fired a tremendous lot of hundred pound shells on us. The noise is terrific & each one you expect to fall on you, so near do they sound. They are fired from a 6 inch gun & are 18 inches high & 6 inches in diameter, & they come a distance of 7 miles in about 15 seconds, so you may know with the weight and the force, they do considerable damage. The tin houses used by all the poorer people simply fall like a pack of cards before them. It makes you shudder to hear the bricks & things tumbling about, & some of the buildings come down with such a crash.

Mother has been very ill since I last wrote; Dr. Ashe says it is from want of proper food & has given a permit for a little beef or veal daily to be made in to broth – there is no Liebig or Bovril in town. Being so weak the shelling yesterday startled her very much. The excitement gives me palpitations badly, so now I have a new name that of "Palps". Lal, I am thankful to say, seems better, though she is as thin as a rake.

A shell has just burst in Cuthbert's shoe shop & set it on fire. I have been to the door to look at it – nothing can save it, but the hose is playing on the shops on either side or trying to save them. Another has set a small place on fire in Main Street. There is the whistle of the engine! & we have so little water we are only allowed to have it from 9-11. I suppose they are trying to fire the town – the brutes, the brutes, they know it is full of helpless women and children. The fire is one huge red roaring mass – Col. Finlayson has just told Lal that Loo is there helping – by the amount of smoke arising the enemy will imagine they have set the town on fire. If only those troops could come.

Feb. 9th. Another terrible morning. We woke to the music of the shells once more, just before 6 o'clock. The shell that woke us hit a shop just over the way, so we ran, each of us with a child in our arms into the safer room at the back. This afternoon a shell – a 103 pounder – burst in the room where our furniture is stored & from the look of the room, everything except a few of the pictures is smashed up. There were only two sides left of my hat box. The blue hat was quite unrecognisable – you couldn't tell shape or colour - & the fawn straw had two holes in the brim, another had the quills all smashed & the last, which didn't matter, is only dirtier than it was before. We cannot tell what else is saved. Captain White came in with Loo to tell us, & as he seems too upset to talk about it, that is all we know. It seems he has sent the pictures up here & I see they are all saved but many of them are minus frames. We feel we have lost an awful lot what with the cows & the horses (all the latter have been sold for a mere song, as there is nothing to feed them on) & damage to property, but it is a mere dot to what some people have lost. Major Mac & Captain White have lost everything but what they stand up in – had to come away with just the amount their horses could carry, in ammunition.

The Major was in command of the Royal Engineers & some of the Cape Police at the big blaze yesterday, & he left & came down to us for dinner & then about 8.30 he took me up to see the show, & to direct Lieutenant Webster. When we got back we found Captain Fisher & Lieutenant Cramp were there. All these brave men kept our spirits up by coming to see us. Somebody is conveying a perfect shell home in a cab – it looks like a hundred pounder. A part of one of these enormous things fell in Hulls garden, within – I'm not quite certain how many yards of Mrs Hull – but dreadfully close. I saw the piece; it weighed 40lbs. In its fall it had widened until it looked something like an old fashioned urn, with the shrapnel segments still adhering to the sides. Mrs Mallet was lying down on her bed and had just turned over, when a hundred pounder burst through the roof on the place where she had been lying the minute before, & so through the floor and in to the foundation & it didn't hurt a hair on her head. The shells keep on, on, dropping all round. You cannot imagine the awful sound they make – it gets on ones nerves. Still I must brace myself together & be a man, as the Major says. It is half past six now, & still the shells come, & they commenced at six this morning. I suppose we shall have them ad. lib. tomorrow, but perhaps on Sunday they will give us a rest. All this is trying – very trying, still the women of Kimberley, so the men say, have behaved like heroines, so we must keep up our characters & spirits alike a little longer. We often find ourselves saying, "Oh Lord how long". Loo has been most thoughtful and unselfish all through, but he too gets awfully down. One sometimes can hardly realize that one is in the midst of wars alarms (in rather a tight hole too). I looked in to the street this afternoon when there was a lull for a bit – everything looked so peaceful, street empty, the sun so brilliant, the sky the bluest of blues & yet to think of such cruelty & murderous work going on in such a lovely world. But what is the good of thinking – what is the good of anything? Thoughts are apt to be mournful nowadays, & make one sick- at- heart, & heart sickness is such a dreary hopeless never-ending sort of feeling. We give it a new name now – that of "Siegitis".

<u>Feb. 10th</u>. They are shelling us today from the Wimbleton side & are erecting another gun on Carter's Ridge. Imagine our feelings when we know that we have only seven 9 pounders and 10 maxims, and that these will only carry between 3 & 4 miles; while the enemy's sending forth shells 103, 40, & 50 lbs in weight, will all carry 7 miles; so we feel helpless & seem to be contesting against a power that is knocking the heart out of us. We don't talk at all mournfully; if we haven't anything cheerful to say, we keep silent – like the gods.

It is lunch time now & they are giving us a little rest. Dr. Ortlepp has just told us that directly they commence firing at us we are going to fire "Long Cecil" into the Intermediate Station, where their women are, & see if that will make them a bit quiet. We have always left it to them to fire on the women folk, but now we must take a turn in self-defence. Poor Labram, the clever fellow who made "Long Cecil", was killed in his room at the Grand Hotel by a hundred pounder. He was the man we could least afford to lose. I see by the paper this morning, which the London Press Correspondents have been forbidden to say that we have had this 6 inch gun turned on us – this seems rather hard on us. Water, they say, is giving out, but I think that is hardly correct, as we are getting it from the mines. Wood is almost impossible to get. The military allow us 25lb per week & we used to burn a 100lb bag in three days, & it's such green stuff that it won't burn. We should have had no breakfast this morning, only a shell shattered the gate of the yard where our dogs are kept, & Loo had the pieces brought over. How those poor dogs did howl! However, we are all going to stand fast & keep the demons out, I hope.

<u>Feb. 13th</u>. We have spent most of the time lately in the strong room because the shells have been most continuous & "prevention is better than cure". We have had no 100lb shells to speak of since Saturday night at 12.30, & today is Tuesday. Mr. Labram's funeral took place on Saturday night & directly the cortege started from the hospital, the enemy began shelling & kept it up; you see 1/3 of the people here are traitors, & they – the Boers – are told of everything that is going on. All our funerals take place at night - even the little babies.

We felt horribly limp on Sunday, but we felt pretty certain we should get a rest, & went to Church – Sonnie and I – on the strength of it. Very few people had turned out & it was an awful day for heat. By about 2 o'clock every person had heard the report in town that the enemy had erected three more big guns on Carter's Ridge & pointed at us. Now we didn't like this; we had had our share; if you think of the 100lb. shells that fell among us all Thursday, Friday, Friday night, Saturday & until 12.30 or so on Saturday night, you will agree with me in stating that we had had enough. At first men hung about the clubs & no one seemed to know what to do. Then Rhodes sent round notices to offer the women & children the option of going down the Kimberley & De Beer's Mines; & so many availed themselves of this plan of safety, that they were lowering them down until 2 o'clock the next morning. They had to take blankets and food for that day, & then Rhodes supplied them with the rest, & they were down there till the following Thursday morning. At first there was a rumour that we should all be compelled to go down, but Loo went to headquarters & found we could please ourselves. There were many people who had been to the expense of having bomb-proof shelters built in their own gardens, but even some of these didn't feel safe enough above ground. The streets are deserted; in this one are the Hamiltons & Mrs Barker & baby who sleep in the strong room at the Bank. Four other ladies in the Queen's, two of whom with their husbands simply live in a shelter they have had made there, & the husbands almost afraid to show their noses outside; the Chemist & his assistant next door & ourselves. The Bank is opposite to the Queen's & we are two doors higher up so we are altogether as it were.

When there is a lull from the shells, we walk up and down the pavement, very thankful to be out in the open air. We have been told repeatedly that we are most plucky – that we look and talk as if nothing out of the common had happened. It certainly is amusing to hear men who live in "rabbit holes" as these shelters are called, telling us it's very risky staying where we are, & think we are foolish. The Major told me last night, that we <u>should</u> be relieved in a day or two, as a continuous line of smoke could be seen in the direction the column was taking. They are saying that if there isn't a big victory here, or at Spytfontein, the column will just be able to keep the line open for a fortnight or so to enable women and children to get away & then Kimberley would be shut up again. In that case, I don't know what we would I'm sure, but as I say to Lal, there will be time enough to decide when the question is settled. I do pity Colonel Kekewich very much – he has such terribly difficult problems to solve; first the food question, then the relief, & now the women question & all the time, Rhodes & some other dissatisfied people who think they know everything, & should be told everything, bothering and haggling with him, until the poor man must think life isn't worth living. Rhodes has done all a man of his position could do for the relieving of distress & making people comfortable, but one cannot forget that all this is to gain his own ends that it's all for the good of De Beers, that the military would do their best to guard the town & not simply De Beers. Although he has done no end of good during this time, yet, I cannot seem to get up any enthusiasm over him, while, as for the Colonel, I often go up to Middlebrook's to show my nephew the great man.

Loo & Son met him the other day walking – as a rule he's too busy - & Sonnie with eyes and ears open & his sweet little face full of animation, slipped his little hand in to the Colonel's in the confiding way of his, to show he was listening to all they said. So you see, although a man of iron will, he doesn't make little kiddies afraid of him. All this time we haven't seen a single woman in hysterics, & during the shelling you hear no screams, & while the fire was raging there was no panic or scene. Now when you think of it, this thing has been going on for nearly four months; we are getting wretched food; typhoid fever is daily increasing; the fear of the shells always on one's mind; all this is apt to make one lose control of one's nerves. The two ladies and their husbands who have been so terrified at Queen's, look awful – worn & haggard & the one lady looks quite ten years older & the other's husband looks quite "ratty".

Among the men a few of the bright specimens go & drown their feelings in "Tangle Fort", as the awful stuff they sell as brandy is called. You cannot help feeling sorry for the soldiers; this stuff makes them tipsy in so short a time, especially coming on comparatively empty stomachs. I should think Bert and Baby will never forget this time. Bert, whenever a shell falls says "that's jolly pretty near". Baby runs and hides his head in your lap & when it is over gives a prolonged "Oh", & says "Bang". As soon as he woke this morning he said to mother, holding his hand up for her to listen, "Shell". He tries to call me "Pegs" but it sounds more like "Pay". We have a white cook now whom he calls "Laly", every white woman is a lady to him. But he is the sweetest little coaxer you ever struck, with such a soft voice, & he sticks his head on one side like a little bird; everybody says what a handsome lad he will be. He takes all hearts by storm, he comes running in to the room smiling – he's always smiling - & says "Ello" (doesn't sound his H's yet) & shakes hands all round & says "Bye", or "Tata"; oh! he's a perfect boy, as naughty & mischievous as a boy, but you cannot imagine a sweeter little voice, or sweeter eyes, or curls, or whiter rounder limbs than his. Sonnie thinks the world of him & it's "Where's my little b'other" all the day with him. He, poor little chap, gets nervous sometimes, you can always tell, he has such a sensitive face; & he's said to me "I'se frightened for the shells Aunt Pegs". They are both fond of Aunt Pegs, especially towards bedtime, when little legs get tired, then little arms go round Aunt Pegs' neck & its "Sing the little ship", or the "little gun", & I have to make up words about these things for him. They are both very fond of music & will sit & listen for quite a long time, though they will insist on turning over the pages when they deem it necessary, which isn't always convenient. Mother & Lal seem much better I'm thankful to say. Now I'm going to have my "cup o 'tea", as Baby says (I'm going with Mother to Ted).

<u>Feb. 23rd. 1900</u>. When we were told on the evening of the 15th that General French & the "Rimington Tigers" were actually in the town, we hardly believed it, until Mr Fitzgerald came along & told us that he had just been drinking the General's health. I leave you to guess what our feelings were, & how excited & joyful everybody was. The women came up from the mines; shops opened; the "Funking Brigade" turned out of their bomb-proofs, & began talking largely as to what they would do if they were French etc etc & everybody wore a relieved look. The New South Wales Lancers & the N.L. & our mounted men went out & tackled the Boers & drove them from the Intermediate Station & from where their disastrous shells had been bombing into Kimberley. Now the siege is raised & people are rushing down Colony by the trains which started to run day before yesterday. Yesterday the English Mail came in. Great excitement - they had to sort alphabetically & we must have gone to our box at least a dozen times before getting any letters. Mother had 28 & I had 8, dated as far back as September; you can guess how delighted we were to have them, but some of the news they contained was terribly sad. We cannot attempt to answer them yet, "the spirit of unrest is upon us", & we can't settle down to write. They make me want to come home & see you all badly, but I must possess my soul in patience I suppose, & the fit will pass.

According to May's letter, the papers make out that we are having anything but a bad time here. True we have had plenty of concerts & sports, all of which have been got up by & for the benefit of the soldiers, & to which we have been invited by the officers, who treated us right royally. But what about the things that happened between the gaieties – the deaths of the wounded at the hospital, or from fever; from starvation among the coloured people, from want of nourishing food among invalids & children. Every day there is a fresh list of deaths – half the town is in mourning - & no one will know the casualties among the coloured population though Loo, from being connected with the supply committee, knows of heaps of cases, that haven't been announced.

It was awfully good of you to write to Mother so frequently, though you were ill at the time. It gave me cold shivers down my back to read your letters – I want to see you all so badly. You are such a brave little woman; you suffer such a lot & yet your letters are full of comfort and cheer. We often wonder how you all are & what the babies are like, & what fun they would have with ours, if only we could come home.

I am so glad Phil was able to get home for Xmas. What did he think of the little boys & Ada's bairns? I wish I could have seen him too; I felt sorry for George, he must of felt sort of out of it. I know the feeling, & don't like it, but George will be home next year won't he? We have been besieged in another way since the relief column came up. All the Australians & New Zealanders have been looking Loo up, as he's an Australian. The first day though we had a "Rimington Tiger" – such a nice man who made such a fuss of our kiddies – said that they were the first he'd seen since he left his own four months ago. Then just as we were going to have dinner an Australian boy came limping up to ask Loo to recommend a lodging house for him. He was riding despatches, & had come in to Kimberley on a dying horse, so of course could not get back to camp, which was several miles out, & as he had a lance wound in the thigh it was necessary he should sleep somewhere. So of course Loo took him in and fed him and he stayed till after breakfast next morning. He told us he belonged to the Dublin Fusiliers, but was at home on leave & for some cause or other, he & another fellow hadn't been recalled. His own regiment was fighting in Natal. So they came out her and got put on as a despatch rider to the N.S.W. Lancers. He left his address & it was Lieut. Je Vese, c/o Col Je Vese, Brisbane, and Melbourne. He thanked us for our hospitality with tears in his eyes.

Last night we had a Mr Saunders in, who was a pressman, but as no correspondents were allowed with these, he'd joined on as a private. Dr. Burns of the N.L.M.I. & two others came also. The first night the soldiers were in town, Mr Fraser came in to have some music & there were about 40 of these men, standing up, & some sitting on the pavement outside. Lal was singing the "Promise of Life" & we heard someone whistling an obligato outside to it. So Lal just kept on with different things to make this chap whistle. He has a splendid bass voice & sings the "Lost Chord" beautifully. The 2nd day after the relief Loo brought in Captain Cox. He said he should only stop five minutes & he came at 4 & left somewhere between 8&9 o'clock. If you remember he led the N.S.W. Lancers at the Jubilee. He's enormous, 6ft 2 and so very jolly. We did enjoy his company I can tell you. He tried to make us all promise to go to Australia to see him – I forget the name of the town, but he said "Ask for Cox - they know me there, as well as they know Rhodes here".

Next afternoon we came in & found Loo regaling Colonel Ricardo & Majors Chevalier & Robin with tea and anchovy essence sandwiches. None of these fellows have tents or anything & there are the Household Cavalry, the Scots Greys & these Colonial Troops – the two Princes of Teck & the Duke of Westminster are here in Kimberley without Tents, either.

<u>*March 2*^{*nd*}</u>*. Yesterday morning about 11 o'clock, Lord Roberts & Kitchener entered Kimberley & it was decided to hold a meeting in the Town Hall to welcome them, at 4.30. It simply rained in buckets full all morning, but towards three, the sun came out & it was glorious. So we put on our things, & Loo got us in at a side- door, & we obtained seats about five rows down, & next to the middle aisle, & so we heard & saw everything. First of all Colonel W - & the foreign attaches walked up the aisle, amid clapping; & we amused ourselves for a while trying to pick out the different nationalities. Then a few more officers strolled up to the tune of louder clapping. After them came Lord Roberts orderly, & two of his Indian Sikhs – most splendid looking men. At a signal from an official, the piano started the National Anthem, at which we all rose and joined in, knowing his lordship's carriage had arrived; but the crowd outside was so great, that we had sung it again before he could get in to the room. Faith! We could hardly see him for tears in our eyes as he walked up, escorted by the Mayor in his ermine robe; behind them , came Lord Kitchener & Rhodes, Lord Methuen and his staff, Colonel Kekewich & a lot of other officers. I thought the cheering and clapping never would cease. Of course the place was packed, & mostly of the male kind too. First of all, the Mayor made a short speech welcoming Lord Roberts, & called upon the Town Clerk to read an address. (They hadn't been long composing it, had they?) Then the dear old chap arose amid deafening cheers & clapping & made a most beautiful speech, bringing in everybody - & speaking most sympathetically about the women and children. I wish I could remember every word he said; but I know he mentioned how our bravery had been commented on & how all the world honoured and respected us for it. He seemed awfully pleased with his reception, & well he might be. The Mayor then in a few words welcomed Lord Kitchener, which was the signal for more vociferous cheers. The great hero of Khartoum only said a few words – "short, terse, & to the point", but he was simply*

beaming the whole of the time, & each individual thought he was grinning at them – it was very funny. Isn't he a contrast to dear old Bobs? I wanted to give the latter a good hug.

As soon as I saw his face I thought of the son he had lost. His hair and moustache are very white & his face sad. As you know he is a slight little man- he talks in a rather low but clear voice. But Kitchener is enormous & very broad & his face was so tanned & burnt by the sun & his eyes gleaming, & as I said before he seemed to consider the whole a huge joke. Most of the men & women shook hands with them. Loo did too, but we felt shy; but they both saluted us. Nobody mentioned Lord Methuen; most of the military men seem to consider him responsible for many deaths; & you hear on all sides the opinion of the "Tommies", who say, that if he goes into action he'll be shot from the back & we all know what that means. I felt sorry for him, he looked so ill and worried, & most melancholy. The Major says he's a totally different man since he knew him last some 5 or 6 years ago; then he was almost as jolly & full of jokes as a youngster, & now he seems quite broken down. He says he is the most polished, courteous gentleman you could ever meet.

I do hope our Colonel Kekewich will be made a full Colonel. We are all so proud and grateful to him for the way he has managed us – his big family – so well, is to my mind, nothing short of marvellous. We are getting fish now & grapes from Cape Town & gradually relaxation is being allowed in the way of going beyond the boundaries. Now we can keep our lights as long as we please & next Saturday people may stay out all night if they please. The soldiers are kept pretty strictly – privates have to be in by 6 o'clock and sergeants by 8.

We had Captain Green in for last Sunday; it was most interesting to listen to him. He was present at the surrender of Cronje; & described to us how the brave Canadians drew the Boer fire. The same Sunday night Loo brought in a young fellow named MacNamara - related to the noted soldier of that name. He was the most insufferable bounder you ever struck. His Uncle was Loo's greatest chum in Australia, & he came and claimed acquaintance on the strength of it. He's hardly been introduced before he began relating to us how he had met Lord Roberts & Kitchener while he was in hospital (for fever) at Cape Town; & how the famous "Bobs" sat and talked to him, & when he found out who he was, shook him by the hand as did Kitchener & Sir Alfred Milner. He was no doubt a very estimable young man – but he had an exaggerated opinion of his own importance & as there was undoubtedly good stuff in him, I hope the rough life will knock some of the foolishness out of him.

He tried to talk like a father to the Major & Dr. Green. He'd been in India for 4½ years and had returned to England – stayed there for 14 hours & then embarked for the Cape & joined Robert's Horse as a private, though after his interview with the great man, was created a sergeant. We had a dear old Major in for two or three nights – one of the Royal Irish. He'd been wounded (& made prisoner for a few hours) at Jacobsdaal, but had come up here for better accommodation. I don't think he was old, but being ill made him appear so; I never saw a more gentle or refined face; & when he asked Lal to play, or me to sing, we both felt we could, to such a sympathetic listener.

We didn't have so many visitors after the Australians left. I used to get tea & make anchovy-essence-sandwiches for Colonel Ricardo, nearly every afternoon. He's a very fine looking man & awfully nice of course – but they all call me "child" & treat me as if I were 17 instead of the tremendous age I am. Sometimes Major Chevalier came with him, & sometimes Lieut. Osborne. Now the latter is a nice young man if you like, not a bit of a bounder & he's awfully rich & is going into the Guards after this is over. When he & the Colonel & Loo got talking about people in Australia, where this one was, who had married so & so etc. etc. You couldn't get a word in edgeways; Lal, the Major & I would get in another part of the room & try & make as much noise as they.

The Colonel came in directly after lunch on Monday to wish us "Good-bye" – he gave us each one of those Maltese Crosses that Colonels wear on their collars. I'm going to have mine mounted for a brooch as soon as I can afford it. One of the Captains gave me some emu feathers to put on the side of my sailor hat.

Did I tell you that Lal has been under fire? She rode out with the Major to Ottos Kopje & there were a few hundred yards midway when they were within range & sight of Boer guns; all the rest of the way they were pretty well sheltered by the kopjes. Just before they reached the spot, the Major's batman *said "I think we had better hurry over this sir", so the Major turned to Lal & said "Now my girl, brace yourself together & ride as hard as you can till you get to the next kopje & if you hear a shell coming, you must get under your horse". They cantered very quickly & just as they had covered the distance, a shell was fired. It didn't fall anywhere near them, but Colonel Chamier, who was in the Conning Tower at the time said it was aimed at them. Then after they reached Otto's Kopje another was sent there, & they just had time to bundle into a splinter-proof before it burst. The Major brought Lal a part of the copper band off this shell. Before most of the people went underground, when the shells were flying, we used to be warned. As soon as the puff of smoke which indicated the sending off of a shell, was seen from the Conning Tower, a man stationed there waved a flag, which was seen by another man, on the Market Square, & he blew a whistle. This gave you 15 seconds to lie flat if you were out of doors or to gain shelter of some sort if you were near it. We, personally, only heard the whistle twice & instead of running to the safer room at the back, we waited to hear how soon & where the shell would fall. We hardly seem to realise it is all over & the reaction makes us fearfully limp.*

We had a very jolly evening last night; the Major and Captain Shute & young Johnson came in. The Major took us in awfully about this boy the first time he came; said he sang most beautifully, & played all the accompaniments at Government House etc., & of course we asked him to sing & kept plaguing him all evening to do one or the other; & he protested that all he could do was play the violin. We didn't believe him until the end, when the Major confessed he'd been paying off an old score. But to quote the Major "Johnson is an awfully nice youngster, he's about 6ft. & as slim as a girl, is a lieut. in the R.A. & as plucky as they make 'em".

<u>*March 9th*</u>*. Yesterday afternoon the Major came in to bid us good-bye, as today he goes with his maxims to Barkley. We said "Good-bye" to him; but he turned up as usual last night – to wish us "Good-bye" again. (He's left his wife's and son's addresses with Lal in case he is shot), Captain Shute and Johnson came too. Tonight it seems very strange without him, but Katie Thompson came round & afterwards Loo brought in Captain Wright. He reminded me of Uncle Lionel – about his height & the same funny way of saying things to you. He's an old Naval Captain, "a perfect gentleman", & came up as Correspondent with some of Methuen's forces. He said he had a daughter about my age & made me sing the Geisha songs she sang. He made me blush lots of times, said the most awful things – being old he was privileged. He grew quite poetic in describing a scene in which the principal colour was baby running with outstretched arms to meet me – (the little darling), & he kept on saying to me "Take that dimple away it annoys me". He was quite old you see, so you mustn't be shocked. Tomorrow I leave with Mother for Cape Town, & from there to Ted★ at O'okiep.*

★Ted is Mabel's brother (AEG)

<u>*Cape Town March 12th. 1900*</u> *This place is crowded beyond endurance, full to overflowing – soldiers walking on each other's heads, so to speak, & all sorts & conditions of Jewesses, & Jews – fat, thin, dark, fair, beautiful & the reverse, short (mostly) & tall; & all the fair sex in the most beautiful of raiment & sparkling diamonds. (You should see some of them at a dance – they are literally ablaze with 'em). Heaps of refugees are encamped on the beach & here are crowds of people of all nationalities. Every house is packed & we shouldn't have been able to have a room here at the White House, only someone happened to leave that very day & we only wanted it for one night. We arrived here at about 8 o'clock this morning, after a very interesting journey down. Saw, or rather were in, the vicinities of all the battlefields up this way, & saw several of the Boer, rifle-pits – they evidently expected our men to come up the line. You want to see the nature of the country, to judge the splendid, dogged perseverance which our brave fellows must have had to have stormed & taken, kopje after kopje, as they did. We came across many a little cemetery, with rough crosses to mark the resting places of the fallen, or in some cases, just the name spelt in stone on the sand. All the way down at short intervals there were soldiers placed & at all the bridges & they came up & asked us news of the Siege in most places & were awfully interested in anything we could tell them. We met lots of trains of soldiers, ammunition, horses & provisions going up. We saw most of the Canadians & they all, men & officers alike, came to see us women who'd come down from Kimberley.*

At Modder River, just as the train was about to start, we

heard a great wailing noise & a Dutchwoman came along with her baby. Instantly two or three of the officers ran forward asking what the matter was & what they could do for her. She wasn't crying or sobbing – just wailing out oh! oh! But she jabbered something in Dutch & the officers said to the men "Find her an empty compartment & wire to Honey Nest Kloof to tell them to look out for her". Instantly half a dozen Tommies sprang foreword to hold the baby while she got in, oh! These soldiers were gentlemen at heart, as well as brave. One of them told me her husband had been brought to the hospital that morning a prisoner & had since died.

We came through awfully grand scenery – particularly the Hex River Mountains, which we passed in the moonlight. Mr. Randall, who was travelling in the same train, knocked us up & we wrapped up & stood on the balcony in the front & for an hour or more, we saw the grandest, most weird, tremblingly glorious mountains that I had ever set eyes on. One time you were bordering on tremendous precipices & then again being whirled round another great mountain with moonlight shining on the rails before and behind, & you wondered how you could ever have come such a circle & how on earth you could possibly get round on to the rails ahead of you. We passed one station & several solitary tents where a few soldiers beside enormous fires, which looked cheerful & picturesque though lonely, kept guard through the night.

Now, I am wondering whether you will ever drag through this weary drear letter, but I have tried to tell you in it, just what I should have told you, had I been able to talk to you, & as I have written it under many & various circumstances, during shelling & what-not, you must excuse the imperfections thereof. My eyes have been troubling me lately & as I shall never get another pair, I must needs have a care how I use them, so I shall do as little writing as I can, for a while, & must answer the letters I have received by degrees.

Tomorrow we start by the Nantilus for Port Nolloth – it takes 3 days, then we stay there till the next morning, when we go to Klipfontein & break the journey there for a day or two, before proceeding to O'okiep. [Old spelling of Okiep]

These intrepid ladies were no doubt greeted very warmly by AEG, who had secured a job as store manager with the Okiep Copper Company. It must have been a huge relief to arrive in this quiet backwater away from the fighting – this was not to last.

Pretoria fell in June 1900 and the Boer War took on a new phase, of guerrilla warfare. General Smuts bravely led a 300-man commando and amazingly broke through British lines and out into Cape Colony. They rode north west through the Karoo to the mining area inland from Port Nolloth, captured Concordia and Springbokfontein and surrounded Okiep, which was heavily fortified and defended by regular troops and mining company employees. So poor Elizabeth, her daughter Mabel and son AEG were again besieged; this time for only about three months in Okiep. Relief came in two ways, firstly a column sent by sea to Port Nolloth from Cape Town. Secondly General Smuts was given safe conduct to go to the piece conference at Vereeniging and the Boer War ended on 31st May 1902.

By 1910 AEG was painting and teaching in Johannesburg and had a very important part to play in young Albert's upbringing when he went to Jeppe School and then the School of Mines (Wits University), but more of this later.

L-R: Elizabeth Gyngell, AEG, Mable Gyngell at Okiep during the siege of this copper mining town in 1902. AEG was store manager for the mine then stationmaster. In this picture he is in the Town Guard uniform; he held the rank of Lieutenant. They all look rather thin, probably due to the deprivations of two sieges! (Family archives)

AEGAs officer in Town Guard during siege of O'okiep (Okiep). Fourth from left in back row.

PART OF CAPE COLONY WAS LEFT UNPROTECTED.

The Boers Had Pretty Much Their Own Way in the O'okiep Region in the Early Part of April.

LONDON, May 4.—Mail advices have been received here describing the siege of the British garrison at O'okiep, Cape Colony.

These advices show that early in April the Boers had pretty much their own way in the northwestern corner of Cape Colony. They destroyed miles of railroad, burned the sleepers, and dynamited the blockhouses in the district, compelling the evacuation of many small garrisons and blockhouses, and the concentration of the British at O'okiep, while the small garrisons at Springbokfontein and Concordia surrendered. The former garrison only gave up after a stiff fight, in which the British had four men killed and six wounded.

The refugees from outlying places poured into Port Nolloth, to which point two British gunboats were sent. Gen. Smuts demanded the surrender of O'okiep on April 4, but, although Col. Shelton had 6,000 persons to feed and provisions for only three weeks, he firmly declined to give up.

Contemporary account of the siege of O'okiep.

Chapter Two

POST BOER WAR, 1900-1914

The Anglo Boer War caused much damage to be done both materially and to society, as it was basically a bitter civil war. Not only was property shattered and looted but Boer was turned against English and the indigenous people were marginalised. The Boer discontent, the deeply-felt dislike of British rule and the loss of their Republics had led to a very difficult time after the Anglo Boer War.

The family stayed in Kimberley living at 'The Homestead', which was a suburb of the town. Here they had two more children, Josephine (Jo) and Alice. We do not really know why, but Thomas had a great wanderlust. He developed a mobile dentist's surgery and moved many times, from town to town. Maybe dentistry, in those days, consisted mainly of teeth extraction, and there were only so many teeth to remove in an area and then you had to move on.

There was a great recession in 1906/7 which did not help, but as the correspondent in the *Transvaal Leader* wrote, 'Kimberley remained the most prosperous town south of the Zambezi'. However the Lewis-Roberts family started to move and as you will see from Josephine's letter to Marjorie L-R in 1973, it was quite an unusual time for them.

My father Thomas Aran Lewis-Roberts had a flourishing dentist practice in Kimberley before the Boer War. He and my mother entertained a great deal and lived at 'The Homestead', a farm like residence I think about 5 miles outside Kimberley, near Oliver Schreiner's home, my dad having his surgery in the town of Kimberley itself. Bert and Arthur were born before the Siege of Kimberley and Alice and I born after the Siege. Dr Ashe, a great friend of the family, brought us all in to the world. When Bert was at the School of Mines in Johannesburg, he and other students went to Kimberley and Bert went to see Dr Ashe. He at once said, 'oh I can see you are a Lewis-Roberts. Aunt Mabel's account of the Siege of Kimberley gives the hardships she, my Granny Gyngell and the family went through at that time. Cecil Rhodes wanted Dad, with other men, to go to Rhodesia. Dad told him, 'I have married a wife'. Rhodes said, 'more fool you'. - Things were bad in Kimberley and Dad decided to go to Malmesbury [just North of Cape Town] and then to Paarl. I recollect very little of these places. Except I was told that Alice got Infantile Paralysis [now Polio] at Paarl and that there she was singing and playing a lot and had to give everything up and nurse her.

Dad's next venture was at Oudtshoorn. For our sea holidays we went to Gordon's Bay or Mossel Bay, the latter near the Wilderness. As no railway was built then Dad hired a coach and six mules and the trips were done by road. Once the coach got stuck in a swollen river, water came right up to the lamps. A native party working nearby helped us out – luckily because the river was still coming down strongly. Dad had travelling dental equipment and used to go by Cape Cart drawn by two horses to various places where there was no dentist. Sometimes he went by train. He always wanted to be on the move. He said he had a roving spirit and should never have married, moving so often cost money. His idea was to better his practice by going to these different places. Much money in bad debts was owed to him and he often said it would have helped him a lot if it had been paid.

From Oudtshoorn we went to Ficksburg in the Orange Free State. This was a very small place and nothing much doing. We left Ficksburg in early 1913 I think for Benoni in the Transvaal [now a suburb of Johannesburg]. It was from there Bert went to Jeppe High School. Then the war came and eventually both Bert and Arthur joined up – an anxious time for us all – Dad's practice in Benoni was fairly good.

But on the mistaken advice of a friend he was told that Dundee [in Natal] had no highly qualified dentist. This friend who was the organist at St Dunstan's Anglican Church in Benoni [mother was in the choir and sometimes played the organ] went to Dundee as the organist there. He had a boarding house and said Dad, Mum and I could stay there, never telling us there was no house available. Anyway Dad decided to go to Dundee in 1922. Mother and I followed a little later. This was just before the Rebellion and Benoni and the Reef were very hot spots. Our neighbour was shot dead and Dad said he would probably have been shot too had he stayed.

When Dad arrived in Dundee he found the dentist had been there for years and had a very flourishing practice. He said afterwards he should never have gone to Dundee. By this time Bert told Mother she must remain in Dundee. Dad continued to practice and both boys helped financially. Finally Dad made one more move and came up to Johannesburg to work for a dentist up here. He developed pneumonia and died. I was with him towards the end. A great shock to Mother and Alice, as he was only ill for a few days. I wish he had written his life history right from the beginning. It would have been interesting. Mother did try after he died to record some of his earlier life. Today pneumonia can be treated but when Dad died there were no sulphur drugs or antibiotics and pneumonia in Johannesburg was looked upon as a fatal illness.

Joe.

Young Bert grew into a fine-looking young man, very sporting and keen on outdoor pursuits. He developed good riding and shooting skills, encouraged by the Cadet Corps at school. He must have gone to several local schools during their perambulations, but he attended Jeppe High School in Johannesburg from 1909 to 1912. Jeppe is a well-respected public school still proudly going to this day.

In 1912 he won the Cadet Bisley Interprovincial Cup, recorded by a gold medal from the Transvaal Rifle Association. The Worcestershire Chronicle in England commented that he would be 'remembered as a famous rifle shot when under 17, also as a keen all-round sportsman'.

From 1913 to 1914 he joined the South African School of Mines and Technology, now Witwatersrand University, completing the first year Diploma in Mechanical Engineering, Mathematics, Electrotechnics, Chemistry and Geology. He never finished the degree, as war loomed in 1914 and Bert joined the 2nd Imperial Light Horse; he was 18 years old.

The Lewis-Roberts Family at Paarl, about 1905. Alice, Josephine, Mother Alice, Bert behind, Arthur and Father, Thomas.

Bert's school report from Paarl Boys' High School, 1906, when he was 10 years old.

The winning team of Transvaal Rifle Association Cadet Bisley Inter Provincial Cup 1912. AO is back row, fourth from left.

CHAPTER THREE

THE BOER REBELLION AND GERMAN SW AFRICA, 1914-15

The Union of South Africa came in to being on 31st May 1910. It combined the previously separate colonies of the Cape, Natal, and the former Boer Republics of Transvaal and the Orange Free State.

The First World War was declared by Britain on Germany on 4th August 1914.

In South Africa the first move was made by the Germans, who crossed the border from German South West Africa (Namibia) at Nakob on 14th August and advanced towards Upington in the Northern Cape. But it was to the Royal Navy that the Cabinet in London turned to protect the sea lanes that maintained the island nation of Great Britain.

Strategists studying the German high seas fleet soon turned their eyes to German South West Africa and its support of the threat. The colony had two seaports, Lüderitzbucht and Swakopmund, which could be used by raiders in the South Atlantic. The Germans also seized the undefended British enclave of Walvis Bay early in the war. However, much more concern was declared about the radio station at Windhoek, which stood 350 feet high on the central plateau and was the second most powerful transmitter in the world. In favourable weather conditions it could maintain contact with Berlin. In bad weather contact could be continued via a relay station in the German colony of Togo in West Africa. Smaller stations at Lüderitzbucht and Swakopmund could maintain contact with German warships in the South Atlantic and thus threaten the vital sea routes from India round the Cape of Good Hope. Depriving Germany of the use of the South West African facilities became an important and urgent objective from the first day of the war.

On this day the Prime Minister of the Union of South Africa, General Louis Botha, sent a message to London saying they were confident in defending themselves and that the imperial troop garrison could be withdrawn for more important service elsewhere. Only two days later acceptance of the offer was confirmed by London, along with an enquiry as to whether the Union would be willing to capture the wireless stations in German South West Africa.

On 6th August a British Government cable to Prime Minister Louis Botha said: 'If your ministers at the same time desire and feel themselves able to seize such part of German South West Africa as will give them command of Swakopmund, Lüderitzbucht and the wireless station there or in the interior, we would feel that this was a great and urgent Imperial service'.

On the 10th of August the Union cabinet agreed to send an expeditionary force against the German colony. Political ratification was more difficult and created a serious and damaging split in parliament. Only five weeks later Union forces crossed the Orange River under the command of Brigadier-General Tim Lukin. Two days later, on 18th September, the first seaborne landing took place at Lüderitzbucht.

Within weeks open rebellion inflamed the Northern part of South Africa, followed by the Free State, and on

October 9th a revolt was declared by the Boer commander, Col. Salomon Maritz, military commander at Upington. Martial law was declared throughout South Africa on 12th October by the PM, General Louis Botha, supported by his Minister of Defence, General J.C. Smuts. Being at war with Germany was deeply unpopular with many discontented Boer sympathisers, who also saw this as an opportunity, as Germany had been very supportive to their cause in the Anglo Boer war of only 12 years earlier. However the rebellion was quickly crushed and fizzled out after the remaining leaders surrendered near Upington on January 30th 1915. Maritz escaped with some of his men and SA prisoners to German SW Africa; here he found himself not very welcome and he eventually retreated to Europe via Angola.

In the main, Boer troops (commandos) were used to put down the rebellion by their kinsmen and now, having buried their dead, they rode off to war side by side with their English–speaking countrymen, a truly remarkable achievement for a truly remarkable army of some of the most battle-hardened and mobile troops anywhere.

The overall plan evolved around a swift and complete occupation of GSWA by South African forces from four main directions. There were two compelling reasons for this style of campaign; firstly to stop the Germans adopting protracted guerrilla warfare and secondly to put the German radio stations out of commission as soon as possible. Four forces would attack: in the north by sea through Walvis Bay and Swakopmund. The central force landed at Lüderitzbucht on 18th September. Two more columns attacked overland from the south and south east. Farther consolidation was delayed by the Rebellion in the autumn of 1914 and at the same time the Germans invading the Union towards Upington. As a separate action in the North a small force of Rhodesian Police occupied, without a struggle, Schuckmannsburg in the Caprivi Strip.

Seldom can an opposed landing on an enemy shore have been so easily accomplished as that at Lüderitzbucht. A small party was landed under the guns of H.M.S. *Astrea*. After a brief skirmish the port surrendered and the majority of the German residents retreated up the single-track railway to prepared defensive positions at Aus, about 100 miles across the torrid coastal desert strip. The railway lines were dynamited as they retreated. A not very formidable force of about 2000 landed from four transports. One, the *Monarch*, was remarkable, as she was, at that time, the largest ship to trade with SA weighing 12,500 tons. Her cargo consisted of 4,000 horses and mules, 500 tons of meat in cold storage and 750,000 gallons of water!

The newly-recruited 2nd Imperial Light Horse in 1914. Bert is fourth from the right in the third row from the front seated. It is interesting to note there is no standard uniform; their hats vary from a Stetson through pith helmets to slouch hats, variously personalised. Bandoliers and army issue rifles are however standard! The age of recruits clearly varies from boys to grey-bearded Boer War veterans. Bert joined on 13th November 1914 age 18, pay 3 shillings per day!

Camp on the shore at Luderitzbucht. Desalination plant in the background. Bert's tent marked.

Bert in troopers' uniform, 2nd Imperial Light Horse aged 18

The 2nd Imperial Light Horse (2ILH) was reformed in October 1914 under the command of Lt. Col W F D Davies; many recruits were drawn from students at the School of Mines. Young Albert joined 2 ILH on 13th November 1914, aged 18. From the time the regiment was reformed it had been training at Milner Park Show Ground in Johannesburg. After six weeks there they rode to Potchefstroom to entrain on 22nd November for Upington, to help quell the rebellion. The journey to the railhead at Prieska took four days and must have been torrid; eight men were crammed into each compartment and the horses were carried in open trucks.

On arrival the regiment found it was no longer needed, as the rebellion there had collapsed. After a short sojourn by the Orange River they retraced their steps, this time to Cape Town. Thus Bert's service record defines his service as for the Rebellion and in G.S.W. Africa. In modern terms he seems to have received very little training. They were expected to be able to shoot and ride before joining up!

The first forces having landed in the German port of Lüderitzbucht on 18th September 1914, largely unopposed, Albert arrived in mid-December. They came by sea from Cape Town in the ship *Gaika*, the horses in another vessel, arriving in about three days; it must have been quite something to load hundreds of horses individually by sling and crane in to the hold of the ship to be unloaded into the sea to swim ashore at Lüderitzbucht!

The commander of the Central Force, Brigadier-General Sir Duncan McKenzie, found the advance inland from Lüderitzbucht was delayed because the main fighting had been against the formidable enemies of thirst, the desert sand and the uncertainties created by the Rebellion. From the coast the railway runs 104 miles inland to the well-defended town of Aus through extremely deep sand dunes. The only way across this inhospitable desert was with the help of the railway, but the railway was dynamited and booby-trapped and what wells there had been were poisoned and mined by the retreating Germans.

Bert's first letter home was dated December 15th 1914 and announced his safe arrival:

Lüderitzbucht

My dear Mother and Dad,

…we landed amidst a dust storm. This place is decidedly worse than Upington, really no sign of grass or vegetation anywhere, nothing but soft sand. We have our camp near the sea, and bathing parades are really very enjoyable.

Up till now we have not seen any fighting, but I think it will not be long before everybody has his fill.

…I am writing this letter in the tent, and it is a bit difficult writing for everybody is indulging in heated discussions. As soon as the horses are fit we expect to be trekking in real earnest.

… am going to bathe my horse's legs. He is quite a good horse but is slightly lame owing to being kicked while on the ship.

20.12.1914

Men and horses are being made as fit as possible, and if we are allowed to spend Xmas here, it will not be long before we are off.

27.12.1914

My Dear Mother and Dad

Xmas eve afternoon we had a big parade in full marching kit, and it was the worse day we ever had for wind and dust since we landed. At one spot in amongst the hills, I thought my goggles had been cracked, the grit and sand absolutely stung like shot. It was only with the greatest difficulty that we heard our officer's commands. We were indeed grateful to return to what little shelter our tents afforded.

On Christmas day it was still blowing, though not as bad as the previous day. That day we held our sports, running and horse-wrestling, tug-of-war, etc. These were very fine, and I longed to join in with them but I thought I had better not take any risks with my knee. At dinner time we enjoyed ourselves; we did not do badly on the stew, plum pudding, stewed dry fruit, strawberry jam nuts and biscuits…

When Mother sends my veil could she please pack in with it one of those Balaclava woollen caps. The weather, although fairly warm during the day, is very often bitterly cold, especially when the wind is blowing. Granny knows the sort I mean because she was knitting one just before I left…I have been kept very busy what with aeroplane pickets and various guards… The hospital ship (the Ebani with Bert's school friend nurse Kathleen Niven) has just come in from Cape Town and she will most likely be carrying mail.

In a letter on 25.1.1915 he describes a working day, it is now nearly two months after landing:

We are still having plenty to do. We now do all our work before noon. Reveille sounds at five, and we have our horses saddled and ready for parade at 5.30. We spend two and a half hours indulging in skirmishing tactics amongst the hills. Returning we have healthy appetites for breakfast, and as there is plenty of porridge, we do not do badly.

After 'stables' we have our rifle inspection and dismounted infantry drill. We barely have time to finish this until off to the condenser station (plant to condense sea water into drinking water) to water the horses. This leaves us with the afternoon free until 5.30 when we have 'stables' again……

I am trying to obtain leave to go into the town, Lüderitzbucht. Everybody so far seems to have had his turn.

My horse's near hind heel has almost healed. He is now practically in the pink of condition.

8.3.1915
In my last letter to Art I told him we were about to leave for another patrol. We marched off that same day at about one o'clock, and arrived at our destination, a place by the name of Rossetental. Here we found the remains of a diamond mining camp.

The next day we were allowed a couple of hours off to hunt for diamonds. I started on my own and managed to get a sieve and started on some concentrated stuff which was about to be sent through a rotary machine. I did my washing in a tub of salt water. Tipping the remains of my washing on to a clean board. I found numerous small garnets, but no diamonds. I tried other places but did not come across any of the gems. There were only a few of the fellows found any diamonds and these were small and of little value… In the afternoon we returned to our camp at Whale Island, it was hot and stuffy, and after feeding and watering our tired horses we made a beeline for the sea. You can hardly imagine the ease and sense of contentment after plunging into the cool breakers… I am writing this by the light of a candle. hope it will not be long before we are back again. Your loving son Bert

So, there were two immediate problems to be solved. One was the provision of water, the other getting it to the troops in the desert. It was impossible to use animal transport, so the railway was the only way, and it had to be rebuilt before advances inland could commence. A water-condensing plant was erected at Lüderitzbucht with a 300,000 gallon reservoir, supplemented by water bought from Cape Town by sea. A garrison camp was built and an air of permanence set in. Within about two months 50 miles of track were reconstructed, but work speeded up when a specialist railway construction and management regiment was formed from troops with experience of the work under the command of Lieut-Col Fairweather DSO. Work proceeded at a truly amazing rate, and in the ensuing two months about 200 miles was reinstated.

The railway gauge being the same as the Union at 3'6," rolling stock was bought from Cape Town and landed on special pontoons with tracks that allowed it to roll directly on to the land-based railway. It was only four weeks from landing before the first train steamed out of Lüderitzbucht! The Germans felt safe in the belief that no advance inland on Aus was possible without the railway; they were surprised by the speed of the reconstruction. Aus was heavily fortified with trenches, gun positions and underground bunkers. It was a daunting prospect to take and heavy loss of life was expected.

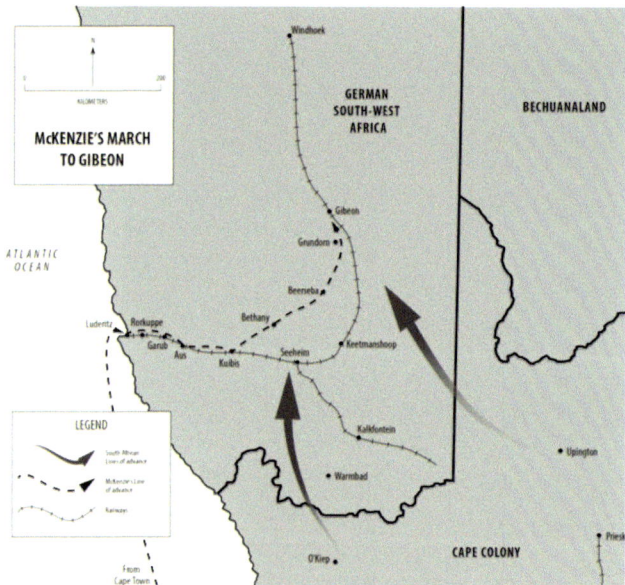

Map of GSW campaign showing central force advance to Gibeon.

On March 24th 1915, three months after landing, Bert describes the order to move in a field postcard home:

My dear Mother and Dad,
Have just been given the order to move. We leave tomorrow at 11 a.m. so it is a bit sudden. The last few days have been kept hard at it, and have had little time for writing… My horse is in good condition and I have finished up his heels; this has eased my mind a great deal…Bert
Tschaukaib

29.3.1915

Am quite well and fit. We have just finished a hard trek of about fifty miles through the sand. It has been very hot and dusty weather. We are moving off again at 7 p.m. tonight. I am having a very busy time so please excuse the short letter.

The force had now reached 6500 in number. Bert, having landed in December, moved inland with his regiment, 2ILH, to a foreword base at Tschaukaib, the official "front" 45 miles up the railway. He found temperatures up to 137F and drifting sand dunes as far as the eye could see; keeping his horses fit and well watered in such a climate must have been challenging. A trooper described himself as being loaded up "like Father Christmas", a remark well founded for man and horse alike. In full marching order a horse had to carry a heavy military saddle, blanket under the saddle, nose-bag and feed, mess tin with "billycan", gun bucket with rifle, two wallets in front and greatcoat with waterproof sheet at the back. The rider carried two water bottles, two full bandoliers, one over the left shoulder and one round the waist, a haversack over the shoulder and a bayonet on the left side of his belt; all this in the fiery Namib desert, in deep sand and through scrub bush.

The wells, having been poisoned with sheep dip or dead animals, were surrounded with booby traps (IEDs in modern terms) making advances on horseback even more problematical. The next advance about 20 miles to Garub was achieved, unopposed, on February 22, 1915. A great prize here was a rich underground supply of potable water. It was estimated that 10,000 men and 6000 animals would be needed for the assault on Aus. The South African forces set to work to improve the supply by building large underground storage tanks, giving two weeks reserve of water. A loop in the railway was constructed to allow the rapid filling of water trains. All this took some time, and the inactivity was hard to bear as these forces were within sight of German outposts on the high central plateau but also from the air.

Perhaps for the first time in warfare, and certainly on the African continent, aeroplanes were used offensively, as well as for aerial recognisance and photography. One of the two German airplanes, an Aviatik P14 piloted by Lieutenant Alexander von Scheele, flew its first reconnaissance over South African forces in Lüderitzbucht on November 21st 1914 only three months after the outbreak of the First World War. He observed and counted the ships in the harbour, then turned and flew back inland towards Aus. He flew over the South African camp at Rorkuppe, where he dropped propaganda leaflets to try and persuade the South Africans to join in the rebellion at home. He turned and flew low again and dropped improvised bombs made out of artillery shells, trailing strips of cloth to keep them straight.

The troops on the ground shot at him with rifles, hitting the plane several times, so discretion got the better of him and he withdrew, to fly the 70 miles back to the landing ground at Aus.

Later they were bombed and photographed by another German airman, Lieutenant Fiedler, flying an LFG Roland. The result was dramatic, as bombs fell amongst the 1700 cavalry horses tethered in the horse lines. Panic ensued and horses disappeared in all directions, many not to be recaptured, and they eventually became the famous wild horses seen in this area. In 2011, while Mary and I were staying near Aus in a remote lodge, a wild horse visited us and drank the water we had put out for the birds! These beautiful animals reminded us of Bert's visit to this area nearly 100 years before. We also wondered whether this first encounter with aeroplanes influenced Bert's choice later in his military career.

It was undoubtedly true that Aus had been heavily defended; even today one can see the remains of bunkers and trenches giving in-depth defence including heavy guns. Great loss of life was expected in any assault by the South Africans, so much time had been taken to consolidate their position and to end the Boer rebellion at home.

However, towards the end of March 1915 things began to happen fast. Following Lord Buxton's visit on 22nd March and General Botha on 26th orders were given to move. The mounted men, including Bert's 2 ILH, were given orders to proceed inland and General McKenzie's headquarter was moved up the railway from Lüderitzbucht to Garub.

General Botha's inspection South African Units before the advance from Luderitzbucht

The attack was set for the night of March 30. Bert wrote home after the attack in a heavily-censored letter dated 13.4.1915:

Tchakalskuppe

My Dear Mother and Dad

I was so pleased to get your letters, also one from Art and the papers. Since my last letter from Tschaukaib, we have been on the move all the time. All our trekking is done at night now. We passed through Garub and Aus, but at these places I had no time whatever for writing. The day before yesterday the squadron left Aus, and we are now doing reconnaissance duty some distance away from that place. Practically every five yards of the railway as far as we have gone has been blown up by the Germans. The water holes likewise have been treated in the same manner, or else poisoned. Carbolic acid so far seems to be the only material they have used… I had a letter from Aunt Margaret, and with it was a Balaclava helmet which Grannie had made. I was very glad to get both.

Five other fellows and I are on observation duty perched on the top of a kopje. We are on the lookout all the time for strange patrols. I have done my shift of two hours and have just been relieved, and now I am making use of my spare time.

The aeroplane has not been bothering us for the last few days, and I think it has gone inland to do more important work.

I do not know when this letter will reach you as no arrangement has been made for the sending away of letters, but I shall do my best to get it away by seeing one of the motor transport drivers. Your loving son Bert.

The war in the south ended fifteen days later, and clearly Bert had no further opportunity to write home.

The first troops to enter Aus were the kilted infantry of the Transvaal Scottish. Bert and his 2ILH were sent round to the north to take control of Kanus Poort, the road and railway into Aus from the east. At Kanus Poort they came upon the sad sight of three natives hanged from a tree by the Germans, probably for being spies. However, the enemy had gone, leaving the town heavily booby-trapped and stripped bare of everything, including the radio station, and the wells were poisoned as usual. Engineers got to work clearing mines and repairing water pumps to clean up the water. Clean well water was not available for nine days; meanwhile water carts were bought up from Garub.

The Germans had finally pulled out about three days before the South African attack. With their effective aerial observation they could see the SA force under van Deventer coming up overland from the SE, and realised it would only be a matter of time before the rail line to the north would be cut, leaving no means of escape. They were hugely outnumbered by the Union forces and decided to retreat to Windhoek by rail.

This bloodless victory must have been a great relief to Bert and his friends, as they could see the five miles of trenches, gun pits and bunkers which they would otherwise have had to storm, no doubt with great loss of life. From here the 9th Brigade, which included Bert in 2ILH, was instructed to reconnoitre towards Bethanie with the overall aim of cutting off the German retreat somewhere near Gibeon. The advance started on April 15th and had to be carefully scheduled to allow wells to recharge themselves. They were now on the dry, stony central plateau some 1500ft above sea level, no longer sandy desert, so a little more grazing was available for animals. The going was so stony and rough that many horses lost their shoes and riders often had to walk beside their mounts to save them from becoming lame.

However water still remained the major problem, as the wells at Bethanie were found to be alkaline, and although bubbling up at 144,000 gallons per day at 82 degrees F. it was more suitable for a spa bath than a drink for man or beast!

The day after reaching Bethanie they set off on the 44-mile ride to Besondermaid, where they found the welcome sight of clean open water, which they could revel in for the first time. So far Bert's column had covered 115 miles in four days. Information was received that the enemy were moving in some numbers to Berseba ahead of them; after a six-hour bivouac they pushed on and at dawn closed on the town. German pickets raised the alarm and the action developed into a chase through the town and into the country beyond. Nearly all the Germans were rounded up – two officers and 28 men were captured and one killed. As well as arms and ammunition, 700 head of cattle and 5,000 smaller stock were also captured.

At the Fish River, the 7th, 8th and 9th brigades joined forces and the reunited division rested for a few hours to allow the worn-out horses to take advantage of the better grazing by the river. By now the troops were on short rations – a quarter pound of biscuits, two ounces of mealy meal, a quarter ounce of coffee and an ounce of sugar per day for each man. McKenzie pushed on; near Aretitis they struck the main north-south railway and started to follow it toward Gibeon. At Grundorn the engineers had an incredible stroke of luck; they found the telegraph wire was intact and tapped it! From German messages they discovered that they had no idea how close McKenzie was and could not believe he was nearing Gibeon. However it became clear that the Germans intended to evacuate Gibeon that night.

Scouts bought in the news that a train was standing in Gibeon station and being loaded; McKenzie had to move fast to try and cut off the German retreat. He planned an immediate strike, and at eight o'clock that night he sent a party of scouts and engineers to skirt round Gibeon station with orders to blow up the line to the north to prevent the train getting away. Royston followed 45 minutes later with a regiment of the 8th and the whole 9th Brigade, including Bert in 2ILH. His orders were to skirt round the station and deploy his force to block the retreat of the Germans when McKenzie made his attack from the south at dawn. The scene was set for the battle of Gibeon.

Scouts and engineers had been sent forward to cut the railway line to the north using dynamite. Three mounted rifle regiments, the Umvoti Mounted Rifles, Bert's 2nd Imperial Light Horse and the Natal Light Horse, under the command of Col J P Royston (known as mad Jack), moved in after the demolition team. Royston's orders were to cut the German's line of retreat, but he made a serious error by deploying his force parallel to the railway instead of across it. The German patrol sent to investigate the explosion soon located the force and bought machine guns to bear from culverts under the railway. The 2ILH were ordered to withdraw to their horses under fire, and sadly in the confusion and darkness most of the Natal Light Horse were pinned down and captured at dawn. Royston withdrew his men some 4.8km to regroup, await daybreak and the arrival of the rest of Brig-Gem McKenzie's force.

The Germans believed they had destroyed the main force and were unaware that McKenzie was about to attack from the south. By dawn they were closing in on Gibeon station. 15-pounder guns of the 12th Citizens Battery opened fire on the German train, with steam up in the station. The train crew surrendered immediately because the train was packed with a large quantity of explosives!

A running fight ensued when McKenzie tried to pin the Germans with his centre as well as outflank to the left and right, and the battle was forced to the west. The pace of the action forced the Germans to abandon their artillery and four of their six Maxim machine guns. Eventually, after losing a quarter of their force, they made good their escape to the north by road.

The action ended at 11.30 am on the 27th April. They had been in action incessantly since the 16th without much sleep and covered 210 miles of very rough country, with dwindling rations; now most men lay down and slept where they stopped. The South Africans lost 24 killed and 66 wounded, but recovered the captured men of the Natal Light Horse. The result of the action was that it cleared the whole of the southern region of German forces and prevented them taking to guerrilla action on the flank of the SA advance in the north.

On the 28th April, Gen Smuts announced a proclamation that South Africa was in control of all enemy territory as far north as Gibeon. Orders were issued for the early return of SA troops to the Union by sea from Lüderitzbucht, the first transport leaving for Cape Town on May 19th 1915.

Bert's service in 2ILH ended in Cape Town on 12th June 1915. There is a lovely photograph of him sitting on the transport ship in civilian clothes, clearly very well, but I suspect very excited by his seven months of active service. He had grown up and now returned to the School of Mines, where studies must have been rather unattractive after such an adventure. Where to next?

Bert, in civilian clothes, on a troop ship at Cape Town on return from the German South West campaign, June 1915.

Chapter Four

EAST AFRICAN CAMPAIGN, 1916-1917

Bert returned by rail from Cape Town to his home in Benoni, near Johannesburg, where his father had his dental practice. Arriving home in June 1915 he had the opportunity to return to the SA School of Mines (now Wits University) where he had already completed the first year diploma with good results, however things in the wider world were beginning to intervene; he never finished his degree in SA.

While SA troops were occupied in GSW Africa, war had been declared in German East Africa. The main threats were twofold, firstly GEA naval bases threatening our sea routes and secondly land forces threatening British East African territories of Kenya and Uganda to the North. Germany's military commander, von Lettow-Vorbeck, turned out to be the most able guerrilla commander of WW1 and was never defeated during the war. There were very few clearly-defined clashes of arms, and these were of a largely indecisive kind. As Gen Smuts stated: 'The campaign was a protracted, harsh test of endurance and pursuit, in which the German force only surrendered some ten days after the Armistice in Europe'. Lettow-Vorbeck built up a force of 1800 Germans and some 12,000 Askaris. The Imperial Government accepted the Union's offer, in 1915, to help with forces in E Africa (and Europe). General JC Smuts took command of the East African Theatre on 12th Feb 1916 with the remit to defeat Lettow-Vorbeck. It was clear that a military campaign in the dreadful climate of Equatorial Africa was going to be very difficult and quite different to the GSW expedition. The combination of heat and rain, exacerbated by human diseases such as malaria and dysentery and the animal disease of horse sickness and tsetse fly promised massive losses in unacclimatised men and beasts. Poor roads and vulnerable railways led to huge supply problems and frequent shortages of food and ammunition.

Bert at 19, in his new uniform of D squadron, 4th South African Horse. He was about to leave for German East Africa from Durban, autumn 1915.

Brig. Gen Collyer wrote in his book:

'As they fought their way through and lines of communication rapidly lengthened, hospital equipment, transport, and supply arrangements proved inadequate, reduced rations became an effective ally to malaria and the host of other tropical diseases. Bush and forests, mountains, rivers and deserts proved far more formidable than the enemy army. The equatorial sun blazed on them from above, disease and hunger sapped them from within. All around spread the endless bush, cutting off vision, full of lurking invisible danger, fear-inspiring, and heart-breaking.'

In South Africa, General Botha and General Smuts set about raising a volunteer army, and in the autumn of 1915 they recruited some 13,000 South Africans and 7000 Indian and African Troops. They were of Boer, British and Rhodesian origin and tended to be segregated into different battalions. Some ten battalions of mounted infantry joined up, as well as infantry etc. For instance the A squadron of 1st SA Horse and the whole of 4th Battalion of SA Horse (4th SAH) were mainly of British origin; it was in this unit that Bert enlisted as a trooper on 8th Dec 1915. He was paid three shillings a day, with an advance of £3-10-0 and a gratuity of £6-0-0 on discharge!

He embarked for E Africa from Durban, the 1500 mile journey taking six or seven days by sea. They travelled in a troop ship carrying, as well as the whole battalion, a thousand horses; this made the atmosphere below decks intolerable, so many men slept on deck. Some animals expired with the heat and were dumped overboard before docking.

4th S.A.H. entraining at Kilindini in 1916 to be packed like sardines with their horses on the train to Voi.

When the transport arrived at Kilindini, the deep-water port three miles from Mombasa, the horses were unloaded by slings into lighters and entrained for the journey up country. They were sent directly to the base at Kajiado on the Longido front, just in German territory, and where the country was more open, considered better for cavalry manoeuvre. Bert sent a postcard home from Kilindini dated 3-2-1916, which says:

Kilindini 3.2.1916

Dear Mother and Dad,
Arrived safely with all kit. It was a great job getting kit from the ship to the shore in the sweltering sun. We are now in the tropics and with vengeance too. We are just about to board a train for up country. We are being treated to tea and lemon squash by the ladies of Kilindini, who were very nice to us. Send this on to Uncle.
Love and kisses Bert.

The official order of battle puts the 4th SAH (commanded by Col Eliott) in the 2nd Div commanded by Major General M J Tighe, while most of the other mounted troops were in the 1st SA Division commanded by Brig. General J L Van Deventer. Smuts' strategy was to try to surround von Lettow-Vorbeck with large sweeping manoeuvres. Frustratingly, this was never achieved, but the plan did lead to a very confused campaign which saw Bert's Battalion moved between the 1st and 2nd Division as conditions required. It is very difficult to find out exactly where he fought, but from one letter it is clear he took part in the intense action at Kondoa-Irangi in support of Deventer's 2nd Div. on 19 April 1916. His letter dated 27th August says: 'I have just heard that when I left Kondoa-Irangi, of the original D squadron there are only 35 left(normal compliment of 150 to 170), the rest having been killed or laid up with fever. This has been remedied to a large extent by numbers of details being sent up.' For this battle the regiment was commanded by Col Deneys Reitz; he wrote a harrowing and vivid account of the battle in his book 'Adrift on the open veldt – Trekking On' starting at page 234 – well worth reading!

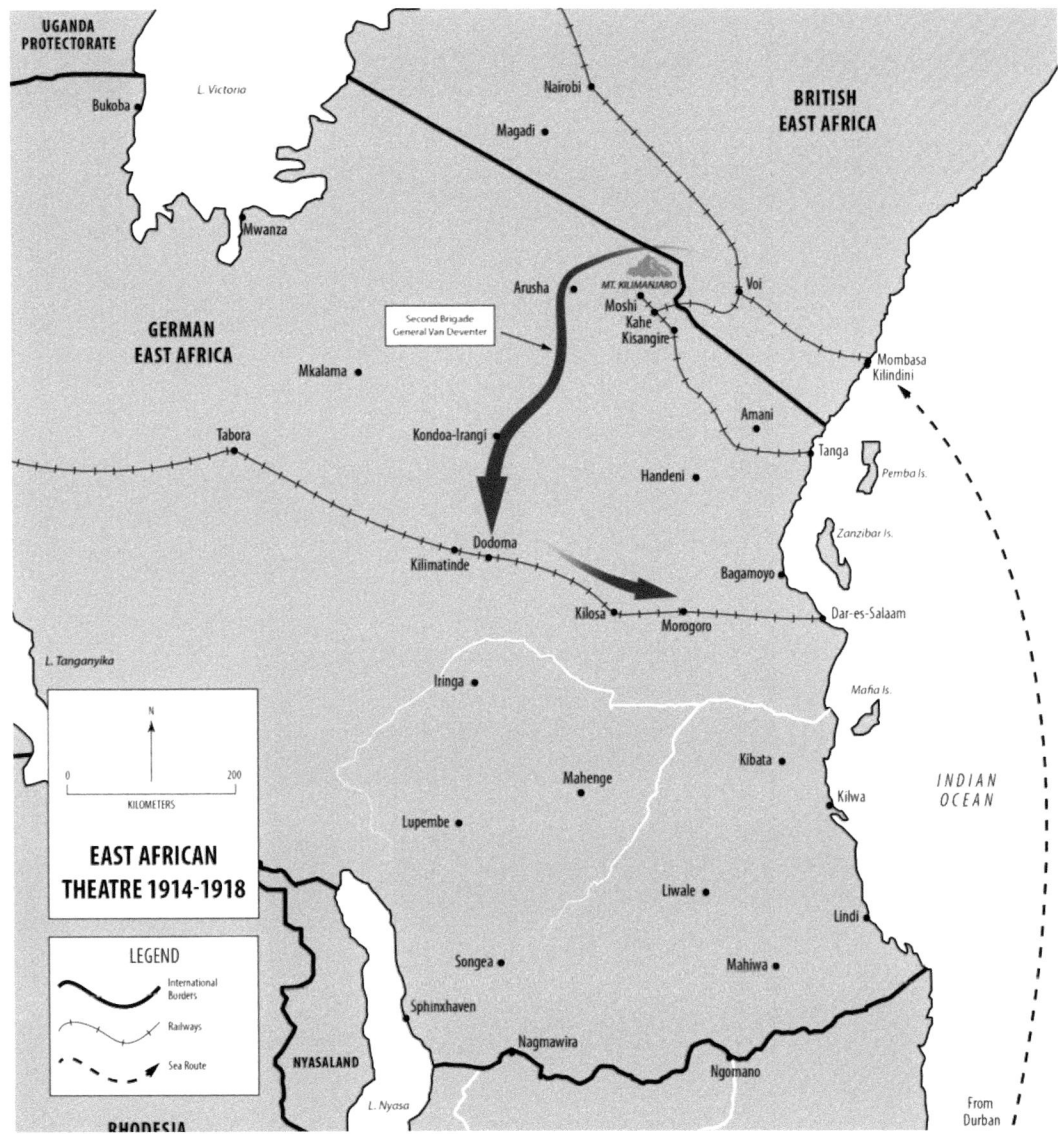

Map of campaign in GEA showing Van Deventer's second brigade's approximate route. Bert landed at Kilindini and was invalided to Nairobi.

This was a terrible period for Bert, because as his mounted regiment progressed their horses began to die from African horse sickness and tsetse fly, and they lost all bar 10 out of 600 or so. Once your mount was dead, you just had to try and keep up on foot. Weakened by poor rations, first dysentery and then malaria took a hold and he was hospitalised on June 17th 1916 at the 14th Casualty Clearing Station, Ufiomi. He contracted malaria and was moved back to 19th Clearing Hospital at New Maschi on June 19th, then to the SA General Hospital at Voi on July 7th and four days later by rail to the SA General Hospital at Muthaiga, near Nairobi, for convalescence, from where he writes home on 27th August: 'I have been sent up to the convalescent home for fever patients. It is about 120 miles from Nairobi in amongst the mountains, at a height of about 9000 feet above sea level… The fever so far has left me completely and am almost my normal self again. The bracing climate with plenty of exercise and good food has done wonders'. His medical record shows he was only fit for active duty for four months!

He was 'discharged to duty' from the convalescent home on September 1919 and with the rest of his contingent, at General Smuts' instigation, was soon returned to SA.

At this time his younger brother, Arthur, had joined up and was a motorcycle despatch rider in E Africa. He must have been very young, 16 or 17; Bert tried to see him but, it appears, was unable to track him down before he returned to Durban. Arthur survived the war unscathed, serving his time all in EA.

The 4th and 8th Horse and 6th, 10th and 11th Infantry in German East Africa were practically destroyed by disease, starvation and exhaustion. The official history states:

The health of the white personnel as well as that of the Indian troops of the Expeditionary Force had [by September 1916] become gravely undermined, and wholesale weeding out of those who, from repeated attacks of fever and dysentery, had practically become physical wrecks, was an urgent necessity… All white troops declared by medical boards to be medically unfit were returned to the country of their origin. Under these arrangements approximately 12,000 white troops left East Africa between the middle of October and the end of December, 1916.

It is clear that Bert was very lucky to be alive and it is certain that it was material in his recovery that he convalesced at the Elementeta Convalescent Home (SA General Hospital) in the Muthega hills of Kenya and was soon returned to SA.

He disembarked from HM Transport *Aragon* back at Durban on Christmas day 1916. He was declared temporarily medically unfit for military service and discharged in Durban on December 30th 1916, although being finally discharged from the army on March 1st the following year, having served one year and 84 days. His discharge document declares his military character to be 'Good', and this was to stand him in good stead for his next adventure.

Chapter Five

THE ROYAL FLYING CORPS IN FRANCE, 1917-1918

Bert arrived in Durban by sea from GEA on December 25 1916 still far from fit. Large camps were set up, and he rested and recovered in one before being finally discharged on March 1st 1917. The SA government was very worried about the political outcry caused by so many men returning so unwell, so large recuperation facilities were built around Durban to help as many as possible to recover before returning to civilian life or war service. Bert, having been declared unfit for further war service, looked around and listened to the recruiting campaign of Major A M Miller DSO from the Royal Flying Corps (RFC) in England.

A small band of South Africans had joined the RFC in 1914 and a steady dribble of volunteers followed as the war progressed. Not the least of these was Arthur Harris, later to become famous as 'Bomber Harris'. Such was the excellence of these young pilots that the British Government requested and received permission from the Union Government to conduct a recruiting campaign for the RFC in South Africa. The task was given to Captain Miller, who arrived in Cape Town in October 1916 to recruit 30 young men to become commissioned officers in the RFC.

Miller was so successful that he finally recruited over 400 young men in the first contingent and 2000 in the second. Bert was in the first; Major Miller set such a high standard that all the first contingent were commissioned and of the second 98.5% passed. He was a great phenomenon in SA, and as he toured round he was greeted by crowds where ever he went. He visited Johannesburg at the time Bert got home from GEA and this is where he was interviewed by Major Miller and accepted as potential RFC officer material.

A Jeppe school friend, N H Anset, was already in the RFC and training in England and wrote to Bert from Lincoln College Oxford on March 9 1917 in glowing terms. His friend from Jeppe and GSW, W A N Niven, had sadly been killed flying in the RFC in France on 28th October 1916. However many other friends of his had joined the RFC, and the offer of a commission and the prospect of flying was exciting. He signed up to go to England as one of 'Major Miller's Boys' as they were called. It is also worth saying that they were motivated by deep patriotic feelings to the Empire and talked about England as the 'motherland' and 'going home'. I enclose, below, a copy of the reference from his former squadron commander 2ILH and 4th SAH, dated 27.3.17. He left for Europe in May from Cape Town.

Many references were written to contacts in England should Bert need any help. One kind note came from Dr Ashe, who had delivered Bert and saved the child's life in the siege of Kimberley:

9.4.1917

Please give him the enclosed and tell him I admire his pluck immensely, and wish him the best of luck over the water.

With kind regards

Yours sincerely

Oliver Ashe.

This sums up what many felt as they said goodbye to Bert and his friends going off once again to war.

Letter to Captain Miller from Captain Cross in support of Bert's application to join the Royal Flying Corps.

He bade goodbye to his family in Benoni and went by train to Cape Town, from Johannesburg, with his fellow recruits to the RFC, I quote his letter:

Cape Town

5.5.1917

My dear Mother and Dad,

We arrived here this afternoon at 4.30. Andrews and I at once proceeded to the Castle where we saw Capt. Miller. Our papers were soon fixed up and we had our final instructions. We are due to embark on the S.S. Nestor, Holt Blue Funnel Line tomorrow morning at 9.30. So I am spending very little in Cape Town. What little I have seen of the place has been quite sufficient for me. What with this half and half population, you do not know where to draw the line. The coloured man to my mind holds more privileges than the white man. He monopolises the trams, pavements and practically everything. They are within their rights, so we were told, and you cannot do anything. We were very fortunate in finding Kathleen Niven. We tried to get in to four different theatres and bioscopes, but they were all full up. In desperation we took a tram ride out to sea point and back again, had tea and motored back to the hospital. Kathleen Niven had to be back by ten. I tried to get in touch with Mr Allan Thompson, Uncles friend, but was unsuccessful.

I had not forgotten old Arthur when I left. I know talking about him would have done us no good. I told Alice at the station that you and Dad were to give him a big kiss and hug from me.

Now dear Mother, I want you to please buck up. I shall be well looked after and Andrews who is with me, seems a decent fellow. Mr Niven introduced me to him, he is the nephew of Sir T. Cullinan. I want you, after things have settled down a bit to go to the Blores for a bit of a holiday. (Ficksburg) As regards those photographs, will you please send one to Mrs Niven and one to Kathleen Niven, Alexandria Hospital, Cape Town.

My address in England will be

Cadet A.O. Lewis-Roberts

Denham Cadet Battalion

C/o Adastral House

Blackfriars

London

So far I have not seen anything of Hudson Evans. Will you remember me kindly to Mrs Hudson Lamb, her sons, the Evans and their friends, explain to them the rush and my inability to see them.

Lots of love hugs and kisses to you both, Alice, Joe and Grannie.

Your loving son

Bert.

Having embarked on the *Nestor* they waited for the other ships to join the convoy being formed to run the gauntlet of German submarines, Bert had time to get another letter off to his mother:

S.S. Nestor

7.5.1917

My darling Mother,

We have embarked on the Nestor, but we have not left nor are likely to leave for a day or two. We seem to be waiting for other boats to complete a convoy.

I met TC Moore, an old friend, on the quay; he has got into the Flying Corps but leaves in another boat the Ceramia. We shall probably land in England at the same time. On board are some fellows I knew at school.

The fellows on the whole appear to be a decent lot. Andrews and I have a two berth first class cabin to ourselves. We are very comfy and ought to have a jolly trip home to England.

I was immensely pleased to get Dad's letter this morning, Captain Miller brought it on board with him. I am sorry he is not coming with us, he is quite a good fellow… When you write again please give me the Panruckes' address also Miss Bennett's… I am well and fit as the proverbial 'fiddle'. Kind regards to Mr Paget. Lots of love and kisses to you Dad, Joe, Alice and Grannie.

Your loving son

Bert.

The convoy sailed on the 15th of May and made steady progress. Due to antisubmarine zig-zagging it took seven days to get to Sierra Leone, where Bert got off the next letter to home:

21.5.1917

My dear Mother,

We have just finished dinner and I am writing this epistle in the drawing room or smoking lounge as it is used. There are a crowd of fellows around the piano making futile attempts at playing a tune. As far as I know there is not a single person on board who can play the piano, so far nobody has come forward to show us how the piano ought to be played.

It is almost a fortnight since we left Cape Town and it seems interminable ages. We have fallen too easily for my liking into the humdrum ship routine.

Andrews and I are up first thing in the morning for physical drill, this as a rule takes half an hour, and does us an immense amount of good. There is always the scramble for the bath rooms, Andrews and I are as a rule fortunate in finishing our tubs long before the bugle sounds for breakfast. I consider myself fortunate I have not felt the least bit sea sick, am as fit as the next man and am enjoying the voyage immensely.

At the commencement of the voyage a sports committee was formed, the ship's doctor surgeon Brown as chairman. He is a man of fifty years, middle height, with a face tanned to almost crimson. He is to my mind the life and soul of the ship, one of those jovial, busy body folk whom one meets at rare intervals: a man who has travelled the world, been through some wonderful experiences, and yet shows remarkable modesty when relating some of those exploits.

The great game at the present is deck tennis; rope quoits are used instead of balls, these are thrown over a net and the usual rules of tennis are observed. My name is down for almost every competition including boxing, cockfighting etc. etc. Partners were drawn for deck tennis.

Wetherby and I have come off best in the finals. Our final game was a truly titanic struggle. In the first set we were beaten 6-4, pulled through the next two 6-5, 6-5.

Dear Mother, please excuse the disjointedness of this missive, it is an almost superhuman task writing amidst the din of a thumping piano. I should have written in my cabin, only that I should be cramped for elbow room.

We are in the tropics and everybody is in shirtsleeves, the moist heat is at times quite trying, but what a tremendous difference it is, travelling in a first class cabin to a stuffy hold in a troop ship as was my lot going up to G.E.A. [German East Africa]

22.5.1917

I hope you have had my letters written at Cape Town. The day before we left Cape Town Andrews and I got the Padre to purchase a camera and films. He was one of the few persons allowed to go ashore. I think it was a quite good investment, I shall now be able to send you some snaps.

We may be stopping at Sierra Leone in a few days, I shall endeavour to get this letter away. No information of the ship's movements or what we see at different stations is allowed. The censor as in G.E. is always to the fore. I have since gathered that on our arrival in England we shall have six weeks training in the Denham Cadets Battalion. After passing the final examination successfully you are given a commission and then proceed to start for the exacting training for the R.F.C.

I ought not to have any difficulty in passing these exams. I feel strangely eager and confident in starting them.

I have met some very decent fellows on this boat, Yates was at school with me, his brother Jack is with him, he won the Military Cross in the night attack on Kondoa Iranji, bringing up ammunition for his platoon. Both brothers held commissions in G.E.A.

Major Macneille, late mayor of Bocksburg is on this boat and is chief medical officer.

I have not seen or heard anything of Mr Centran [?], Moberly, or Hill; they may be on the other boats. I have not found out whether Evans came down to Cape Town to see Captain Miller. It is quite likely we shall all meet at some time or other.

I have written Arthur a long letter and have asked him to write to you regularly. I hope it will not be long before he gets home safely. I want you, after things have settled down a bit to take that holiday down to Mrs Blore [Ficksburg]. The change will do you an immense amount of good, even if it only takes you away from Benoni for a while.

I hope everybody is keeping well.

My darling Mother, I do not want you and Dad to worry over me. I am with good fellows and we look after each other satisfactorily.

Lots of love, hugs and kisses to you all.

Your loving son

Bert.

As Bert and his friends headed for England and the First World War in Europe it is worth reflecting on what was happening in the battlefields of France and in the air above.

Through the war the numbers of pilots increased

> **WORCESTER ARTIST'S GRANDSON.** — The "Johannesburg Star" of May 5th, says: "Mr. A. O. Lewis-Roberts, son of Mr. and Mrs. T. A. Lewis-Roberts, of 37, Ampthill Avenue, Benoni, Transvaal, left for Capetown on Thursday evening, to join the Royal Flying Corps. Mr. Lewis-Roberts is an old Jeppe High School boy, and will be remembered as a famous rifle shot when under 17, also as a keen all-round sportsman when at the School of Mines. He served through the South-West campaign in the 2nd I.L.H., the Rebellion, and in East Africa with the 4th African Horse. With such a fine patriotic record the best wishes of a large circle of friends will closely follow his fourth effort for the Empire." Mr. A. O. Lewis-Roberts is the grandson of the late well-remembered Mr. Albert Gyngell, artist, of Bath road, in this city, and is the eldest son of Mrs. Lewis-Roberts (Alice), eldest daughter of Mr. Gyngell, who went to Africa many years ago. It is possible that Mr. Lewis-Roberts will visit this city, and make acquaintance with his mother's friends in the old homeland.

The Worcestershire Chronicle announces Bert's arrival in England.

dramatically; in 1914 there were about 60 aircraft and 2073 personnel, but by 1918 the numbers had increased to about 4000 combat aircraft and 114,000 personnel, including 5182 pilots. Hence Capt. Miller's mission to South Africa to recruit young pilots.

In April 1917 the British Army, in conjunction with the French High Command, planned a massive attack. The Royal Flying Corps (RFC) supported British operations by giving close air support, aerial reconnaissance and strategic bombing of German targets. Hugh Trenchard, commander of the RFC, was a believer in the offensive use of air power and pushed for operations deep into German-held territory. To fulfil this purpose large numbers of Allied aircraft were assembled over the front line. Sadly the aircraft were, in the main, inferior to the German fighter aircraft. Even more crucially, pilot training was not only poorly organised and patchy, it had to be drastically curtailed to keep squadrons from suffering heavy losses up to strength. Instances are on record of pilots joining the fight with only five hours' flying time; many new pilots lasted just a day or two.

The Battle of Arras began on 9th April 1917. During April 1917 the British lost 245 aircraft with 319 aircrew killed missing or captured. The Germans recorded the loss of 66 aircraft during this time. It became known as 'bloody April'. This period marked the lowest point of the RFC's fortunes. However, in spite of the terrible attrition the Germans did not stop the RFC achieving its prime objectives. The RFC continued to give valuable support the Army throughout the Arras offensive with aerial photography, contact patrolling, reconnaissance and harassing bombing raids. Of particular value was the spotting support for the artillery, which allowed them to achieve superiority throughout the battle.

In the aftermath of this battle, the RFC learned from its mistakes. Advanced generations of fighters (such as the SE5, Sopwith Camel and SPAD SXIII) became available within a month or two. New policies in training and tactical organisation were instituted. The casualties in the air were never again so one-sided and the Germans never again possessed real air superiority for the rest of the war.

The carnage earlier in the war amongst RFC pilots, both in action and during training, shocked many officers; one, Major R R Smith-Barry, was determined to do something to rectify the problem. He wrote a detailed curriculum based on a balanced combination of academic classroom training and dual flight instruction. Philosophically the 'Gosport system', as it became known, was based not on avoiding potentially dangerous manoeuvres but exposing the student to them in a controlled manner, thereby gaining confidence and skill. This system was eventually adopted worldwide.

It was in to this tactical situation that Bert arrived in the summer of 1917; the Gosport system gave him far superior training starting that autumn than he would have received if he had arrived earlier in the war. This timing was fortunate and must have contributed greatly to his chance of survival.

After running the gauntlet of German submarines, which were at the height of their powers in 1917, they arrived safely at Devonport on about June 6th 1917. Nearly a month from Cape Town! The first letter home follows:

Denham Cadet Battalion (Note. Bert never actually got to Denham!)
Adastral House
Blackfriars
London

My dear Mother

We have landed safely after braving the submarines etc.

There is a likelihood of mail leaving for South Africa immediately, so am sending this off.

Andrews and I are tremendously fit and are as brown as berries.

When you write please give me Miss Bennett's full address also Aunt Mabel's.

You must excuse the shortness of this letter, will write a longer letter when we have been fixed up. I hope you are well.

Heaps of love and kisses.
Your loving son Bert

He wrote a letter to Aunt Mabel to let her know he had arrived, and after six weeks' infantry training at the Cadets' Camp in South Farnborough they would start flying training. He laments in the letter:

Our work as far as I can see is going to be exacting and most thorough.

We shall soon be kept hard at work on infantry work. All my cavalry work will have to be forgotten.

His movements are explained in more detail in his next letter home:

14.6.1917

My dear Mother and Dad,

After we had landed at Devonport, we fully expected to go to the Denham Cadet Battalion, instead all (including those who were on the other boats) have been drafted up to Farnborough.

We have been in a bit of a muddle these last few days, but are gradually being sorted out. The country we passed through is beyond description; what little I have seen of England has pleased me very much. Once you get clear of towns, the country is one huge park, split up into gardens, we are in the middle of summer, yet flowers and trees are as fresh and as green as if an eternal spring bloomed. You cannot imagine anything like it in South Africa.

I am afraid camp life is proving a disillusion to some of our fellows; they expect to qualify for commissions straight off the reel, without doing the real hard work. It will not take them long before they get in to the swing of things.

As far as I can see our training is going to be extremely thorough and may last eight months ere we graduate. It rests with each individual whether he is a success or not.

I managed to get a cable off yesterday afternoon. I hope it reaches you soon, as I know how anxious you all are.

We were told after we landed that we had had a narrow shave from a Hun submarine. We did not see the submarine, but got up on deck in time to see the escort the t.p.ds [?] chasing round furiously. On the whole our trip over on the Nestor was a pleasant one. I came off second in the singles deck tennis. Andrews beat me by a game.

Quite a number of us took the oath this morning, I have made out a separate allowance for you.

While waiting for our train at Devonport, I managed to see Mr Moberley; Outram and Hill were busy, but I learnt that they were both well.

I hope you are all well at home. When is Mother going to Mrs Blore's* for her holiday? I wrote dear Arthur a long letter. I hope he is keeping well. I have since found out that we may not go to the Denham Cadet Battalion.

My present address is:
Cadet No. 84451 A.O. Lewis-Roberts
Recruits Depot
Cadet Camp
South Farnborough.
Lots of love and kisses
Your loving son
Bert

*She finally got to the Blores in Ficksburg on 18.10.1917 for a month's stay.

A few days later he wrote to his Aunt Mabel in Dawlish giving more insight in to his RFC training and indeed his delight in the English countryside:

Cadet No 84451
Recruits Depot
Cadet Camp
South Farnborough
19.6.1917

My dear Aunt Mabel,

You cannot imagine how pleased I was to get your two letters. At present we are still in Cadets' uniform, nothing seems definite as to when we leave for Denham, Winchester or Reading. This morning I was placed in a batch of 'Africans,' as we are called here, fellows who had seen active service in G.S.W. and G.E.A. We were paraded before Major Parkin our OC and a Staff Officer; our names were put down on a roll and we were told to hold ourselves in readiness.

If we leave within two or three days I shall be well satisfied. It means we shall be given the opportunity of qualifying for our commissions in a much shorter period than those who have just started their military experiences.

Andrews, being only eighteen and not having seen active service, was not included in our batch. This is most unfortunate as he is straight, and one of the best fellows. Mr Niven introduced him to me the night I left Johannesburg, ever since then we have been together.

Should we proceed to the officers Training Corps I may find myself forced to borrow a small loan, until I get my allowance. Our pay at present is 1/- a day. It was extremely kind of you and Uncle Earnest to suggest it. The food in this camp is really none of the best, and at times Andrews and I are obliged to satisfy the inner man at the canteen with sandwiches, bread and jam. Otherwise my expenses are nil.

I have had to go through the old inoculation and vaccination business again, my arm at present is feeling rather sore. I think it a very excellent idea that I should have one permanent address [with you]. Moving about from place to place I may experience difficulty in getting papers and parcels.

Last Saturday I went for a long stroll into the country and

enjoyed myself thoroughly. Everything seemed so beautifully green, fields, parks and meadows. I can compare nothing to it in South Africa, the country must be a veritable Paradise during spring.

Up to the present there seems little hope of any leave being granted, but we are bound to have it sooner or later, and I shall let you know when it does come. I hope you and Uncle Earnest are keeping well.

*Lots of love
Your loving nephew
Bert.*

Cadets at the No1 School of Military Aeronautics, Reading.

The No. 1 School of Military Aeronautics was established in buildings commandeered from Reading University in 1915, primarily as an instructor training college, but expanded the following year to include cadets. The training included the theory of flight, gunnery, map reading and engineering. A small airfield was added at Coley Park nearby. Technical trades were split off from the flight school. The instructors were mainly time served pilots from the front, very little different in age to the students! Bert moved there in June 1917 as this next letter describes:

*Cadet Wing RFC
Reading
26.6.1917*

*My Dear Aunt Mabel,
I had your letter just before I left for Reading. We are in tents and as far as I have seen, we shall be much better off than we were at our last camp. Our course at the military school of aeronautics is supposed to last six weeks. All our time, as you can imagine, will have to be devoted to our work.*

*This afternoon we were measured for our new rigout. What funds I have in hand are not quite sufficient to see me through until I obtain my allowance. Could I please borrow a loan of £3? Mother promised to send me a few pounds, but at present we have had no South African mail.
I hope you and Uncle Earnest are keeping well. We are having lovely weather*

*Lots of love
Bert*

5.7.1917

I received you registered letter with the £3 yesterday. I really do not know how to thank you for this loan. We were measured a few days ago by military tailors, and this afternoon we are to have our joy rags tried on.

At present we are having an intensely busy time. We are to be examined this Saturday on several important subjects, Rigging, Theory of Flight, Bombs and Instruments. I have had no letters from home except from Uncle Ted and Alice and I am beginning to think that some have gone astray. I have written to mother to direct all her mail to you and you could send them on to me. I shall be moving from place to place in the future... Bert

26.7.1917. The last fortnight, fellows in our course have been simply rushed off their legs as regards work. Last Saturday we finished off 'Engines'. The papers could not have been called difficult, and I think most of us have done well. The instructors are pleased with us; they say our course is the best they have had for some considerable time. Tomorrow we are being examined in Signalling, the next day Machine Guns, and on Saturday Artillery Obs. Our course is supposed to finish this week, and then we shall know whether we have qualified for commissions. I have put in for seven days leave, but think my chances of getting it are small. We may be drafted straight to various flying schools, but in any case we are bound to get leave sometime sooner or later. Up to the present I have had only one mail from S Africa and that dated 21st May.

*I will let you know as soon as possible when we get our leave. I have had my uniform from the tailors, and when in it feel uncomfortable. I shall have to get accustomed to tight fitting tunics.
Bert*

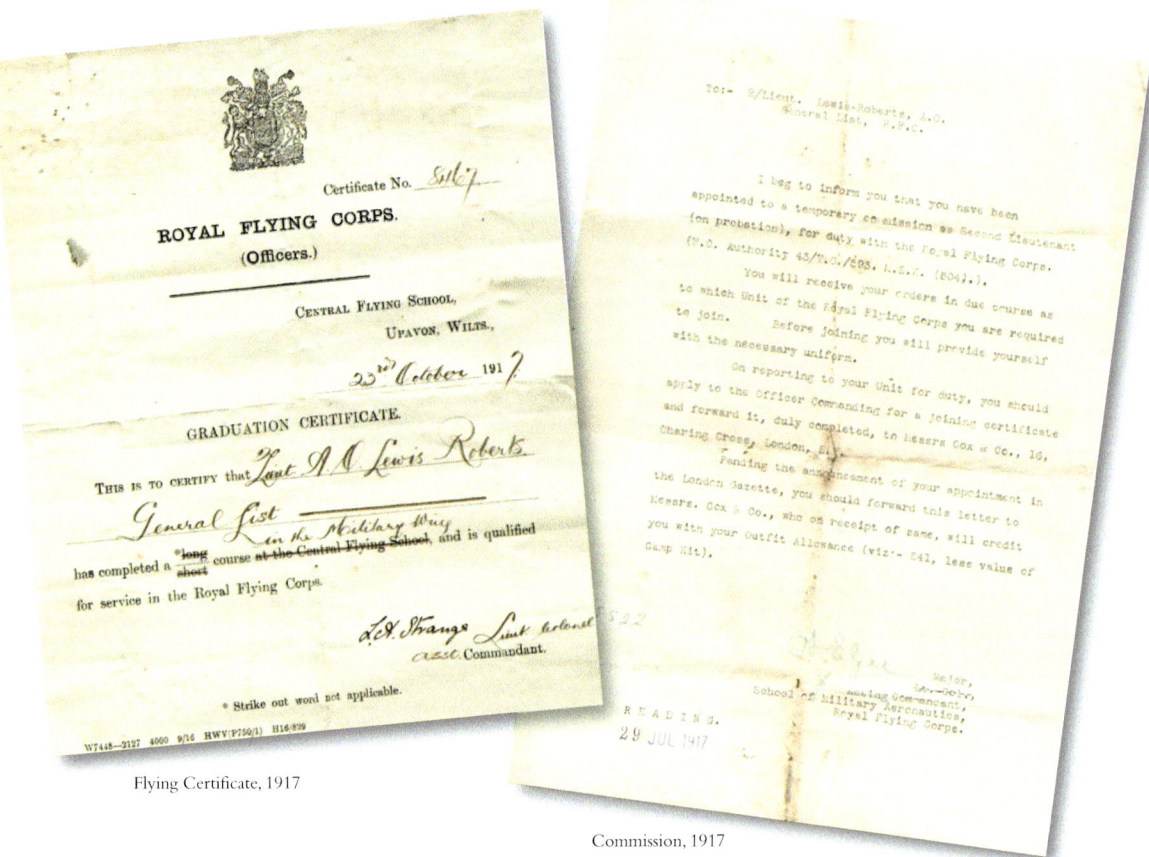

Flying Certificate, 1917

Commission, 1917

48 Reserve Squadron
Royal Flying Corps
Waddington, Lincoln
1.8.1917

My Dear Aunt Mabel

I had your letter early yesterday morning just as we were leaving Reading. I was very pleased to get it. While finishing off our final exam on Artillery Obs. Last Saturday, I learned that I had qualified for a commission, and was expected to put up my 'pips' immediately.

The next day I had to interview the adjutant at headquarters, and he gave me my orders as to which squadron I had to do my flying. I have been very fortunate in having some of my best pals with me. Four of them are in the same flight and squadron as I am in. The whole South African batch has been split up; fellows have been drafted to flying squadrons all over the country, even to the north of Scotland.

We arrived at this place yesterday afternoon, and had to get fixed up ourselves. No officer, OC or adjutant had the common decency to show us to our quarters or to welcome us into the mess room.

This however worried us very little, as it showed us with what type of men we had to deal.

The weather these last few days has been exceptional, one continual drizzle. It reminds me of the rainy seasons we had in E Africa. Accordingly no flying has been done. We shall have to wait for fine weather before anything can be attempted.

Our training in this squadron is only preliminary. After going up several times with an instructor, and feeling confident, we shall be told to fly the machine ourselves, we may be only ten days in this place before we are drafted to another squadron for higher training.

I have, so far, heard nothing about my leave, but am hoping that it will not be long before we get it.

I would have written earlier but as you know we have had very little time to ourselves… Bert

Newly-commissioned portrait

19.8.1917

I am getting on rather well with my flying, and were it not for the bad weather we have been having lately, I should have finished my 'solo'. As soon as I have finished my 'solo' I am entitled to 48 hours' leave. But am afraid that when I do get it, it will be insufficient to see you in Dawlish.

When we have finished the day's work the time hangs heavily. I have been in to Lincoln several times with Yates and Liddell and have found it a very sleepy old town. The cathedral is the only sight worth seeing. We spend most of our time taking long strolls in the country …Bert

P.S. Have had no mails from S. Africa yet.

According to Bert's log book he made his first flight with No 48 training squadron at 10.30am on 6th August 1917. The flight lasted five minutes and he was a passenger, with Captain Brooks as pilot. The machine was a Maurice Farman MF 11, No 2002, commonly known as the 'shorthorn' after its reduced length of front skid designed to stop it upending on the ground. It was, by all accounts, a poor plane to start on as it was very underpowered and had a very high drag factor, being a pusher, with a profusion of wires. In consequence, its stall speed was only about 5 mph under its top speed. It is said that if the pilot stood up the drag would stall the plane. Few pilots had a good word to say about it - in fact Bert crashed on his first solo landing. The first flight was critical, as under the Gosport system instructors were required to note the pupil's reaction and some unsuitable candidates were withdrawn at this stage.

It is clear from his logbook that he passed this test and went forward to a programme of dual control flying in the 'Longhorn', mostly short flights round the aerodrome and never at more than 1000ft. altitude, with many landings, in fact it was mainly take-offs and landings. In one 40-minute flight he did six landings!

After only a week he was ready to go solo. On August 28th 1917 at 7.05 am he did a five-minute flight, but sadly he smashed the undercarriage on landing machine No B2004. He was no doubt shaken, but unhurt. Three days later he had further dual control practice, making three more landings successfully. It should be noted it is the same aeroplane which had been repaired in three days. I expect the RFC riggers were quite used to damaged undercarriages!

He immediately went solo again, but this time smashed the right wing extension on landing after a 10-minute flight. He ran into another plane stuck in the middle of the airfield. Again B2004 was repaired and five days later, he went solo successfully, making eight landings without mishap.

At the end of August 1917 Bert recorded a total time in the air of 9 hours and 5 minutes, including 2 hours and 25 minutes solo. Thus he achieved his solo status and ended his time with No 48 Training Squadron.

He wrote one more short note to Aunt Mabel about going solo. His letter describing his crashes is interesting:

1.9.1917

A few days ago I took my machine up and made a bad landing, on going up in another I made a good landing, but the impetus of landing my machine carried me into another that had stuck in the middle of the aerodrome. I smashed my right extension and damaged the planes of the other machine, but was unhurt myself. These accidents were unfortunate as I have every confidence of myself while in the air, and should have been more careful when choosing my landing ground.

Last Thursday evening I went up again, did four landings and remained aloft for thirty-five minutes and eventually came down on account of rain and air 'bumps'. Friday afternoon was an ideal afternoon for flying. I went up for a joy ride round the country for an hour and enjoyed myself. Yates is just about to finish his solo and we are both hoping to get sent to an advanced squadron for higher instruction. The weather at present is very windy and chilly. Bert

Bert was progressing relatively quickly through his basic training. It was said that horsemen made good pilots as they had sensitive 'hands,' and Bert had of course come straight from a cavalry regiment.

With a total flying time of 9 hours 5 minutes, of which 2 hours 25 minutes was solo, he had completed his basic flying with 48 Training Squadron. The next move was to 200 Depot Squadron for more advanced flying training using the DH1 aeroplane. A better aeroplane than the longhorn, still a pusher, but with considerably more horsepower, the 1A variant had a 120hp Beardmore engine. It was not widely used in combat before relegation to home defence and training; only about 100 were made, as it was soon superseded. There being almost no communication between instructor and trainee, most learning was done by resting the trainee's hands and feet on the controls to feel what the instructor was doing. Later a huge advance was made by developing a speaking tube between pupil and instructor. Until then communication was by signals or physical contact with anything to hand, a screwdriver or spanner for example!

Bert records more flying episodes at 200 Depot Squadron:

17.9.1917

I received your parcel and cake this afternoon and cannot tell you how pleased I was at this surprise packet.

I have been doing rather well with my flying. I finished my ten hours solo this morning. Yesterday I went for my first cross country flight to Waddington. I could not follow the map given to me very much, and steered my course entirely by compass.

This morning I went up and the weather was extremely windy and bumpy. When I was up at about 3000ft. I practiced a few 'Immelman' turns, nose-diving and side slipping. I came down in the orthodox manner, but when just off the ground flattened out too soon. The machine stuck its nose into the ground and hung there with its tail high up in the air. The nacelle and wings were slightly damaged, and on the whole I was extremely fortunate.

Poor Yates has been sent to the military hospital in Sheffield with bad malaria, so am on my lonesome… Bert

As can be seen from Bert's letters, he was very dependent on the 'mail' for his morale. Post from South Africa could take up to five months and more to find him. Letters home were less time consuming, although they had to go through the censor and run the submarine gauntlet; indeed water-damaged letters were not unknown. I enclose the envelope of a letter from Kathleen Niven's father, sent from Johannesburg on 14th September 1917. It shows the last postmark of 27nd January 1918 from Gainsborough, having gone through at least six forwardings and the blue crayon of the censor. It was even more difficult for mail from and to Bert's brother Arthur, who was still in Dar-es-Salaam; about half the letter was taken up with postage issues! Things improved when Bert organised all letters to be channelled through Aunt Mabel, as she would have a better chance of knowing where he was. Even so the post was very slow, but amazingly persistent, because the forces realised the importance of 'letters from home' in influencing morale. Nothing has changed to this day.

RIDING THE WIND - THE LIFE OF A. O. LEWIS-ROBERTS, 1896-1966

The Post Office went to great pains to follow service men as they moved from unit to unit. It is truly remarkable that some of the letters were forwarded more than eight times!

Bert's log book records two flights on 5th and 7th Sept in his DH1, which he described as 'Joy Rides'. An unwise description, as the log book had to be signed off by the flight commander and adjutant weekly; the description 'joy ride' was crossed out by the flight commander and replaced by the description 'Dual Instruction'. Never again was the description 'joy ride' used in any of Bert's many log books!

One last letter from Bert to Aunt Mabel describing more of his training with 200 Depot Squadron, Retford:

10.10.1917

My Dear Aunt Mabel

I had your letter this morning and am replying to it immediately.

I thoroughly enjoyed reading the book you sent me. Yates has read the book too, and laughed heartily over it.

The cold weather has started in already, as far as I can see. A few mornings ago I was up for early flying and found the water in my wash basin frozen an inch thick. We are still in tents and what with the rain, and cold winds, we find it rather uncomfortable. This is not to last much longer as we have been told that we shall move into Ranby Hall very shortly.

I have not been flying much lately as I have had to put in more time with Machine Guns. Nevertheless I have gone up for short spells, when it has been very windy bumpy and misty.

With my thick leather coat and flying boots on together with the excitement I always manage to keep fairly warm.

In another week or two I shall start my night flying – this should prove most interesting.

I have had several letters from home and from Uncle Ted. The winter has evidently been a severe one out in South Africa… Bert

Throughout September and early October Bert continued to confidently fly solo and was allowed to step up to an operational type, the FE 2b. This was still a pusher, powered mainly by a 120HP or 160HP Beardmore engine. Built by the Royal Aircraft Factory and introduced in 1914, 1,939 were built by 1918. In the fighter/reconnaissance role it became obsolete by April 1917 but was still liked by its crews for its strength and its good flight characteristics. The FE2b's use gradually developed into a light tactical night bomber, and it was in this role that Bert became operational when he completed his training.

Meanwhile he moved to 33rd Squadron at Kirton Lindsey on 18th October for bombing and night flying training in the FE2b. For instance on 27th October he did six night landings at Scampton solo and on November 4th three night landings and bombing from 500ft, 1000ft and 2000ft. In a letter of 22.10.1917 he relates experiences with 33rd Squadron to Aunt Mabel:

I have been on the move again, transferred to this Home Defence flight for instruction in night flying and 'Zepp strafing'.

I am speedily being turned into a night owl. All our work at this place is done at night. We never go to bed before 12pm, and if there is anything on as was the case the previous night, it is often in the early hours of morning that we woo sweet slumber. I am in a room in a hut where there is a fire going all day so am quite comfortable.

The day before I left Retford I had five letters from home and very pleased I was to get them.

The next day we were moving out of tents into Ranby Hall and I had all my kit unpacked in my room when an order came that I had to fly a machine over to this place and that my kit would be sent on. This was late in the afternoon and by the time I had my engine started it was after 5.30pm and almost dark, with a heavy ground mist. I got up alright and when about halfway to this place I had engine trouble. Having sufficient height and assisted somewhat by the engine I managed to return to Retford safely. Soon after another order came along that I had to go up as passenger with a night pilot as soon as he arrived from Gainsborough. The pilot arrived about 11.30pm and it was after 12.00 before we got away.

Night flying is most interesting and highly exciting as you can imagine.

I hope to be given some leave after I have finished my six night landings. I shall inform you as to when it comes along… Bert

After only 13 days with 33 Squadron, Bert moved again on 31st October to A Flight of 51 Training Squadron at Mattishall, Norfolk. This squadron specialised in training newly-commissioned pilots in night flying and acted in a home defence roll. As a matter of interest Arthur 'Bomber' Harris had been a flight commander here until 18th June. Harris, as a trumpeter in the Rhodesian Regiment, and Bert, as a trooper in 2 ILH, both took part in the German SW Africa campaign of 1914-1915.

Again a charming letter of November 1st 1917 to Aunt Mabel tells us the story:

Flight
51 Squadron
Mattishall
Norfolk

I had to leave Kirton Lindsey very suddenly for this squadron - advanced night flying. I finish off my training here and I do not think it will be long before I am drafted overseas. As soon as I have finished my long night reconnaissance I am entitled to six days' oversees leave, and the Major says he will see that I get it.

Five of us were travelling all the night before reaching London at 3 o'clock in the morning, put up at the Queen Marys Club for Officers, had an early breakfast catching the train for this place.

We are about ten miles from Norwich and out in the country, and have comfortable quarters.

I was up for two and a half hours last night bombing with an observer. It was brilliant moonlight and it was simply gorgeous flitting from place to place – the countryside bathed in a silvery, sheeny atmosphere.

Not having had any sleep for thirty-six hours it was not long before I went to bed. I slept solidly till 12.30 this morning…
Bert.

17.11.1917
51 Squadron
Mattishall

I must thank you so much for letter and parcel of cake. I took it in to the mess and we all enjoyed it with our afternoon tea.

I have not been able to do much night flying lately; thick mists come up in the afternoons and nights. Testing a 'strafing' machine at fourteen thousand feet the other afternoon, I had a race against time coming down – and was caught in the fog. Luckily having taken my bearings, I managed to get into the aerodrome and land.

I have had several letters from home lately and everyone is keeping well - Bert

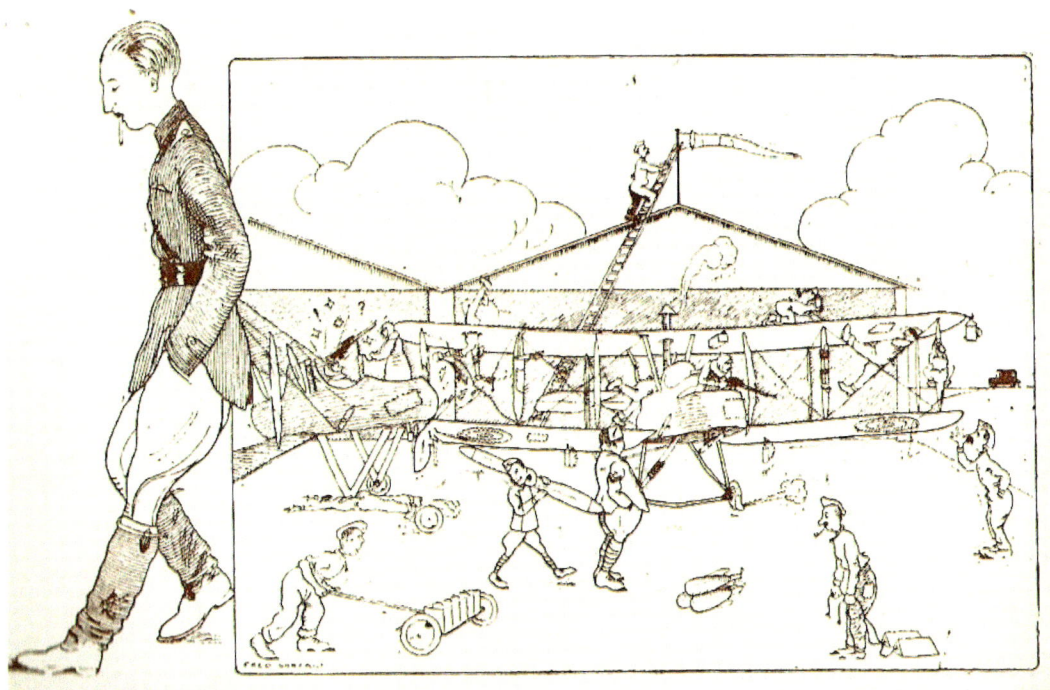

51 Squadron Christmas card

1.12.1917

I hope you will pardon me for not writing lately. It has not been an overdose of duty - what with the present 'dud' weather we have not been able to do any flying at all… I shall probably get the 'push' from this place very shortly. I am waiting patiently for a respectable night to finish off my bombing and reconnaissance. I shall then be able to have my leave… Bert

He moved to B flight 51 Squadron at Lydd St Mary, Lincolnshire, on 3rd December for further night bombing and reconnaissance. On the 5th he had another crash landing, damaging the undercarriage of his FE2b while flying solo. He again moved on to 33rd Squadron on 1.1.1918 at Kirton Lindsey. Having done 68 hours and 20 minutes solo flying, of which 10 hours and 10 minutes were at night, flying training was over and he left Kirton Lindsey.

Flying training had taken five months after theoretical and military instruction. It seems pretty thorough after the training earlier in the war when a pilot might have been thrown into action on an unfamiliar machine with only five hours' solo flying.

Bert was now due some leave, which he got, with little warning, over Christmas. He sent the telegram below to Aunt Mabel warning of his impending arrival and set off on a long rail journey to Dawlish for Christmas. It must have been a joyous reunion and a very special Christmas present.

B Flight, 33 Squadron RFC,
Kirton Lindsey,
Lincs.
30.12.1917

Reaching York at 6 pm Friday night, I reported to the Northern Wing and was posted to this squadron.

Stevenson, an old friend of mine, and I stopped the night at York and left the next morning for Gainsborough. There I was indeed lucky finding Yates at the headquarters mess. The adjutant seemed pleased to see me – this was the squadron I was in before I left for 51.

Stevenson and I spent the night at the mess and after interviewing the C.O. the next morning were posted to different flights.

At this station I am classed as an operation pilot, a stand by for 'Zepps'. I do not know how long I shall stop here – many of my friends are about to cross the water for France. So things are rather uncertain. I sincerely hope my visit has not made you feel nervous as regards myself. You must never feel worried, as I am able to look after myself and never as a rule inclined to be foolhardy.

Yates is at present waiting to be sent over to Egypt for his flying. He is very keen to take it up again and naturally wants his wings… Bert

Bert had many other letters from both South Africa and England during this first six months. Other than family,

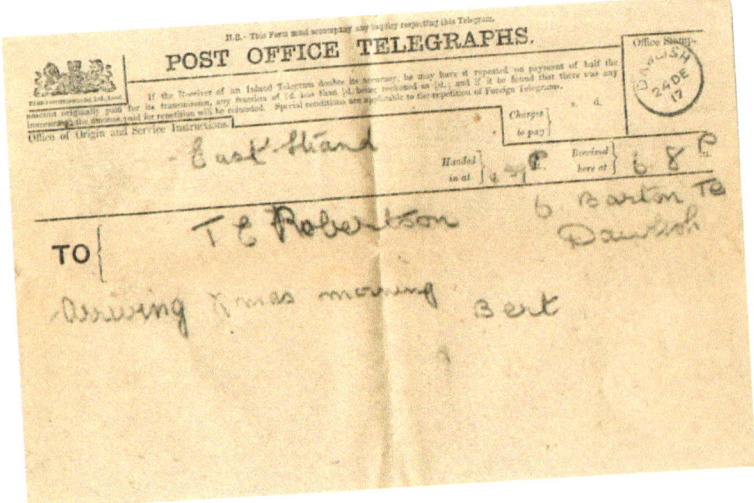

Telegram to Aunt Mabel warning her of Christmas Day arrival at Dawlish.

many, if not all, were from girls who were former school friends from Jeppe High School; others were from the parents of school friends. Some of course are untraceable for me, such as letters signed by 'Winky', Hilda Curties, Babs Kinkead and Doreen Jones. But there was extensive correspondence with the Niven Family from Johannesburg.

Kathleen Niven and her mother were avid letter writers who wrote many letters to Bert. Kathleen was a nurse; during the GSW campaign she was on the hospital ship *Ebani*, but firstly at Cape Town Hospital and then in the South African General Hospital in Dar-es-Salaam. Kathleen also knew Bert's Brother Arthur in East Africa, where he spent most of the war. Arthur was very upset because, not being commissioned, he was not allowed into the nurses' mess. The rules, enforced by the matron, were very strict and they only ever went out in a groups. Her letters gave a particularly charming insight into the life and work of a nurse (they were known as 'bluebirds' because of their blue uniforms); the main problems were malaria and dysentery. After initial hospital treatment, most were sent 'South' to SA.

One sad death Kathleen recorded was their own former headmaster of Jeppe High, Mr Payne. He could not bear to see his former students 'doing their bit,' as he said, without doing the same; as a rather mature officer, he paid the ultimate price by dying of malaria. He was much loved by students and staff alike and was buried at Kilwa.

Kathleen kept up a stream of delightful correspondence to Bert always signed, 'Love and best wishes, from, your pal, Kathleen.' Perhaps they felt particular affinity because Kathleen's 22-year-old brother, William, (second lieutenant W A N Niven) had been killed in action in France on 28th October 1916 with the Royal Flying Corps. He went through school with Bert and the German SW campaign. He is buried at Habarcq Cemetery in France.

Notice of Allan Payne's Death in East Africa.
He was Bert's much loved headmaster at Jeppes School.

83 Squadron badge

Another school friend who kept in touch was Catherine Bennett; she moved to England with her stepmother, who became a nurse in France while Catherine worked in the WRNS at Harwich. She said that after the war she would farm in Kenya, but it is not clear whether she fulfilled her dream or not.

The family of course were avid correspondents, including Mother and Father, sisters Alice and Joe, Uncle Ted ('AEG' the artist) and Arthur. He spent the whole war as an NCO in East Africa mostly in Nairobi and often, it appears, on a motor bike.

Bert, now on the active list, was posted to No. 83 Squadron at Narborough on 21st January 1918. He spent the rest of the war flying with this squadron in France. No 83 Squadron was formed at Montrose, Scotland, on 7th January 1917. Equipped with FE2bs, it engaged mainly in night bombing and reconnaissance missions. They crossed to St. Omer, France with Bert in Feb/March 1918. The squadron badge is a red deer antler with six points commemorating an occasion in the first World War when six DFCs were awarded for one mission by three aircraft during the night of 14th/15th June 1918. Bert piloted one of these aircraft with his faithful observer/gunner, Lieut. Lohmeyer.

The spring of 1918 became a crucial time on the Western Front. The Germans realised that their only remaining chance of victory lay in defeating the Allies before the Americans added overwhelming power in terms of materiel and manpower to the Allied cause. They planned a series of attacks along the Western Front, starting on 21st March 1918, the 'Spring Offensive'. They also had a temporary advantage; because of the Russian surrender, nearly 50 divisions were freed to be moved west.

It was into this maelstrom that Bert and his squadron landed on the 3rd of March 1918 to give vital tactical support to the British Army, which was under extreme pressure. Sadly, almost immediately he was ordered to hospital, in France, with tonsillitis. I pick up his story using his own account of happenings from his letters. He was given embarkation leave, which he again took with Aunt Mabel in Dawlish.

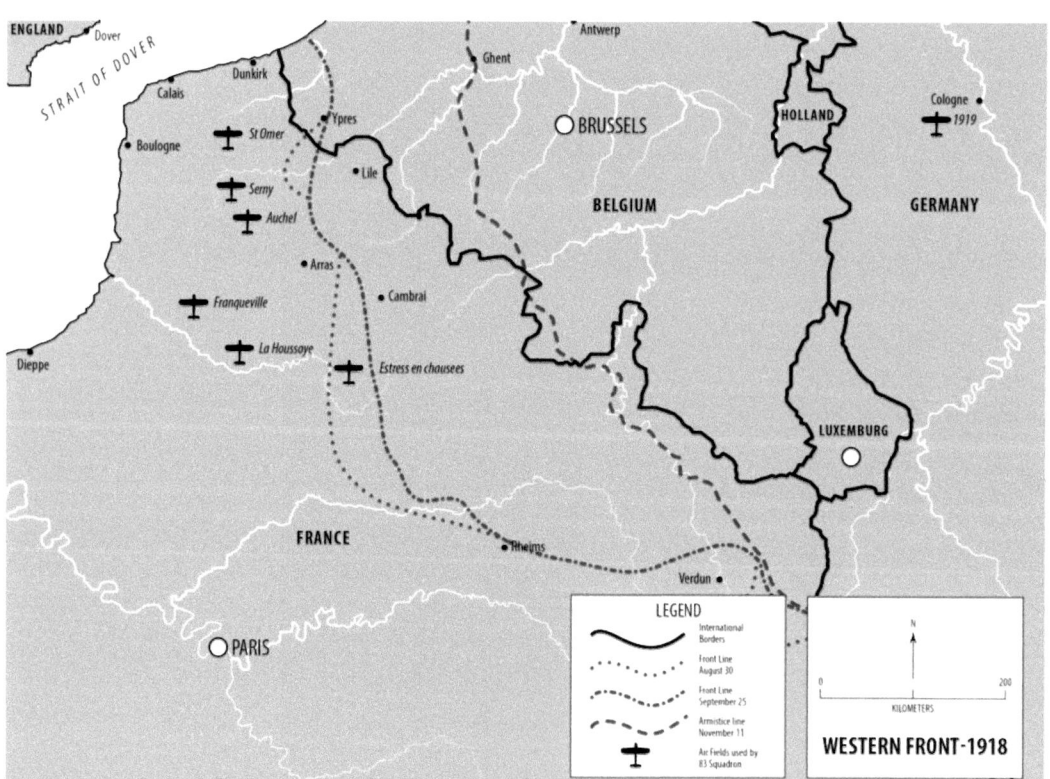

Map of battlefields of France showing airfields used by Bert's squadron, the front line when he came to the front and how it moved until the armistice.

22.1.1918

My dear Aunt Mabel

After leaving Dawlish that night, I met Knuckey [?] on the train and we got in to Paddington at 3.30 am. After reporting at the Horse Guards Parade, Whitehall we were sent to another Head Quarters in Masons Yard. In that place we could find out nothing definite, excepting that we had to report to Narborough. We reached this place rather late in the afternoon.

Our machines have not arrived, and as far as I can make out the squadron is only just being made up, so by the time our machines arrive and everything is put 'ship straight', it will be well on into February before we leave.

There are three other training squadrons here, and about seventy officers training. We all mess together, but have different anterooms. My crowd have the use of the staff anteroom. While I was in town, I had my photograph taken at Lanffier's, 34-36 Oxford St, the place was recommended me by one of our fellows. The proofs will be sent on to you in about four days' time, a full length one and another one head and shoulders. I paid £2-10 in advance. When proofs arrive, send them on and tell me which you like best.

I am writing this in a very noisy anteroom… Bert

1.2.1918

Narborough

took my observer up last night. The moon had not risen and to make flying uncomfortable there was a thick ground mist. We remained aloft for some time, did not see anything, picked up our flares after some difficulty and landed… Bert

15.2.1918

Narborough

I am still alive and doing well. This last week I have been having a very busy time. I went over to Norwich and flew back my service machine. Everybody in our flight is working at top speed getting the machines serviceable. Although we do not fly much during the day we are always up at night when the weather is favourable. I went up a few nights ago when the conditions were far from being enjoyable, plenty of wind and clouds.

Full-length commissioning photograph

Although we are working hard we find time for the occasional game of rugger. I have been picked for the station fifteen and have played in several matches.

I have got to be careful with my knee and have it well bandaged when playing. A good hard game of rugger puts one in fine fettle, and although one may feel stiff and sore for a few days, it helps considerably towards fitness…

I will have to close, Macrae my flight commander wants me to take up an observer for machine gun practice. It is a beautiful moonlight night.

Bert with his rugby team (back row on the left).

2.3.1918

Narborough

I have been on the move again, and this accounts for me not having written.

Last week I flew the OC, Major Leverson-Gower to France, landing at Lympne (near Folkestone) and then St. Omer. We spent a couple of days at a night flying squadron near Auchelle, inspecting their machines. Altogether I spent a most interesting time, I got back early Thursday.

The photos from Lanffier have arrived. I have enclosed slips in each for various people… the others to Mother and she can distribute them as she pleases.

We leave tomorrow morning at 8-00pm for France. Flying weather permitting. I have got to lead the first formation, as I am supposed to know the way. I managed to get in to town last night and bought several things this morning. I have only just got back tonight.

As far as I can make out we shall be working on a part of the line south of Ypres.

P.S. Could you kindly send a full length photo to Miss Bennett, 6 Grey Coat Gardens, Westminster.

83 Squadron

RFC

BEF

10.3.1918

The Squadron left Narborough early last week. I was the first to take off and led my formation of seven machines safely down to Lympne, without any forced landings. We all had lunch there and were soon off again, crossing the Channel and reaching our destination safely.

We were to have left the next morning for our own HQ. The others managed to get away, but had to go into hospital with a bad throat. It had been bothering me for some time, and instead of improving grew worse. My flight commander made me see a doctor and he ordered me to hospital without delay. I do not think it will be long before I shall be allowed to get back to the squadron.

Nurses and doctors in this place have been very kind to me. The weather although inclined to be hazy as had plenty of sunshine. Spring is not far off, trees and plants are shooting out buds and the birds are beginning to chirp and sing… Bert

B.E.F.

26.3.1918

My throat has been cured and I am feeling pretty fit. I hope to get out tomorrow morning when I shall see the O.C. of the place I have got to report to, and get him to send me to my squadron.

Two fellows who managed to get away paid me a visit and they told me some very interesting news. Our squadron has started work in real earnest, and every fine night have been very busy.

The Bosch's push★ seems to be something on an unprecedented scale, the impression given is that this business will show forth some very decisive results.

There is a scarcity of news in this place, we get the English papers thirty-six hours after they have been published, but stirring tales have come through of our heroic resistance, showing that the Bosch has not had things all in his favour. I have no doubt whatever that we shall be able to hold our own.

If I get sent to another squadron, I shall write and inform you without delay… Bert.

★He is clearly referring to the German spring offensive referred to earlier, starting on 21st March 1918. He now has quite a struggle to get back to his friends in 83 Squadron.

YMCA Officers Rest Rooms,
83 Squadron
B.E.F.
6-4-1918

I received your two letters which were sent on from the squadron, and was very pleased to have them.

After leaving hospital I thought there would be no difficulty in getting back to the squadron, and refused very kindly an offer of going to a convalescence home in the South of France, at Monte Carlo or Nice. But I was very much mistaken, for I have been here about ten days and have not been posted.

The Pool is a most uncomfortable and miserable place, there is no mess, our huts are broken down shacks, and we have to walk into town, a distance of about three kilos.

I have phoned and written to our O.C. and Adjutant about getting me back – I know they are doing their best, but there seems to be a general mess up at H.Q. who have charge of all the postings.

Although I am naturally keen on getting back to work I try to look at things 'philosophically', but sometimes fail. I am fit and well… Bert.

I find Bert's enthusiasm and loyalty very touching.

Convalescing in the South of France was not for him; he wanted to get back to the fight, although he knew things are getting rather 'hot' as he would have said. It says a lot about his character, always steadfast and loyal. However, things start to happen as we can see from the next letter, to his Uncle Ernest in Dawlish.

Officers' Rest Rooms
18-4-1918

I have been busy again making enquiries at this end and at our own squadron. I managed to get on the phone to our own Adjutant. He said that he had applied for me through the wing to HQ, that they had sent three others in my place. The squadron of course is full up, and there will now be no opportunity to get back to my own crowd. It is very disappointing after being told that the OC is keen on getting me back. The impression given is that you are not wanted.

I shall do no more worrying but allow the matter to run its own course. My stay in the Pool is proving very expensive, no matter how economical I am – The French know how to charge.

At the Pool we are left entirely to ourselves – we get up at about ten in the morning, have a meal of fried eggs and chips with coffee at a French peasant's cottage at 11.30. If nothing comes through the majority of us walk into the town and spend our time in the reading room of this YMCA club until 7-30 when we have supper at a restaurant. We spend the remainder of the evening at the Club and then stroll back to our huts. Each day is but a repetition, the life begins to pall, becomes deadly monotonous especially at a time like this when you think every man must be doing something.

I had a letter from one of the fellows in the squadron. Macrae, my flight commander, went up in the day taking his flight sergeant. Coming in to land he hit a telegraph pole, crashed, and both were killed.

19th I could not finish this letter, a tender called and I had to go to the Pool immediately. There I found my bag packed – we were moving to another pool.

This place is out in the country, beautiful surroundings, but what with the present cold snap of rainy weather I find it uncomfortable under canvas. I was fortunate in getting a billet, as all my camp kit is still at the squadron. All this morning we were busy at the range with machine guns and clay pigeon shooting.

There are two other South Africans here, one of whom I played against at cricket at Pretoria, and we get on well together.

I hope your brothers have come through this business safely. A number of South Africans in the Division have been posted as missing. I heard that they had fought magnificently… Bert

83 Squadron
R.A.F [note, the RAF started on 1-4-1918]
22-4-1918

Yesterday morning I had the surprise of my life when on going in to the mess-tent I found I had been posted to 83.

The tender did not arrive until tea time, I reached our quarters at dusk and reported to the OC. He seemed pleased to see me.

I was glad to see the other fellows, although I have been away from them for such a long time, and felt rather out of it, especially as some of them had done about eighteen shows. I had my first flip this afternoon to see the surrounding country. I shall have to practise a few night landings, and then I hope to be allowed to do something.

We are close enough to hear and see the work of the guns, and some of their bombardments are very lively.

I was posted to 'A' Flight, Capt. Scott's and would have like to have gone to my old 'B' Flight but beggars can't be choosers. Each flight has its own mess, and they are all very comfortable, also we cannot complain of our quarters.

Bobby Greathead who was with me at School of Mines, is with me in the same flight and is keeping very fit.

I had a letter from Arthur today and he sends his love to you and Aunt Mabel. I wish he could manage to get home from East Africa; he has had several attacks of fever, and it is high time he was out of the country… .Bert.

Bert with his FE2b, 'Spilikins', and Lohmeyer.

This page from Bert's log book shows the start of his active flying from his arrival back from the Pool and hospital on 22nd April. He started bombing operations in a new FE2b against Peronne on May 12th 1918. He was flying at night, depending on the moon, the last flight at 2.20 am on that night. He now enters into a phase of intensive action, with many casualties, until, in the end, he was the oldest flight commander and only three members of the original squadron were left. His letters reflect this activity in a very modest way.

83 Squadron
R.A.F.
B.E.F.
1-5-1918

Dear Mother and Dad

I have got in to the swing of things again, have been up several times, but have not done a show yet. The weather for the last week has been atrocious, rain and thick mist, the sun only showing itself at rare intervals.

Nevertheless, the weather has not kept us indoors. Up till a day ago we could always get horses for riding from one of the remount depots. I cannot tell you how much I enjoy a good hard canter after not having ridden for such a long time. There were several jumps, hurdles, in the clearing near the aerodrome, and I was not satisfied until I had tried my horse at them (one of the smaller ones). I was greatly delighted that he did not buck away but took them in good style.

There is a tennis court next to our quarters, and we have some very exciting games at times. What with an occasional game of rugger, all this exercise and recreation keeps us all fit, hard as nails and happy.

I am orderly 'dog' today and was up till after 2 pm last night, keeping an eye on the weather in case it clears up sufficiently for a show. This morning it turned out a beautiful day, although hazy, plenty of warmth and sunshine, and I would not be surprised if we did something tonight.

I had a long letter from Arthur, telling me he had gone to hospital and was due for S.A. So by the time you get this he will be with you all. He wants a good long rest before he attempts anything again… Bert

83 Squadron
6.5.1918

We are in the dark period now – the moon does not come up until about 2.30 a.m., and as it starts getting light at 3 a.m. it does not help us much.. The dark clear nights are the best for searchlights, and on our particular front they seem to be increasing in number and make things feel rather warm at times – but this is all in the days work.

Our flight commander Scott has had to leave us. We feel his loss very keenly; he was one of those bright and cheery individuals, a 'white man', but too straight for a few individuals, and that is why he has been sent for Home Establishment. The Major has put me in charge of the flight until Weaver comes back from leave, and he takes over.

A week ago we had a spell of bad luck with our machines, sundry crashes and engine trouble, but have got them all working again. The fitters and riggers have done splendidly considering.

Several nights ago, the Bosch machines came over rather early looking for our place and dropped bombs everywhere. The place was in absolute darkness, but we managed to get off and felt much safer when we were up in the air, although we had to be careful steering in amongst our own searchlights and archie barrages.

Yesterday Lohmeyer, one of our observers, and I paid a visit to one of the hospitals on the coast, to see some of the V.A.D.s who were so good to me when I was at St. Omer. Two were off having a half day's holiday on the other side of the town. We managed to find them after some difficulty and took them to tea. The matron at the hospital was very nice, and she told us where they were to be found.

The country round is glorious, everything looking so fresh and green. It is wonderful driving along in a tender down the long straight roads bordered on either side by trees. France in summer during peace must have been a wonderful country to be in.

It is a picturesque sight watching the French peasant women working in the fields with their white 'cappies' and blue or black frocks. I often think now how true to life some of the pictures in the Art Gallery were.

I am sending a cheque to Aunt Mabel to have forwarded to you. Each month I hope now to be able to send you something. It may then be possible to send Alice and Joe to some decent school without relying on government admission to their schools… Bert

Bert on a trip with some friends in the station tender.

Flying in open-cockpit aircraft was extremely uncomfortable. Leather and lamb's wool was the order of the day. Nevertheless, frostbite was quite common.

B.E.F.
France
6-5-1918

My dear mother and Dad,

We had to leave our aerodrome and quarters in a hurry, our one time little haven of rest and comfort eventually became a very hot place to be in. Shells used to come over at odd intervals, but we were not much worried with these, until one morning at about 8-30, the Bosch started sending over some heavy stuff, shrapnel and H.E. about our quarters and aerodrome, making things very unhealthy.

Our main purpose was to get our machines away safely, this we did successfully. My flight commander, I and others left at about 10.30 and landed at another place, which we had to leave again. We became attached to another crowd (squadron) in the meantime, until we heard where our own squadron was being stationed. We were very anxious to get away, as the people we were with showed themselves an awfully unsociable lot. The weather had turned dud, and in trying to get away with Scott, my flight commander, and another chap, I and two others were caught in a bad thunder and rain storm: we tried to stick it, but could not see a thing, the rain caught us like stinging hail; our goggles were useless, and had to take them off as we could not see through them. The three of us luckily landed safely, and clambered out of our machines like half drowned rats.

The next day we managed to get away and join up with the squadron. We are all under canvas in fields and are fairly comfortable when it does not rain. Summer is coming on, the country round is glorious, the fields are blooming with flowers, the woods are covered in clean and fresh greens, and the birds seem to vie with each other to sing their cheeriest song. Nature seems to be doing her hardest in obliterating all signs and impressions of war.

I was very pleased to get your letter dated 15-3-1918. I had no idea that all next-of-kin were informed when one went in to hospital; No7 General St. Omer was the base hospital I was sent to… Bert

83 Squadron
B.E.F.
France
15-5-1918

The weather for the whole of the last week has been fine, and we have been very busy flying and bombing.

As soon as it is dark, this is about 9.45pm as there is such a long twilight, up we get into the atmosphere heavily laden with 'eggs' and slowly gain a necessary height, which is not anything much, before crossing the lines. Everything appears marvellously wonderfully and strange. The multitudinous flashes of batteries of guns are an impressive sight, especially when there is a heavy 'strafe' on.

On crossing into Hunland we are given a very very entertaining reception as a rule in certain areas. Flying along all unsuspectingly, the gloom is suddenly broken by cold snaky beams of searchlights, next a barrage of 'hate', red tracers, 'glowing onions' and Archie is sent up. It is quite exciting dodging all this, and getting out of the beams of searchlights when once enmeshed in them. One's observer is as a rule busy with his machine gun at a time like this. The whole impression is one of a gigantic firework display.

Last night I did two shows, and had quite an exciting time, managed to get back safely to the aerodrome just as dawn was breaking. A couple of nights previously I also had to do two shows, each show taking about two hours.

While going in to a French town a couple of days ago to buy several things, I was greatly surprised and pleased to meet Jimmie Yates; he is in a day flying squadron and is quite close to our place; he flew over yesterday afternoon, and we had a long enjoyable chat.

…I have asked Aunt Mabel to send you some of the latest music. Miss Bennett wrote me a long interesting letter, she is well and sends her love. I am feeling fit and very happy with life in general… Bert.

One of Bert's most treasured possessions was his WW1 flying watch, used to synchronise time before a flight and often stolen, particularly after a crash. It was carried in a clip on the instrument panel in the cockpit.

83 Squadron
B.E.F.
France
27-5-1918

All this last fortnight the weather, especially at night, has been fine with plenty of moonlight, and in consequence we have been very busy flying, doing one and two shows a night and finishing often as dawn is breaking.

We have had little time to ourselves. Nobody gets up before midday and the afternoon is spent in testing machines and overhauling engines. My flight commander Scott went away on leave with his observer, and the O.C. has put me in charge of the flight. I have hardly had a minute to myself – Just lately we have been most unfortunate with our engines, and have not been able to use all our machines on a show, and the major always wants full facts and details. He is a good man, although he always keeps everybody on the move and gives them little rest.

The night before last while on a show, I had just reached the lines when my engine cut out completely with a nasty jar. I managed to glide back several miles, dropped a flare and luckily made a successful landing with a full cargo of bombs in a field quite close to an Archie battery. The machine was not strained in the slightest, but the engine was almost a complete write off, broken pipes, valves etc. The officer's i/c of the battery, rushed out to see if anybody had been hurt, and I never came across a nicer bunch of fellows: Brown, my observer, and I were taken into the mess and given hot coffee. I managed to get on to our O.C. by phone and told him what had happened. We stopped the remainder of the night with these fellows, and the next morning a tender arrived with mechanics but nothing could be done, so we took the engine out of the machine and came home, not forgetting to thank our friends for their kind hospitality.

According to reports we have been doing some good work. At times we have some exacting moments when having been caught in searchlights the Bosch sends up every conceivable form of hate, 'flaming onions', galore i.e. strips of phosphorous balls, 'flower pots' another sort of onion, ' golden rain' a sort of shell which on exploding sends down a deluge of rockets, and red tracer ammunition. At times it is like one gigantic firework display… Bert

83 Squadron
B.E.F.
15-6-1918

I was very pleased to get your letter dated 21st April, it had a good soaking in sea water at some time or other. It is quite likely that some of the mails have been lost and therefore accounts for me not receiving any letters.

You will be pleased to hear I have been given a flight with the acting rank of Captain. I only hope that I shall be worthy of the trust and shall do my best. We are still having a busy time and lately have been doing reconnaissance in the dirtiest of weather.

Last night three machines had to go up, I had to take one up, the wind was almost a gale with low lying clouds. We had the wind at our backs going across the lines and simply 'flew' along, but it was a different thing coming back, we barely seemed to move at all. We were picked up by searchlights and strafed severely by machine guns firing red tracer ammunition. We had to run the gauntlet. The only thing I could do was to stick my machines nose down until we were very low down and dodge the stuff. Thick mist was coming up and we were indeed thankful when we crossed back to our side. We managed to land just before the rain came pelting down. Powerful rockets were being sent up for the other two machines, and they landed safely after a while in this thick drizzle. It was a magnificent effort on the part of the two other fellows and we were indeed thankful. The C.O. was very pleased, and the Colonel of the Wing sent his highest appreciation to all six of us by wire.

I have not yet blossomed forth with my six 'pips' and feel very bashful about it, but will have to shortly… Bert

Painting of the action when six DFCs were awarded for the one reconnaissance, by Darryl Legg

21-6-1918

A couple of days ago General Salmond motored down and congratulated all six of us.

26-6-1918

I have another surprise for you, Lohmeyer, my Observer, and I have been awarded the Distinguished Flying Cross; it is a new decoration for the Royal Air Force, and can only be won by work on the other side of the lines, or work against Hun machines at home in the air raids or out here. In my letter to Aunt Mabel I asked her to cable out the news to you, as I thought you, Dad and Uncle Ted would be pleased to hear about it as quickly as possible.

The award did not go unmarked in the squadron. I discovered a comment in a letter from a fellow pilot A E Walsh to Bert much later describing a 'binge' to celebrate:

I recollect the binge and my passing out on the occasion of your D.F.C. – I tripped over a guide rope and burst my nose – Remember?

29.6.1918

I had to go off on a reconnaissance last night and so could not finish this letter. Lohmeyer and I had been up about an hour and were over the Hun Lines when my engine started worrying me and I made for home. A thick ground mist had come on in the meantime, at about eight miles from the aerodrome, the engine cut out and I had to come down. I managed to scrape over some trees and landed without hurt in a field of barley. It took us quite a time to find a village where there was a telephone, and even then we could not get out to the Squadron. In desperation I 'commandeered' a divisional staff car and drove up. This was about six a.m. and we were indeed thankful to find some hot cocoa and sandwiches waiting for us.

DFC citation in The Times

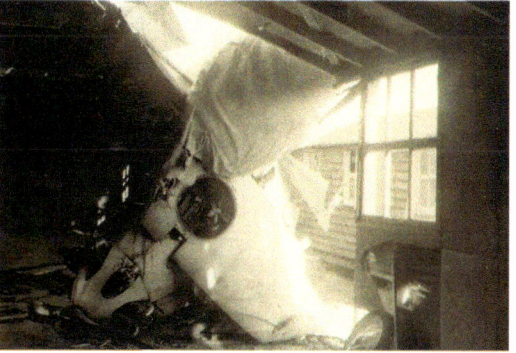

Crashes were not uncommon. Bert had quite a collection of photographs!

I am still having a very busy time with my engine and now have little time for myself, but hope to have things working smoothly soon.

Mrs A.L. Rutter sent me out a beautifully knitted muffler, and wants me whenever I get my leave to pay her a visit; she wishes to be remembered kindly to you and Dad. I have not heard from Miss Bennett for quite a long time.

Dr and Mrs Rutter lived in Bournemouth, but they clearly met Bert's parents in South Africa. He stays with them often in Bournemouth and indeed convalesces there after the war. It seems highly likely that it is through this contact that Bert meets his future wife, Marjorie Gresham.

It is now four months from the end of the war and the tempo of tactical bombing and reconnaissance hots up, as we see from more of Bert's log book and letters.

Bert with Auntie Rutter, showing his new DFC medal riband.

83 Squadron
B.E.F.
19.7.1918

We are still being kept fairly busy, reconnaissance and bombing trips. The reconnaissance trips are usually long shows and at times rather exciting. The Bosch objects very strongly to having his movement spotted, especially when we drop our flares and circle down slowly watching the area lit up; he vents his wrath by sending up every conceivable form of hate and at times it becomes rather hot. I always, if possible, give the recon fellows a night off to recuperate as it takes it out of one slightly.

The weather lately during the day has been dud, but clears up towards night for short intervals. It is rather annoying at times as one cannot tell for certain whether it is going to clear up for good or keep dud. The result was that two others and I were caught in a rather bad thunderstorm several nights ago. It was a very strange experience flying in amongst sheet lightning and occasional flashes of forked lightning. It was an awesome sight watching the elements at war in the air, at times the whole countryside would be lit up like day at the same time blinding one for the moment. At the time I did not waste time philosophising, and 'beetled' as hard as I could: 'you could not have seen my tail for dust'.

A little while ago, having an afternoon off, Lotz and I paid a visit to the S. African hospital to see if we knew anybody there. It was awful cheek on our part; the sisters and V.A.D.s entertained us in their anteroom. We met several who had been nursing out in West and East Africa. We spent a pleasant afternoon and it did us both good talking to them, we got over the feeling of being strangers in a strange land.

This last week or two I had serious intentions of growing a moustache, eventually cultivating it into something of martial appearance, but was finally dissuaded as very flattering compliments were being paid.

I am glad you keep in touch with the Nivens, I think they are nice folk. Thank Alice and Joe for their letters. Is Arthur still in Nairobi, what letters I have written have been addressed to Dar-es-Salaam……Bert?

83 Squadron
B.E.F.
25.7.1918

My dear Aunt Mabel,

Thank you so much for parcel of cakes and book. I do not get many letters and become rather despondent at times, in fact develop a stagnant state of mind. By this I mean one never cares to leave the camp for a change, neglects letter writing, and carries on in a listless fashion. Letters brighten one's existence tremendously out here.

What with the brilliant moonlight nights lately, it is almost like flying during the day. On both bombing and reconnaissance excursions, the Bosch never worries about picking us up with searchlights but pelts us as hard as he can go with Archie and machine gun fire or sends up his scouts to worry us.

On my previous trip we had quite an exciting time of it. At the time we were on the way home up against a strong westerly wind and our ground speed was not much, we had passed a hot belt of Archie and were congratulating ourselves on coming out of it, when a stream of tracers came past from underneath and we had to fight for it. As soon as Hutchinson got his gun working, we were allowed to go on undisturbed.

Our C.O. Major Leveson-Gower has left us, or was forced to, 'funny' people at the head of things and 'Boloism' were responsible. I am, so are all of us, very sorry about it. We thought a tremendous lot of him.

Bert

This letter shows again how important mail was to support morale, and it appears that the intensive and dangerous night operations were having a detrimental effect on his 'nerves'. Stress was common but not widely recognised.

83 Squadron
B.E.F.
4.8.1918

My dear Mother and Dad,

This evening I was down for a long reconnaissance trip, but as the weather has turned out very dud, I am spending the evening writing letters.

This morning I attended the Church Parade, and after lunch we had the Squadron Sports. I had been appointed one of the judges and had a very strenuous time. I could not enter any of the running or jumping events as my knee was in a very shaky condition. I was beaten in throwing the cricket ball by two yards, the best throw was a hundred and six yards, and in Tug of War my flight team beat everybody else. In the final we were up against H.Q. flight and we were struggling for seven minutes before we finally pulled them over. In the second pull we had more success and got them over rather easily, but I never felt more done up in all my life, my legs were trembling for minutes afterwards, and my arms and hands had no feeling in them for quite a time…

With our new C.O. things seem a bit strange and awkward; we have got to accept his ideas and the orders he gets from people Levison-Gower had trouble with. What we have seen of Major Price, he seems a good fellow, but ones imagination pictures more 'hot air' than ever there was. Never the less, I for my part shall do my best to keep things running smoothly…

Kathleen Niven sent me a nice long letter. I think she is a brick sticking out in Dar-es-Salaam in that ungodly climate. I have met one of her school pals who is nursing out here in No.1 S.A. General Hospital… Bert

Bert's long suffering Observer Lt. Ewart Lohmeyer went on leave and wrote a letter to him which is revealing of the strong bond that existed, created by the extremely close relationship, in action, in a plane such as the FE2b.

27-8-1918

Dear old Robbie,

I do hope you had a good leave. Well how do you like France after leave? Rotten isn't it… In many ways I wish I were back with the squadron. It is all very nice having leave but the various brass hats and the 'little tin Gods' with blue uniforms and NO WINGS at the Air Board rather frighten one. Life is not so free easy and happy go lucky as with the squadron. Well cheerio for the present will write again shortly. Give my kindest regards to the fellows of 83. Especially old silver.

Your bit of ballast,
Ewart Lohmeyer.

83 Squadron
B.E.F.
4.9.1918

There have been some tremendous changes in the squadron, there are very few of the original 'crew' left, and I am now the senior flight commander.

On arrival at the squadron I felt like a newcomer at seeing the number of strange faces, and also having to face the new 'hot air' and 'red tape' just brought in by 'brilliant Boloists' [?]

We have been kept very busy working, finishing often after four o'clock in the morning on shows, also my engines keep me occupied during the day, and this helps me to forget a great deal of the unpleasantness.

Lohmeyer my observer has gone on Home Establishment and I miss him.

Bobby Greathead has been sent to the squadron and I managed to get him into my flight, he is one of the stoutest of pilots.

Poor Jimmy Yates has gone missing, I flew over to his squadron and found out particulars from Stokes, a S. African, who was with him at the time. The three machines were ground strafing and the identical job I was on when I had the forced landing. Jimmy's engine must have been shot, because they saw him come down and land without mishap, shortly afterwards the machine went up in flames, so we can only surmise that he is prisoner and safe.

On the whole we seem to be doing well on the front, I hope it continues.

I am feeling very much better even though I am working hard… Bert

83 Squadron

R.A.F.

France

12-10-1918

My dear Mother and Dad

A fortnight ago, the Wing rang up asking us to make up a Rugger XV with another squadron to play some other squadron thought to be 'top notches'. Very few fellows in the squadron came forward to help, the majority of them had never played rugger at all. I had to put my name down as a forward, rather than see the game washed out. My knee had always been shaky, but I thought with a good bandage on I might manage alright.

We eventually got up the team, and met at the spot agreed upon, the majority of us flew our machines over rather than go over by motor tenders.

There were several internationals playing on either side, and the game was a hard and fast one; our side more than held its own. About ten minutes before the finish, one of the opposing three quarters almost got clear, but I happened to be in the way, and in the tackle we both came down in a heap and something went in my knee. I managed to stick it out until the finish of the game, when I had it attended to. Two days after, the Wing M.O. sent me in to hospital.

The M.O. there wants to lay me up for several weeks, which meant I would have been struck off the squadron strength. After about a week in bed I had to call in the aid of the Wing M.O., and after a great deal of 'wangling', we fixed up a compromise, with the result that I went back to the squadron but had to promise to lay up and was forbidden to fly. My knee is now very much stronger and have been up several times in the air.

The wet weather seems to have set in, and although we have not done much flying we have been very busy. We have had to move up to an aerodrome closer to the line, and a move like this is quite a task; things are still unsettled but it shall not be long before we are fixed up. I find the damp and mud rather trying, but hope it will not be long before I shall be sent on Home Establishment. Although I think it is much nicer on this side with a bunch of good fellows than life in a H.E. squadron where 'hot air' and 'red-tape' seem to predominate. There are only three pilots and one observer left of the original squadron, many of course have been sent on H.E., and the present fellows are nothing like the original crew.

We are certainly making things hum for the Bosch, he is fast being driven out of his strongholds, and one can only hope that the advance will continue, although the coming wet weather and cold will not improve things…

I had not forgotten Dad's birthday on the 15th of this month, I send a big hug and kisses and wish him all the best. Cox's & Co are sending out my remittance now, and will you please buy Dad a little present for me…

Bobby Greathead has just gone on leave and I have asked him to send out a 'Sketch' number of 21st Sept. There is a comic picture of three machines out on a reconnaissance trip at night in bad weather. Simpson the artist, who is an A.R.A., sent an officer down to the squadron for material and detail, when the three machines of this squadron went out on that trip I wrote you about some time ago. The result was this comic picture, they have put in the number of my bus on the rudder D.9099, and you may find it rather interesting as it shows the type of machine we fly.

I hear frequently from Mrs Rutter, she is very good writing, the Doctor has been laid up in bed for the past three weeks but is getting better; they both wish to be remembered kindly.

The last three days we have had a slow drizzle all the time, tonight it has started afresh and I do not think there will be any flying, so will be able to have a decent night's sleep. Sleep, to my mind, is the greatest of distractions and after a good night's rest one feels fresh for anything.

You seem to be frightfully busy with all the concerts, entertainment and socials, I hope you are not overdoing it. Talking of concerts, I have seen some of the finest variety shows ever put up, by some of the divisions while on rest out here in France; The talent and technique one meets is really amazing. I went to one of these shows several nights ago, and I doubt whether I enjoyed myself so much anywhere.

The news these last few days has been splendid, we seem to be doing well everywhere… Bert

The war is now less than a month from the end and in the next letter Bert shows an interesting insight in to how things appeared from the ordinary airman's point of view.

21.10.1918
My Dear Aunt Mabel,

In my last letter I spoke of the squadron having to move up nearer the line; we have settled down somewhat, but are still in uncomfortable quarters and what with the mud and slush as a result of the bad weather, everyone hopes we will change to a better place soon. This wish may be gratified in a few days' time, as word has just come through that we have got to move up yet closer. I have been told to start off tomorrow morning, weather permitting, aerodrome hunting.

The place we are in now is in a land of waste and desolation; earth from the air is like a sponge, pitted and scarred beyond recognition – with craters, shell holes and trenches. It is indeed hard to imagine that this tract of land was once a flourishing countryside of little villages, woods and orchards.

Flying over the country during the day, one unconsciously becomes filled with a spirit of awe and sacredness; little places, a wood here, or hill close by, names made famous in history, once the scenes of the hottest and fiercest of fighting where brave men fought and died stemming the flood of a tyrant invasion.

The news this past fortnight has been splendid. One can only hope we shall be able to keep the Hun on the move, a tremendous amount has yet to be accomplished before one can even think of piece. The Bosch with his peace moves, needs all the more watching, he is as cunning as the Devil… Bert.

There was no let-up in bombing missions, right up to the armistice on the 11th November. From his flying log it is clear that Bert was undertaking long bombing trips, mainly against railways at La Louvaine and Charleroi. On the last day of war he took off at 2.45 pm with his Observer, Lt. Greathead, but landed after an hour flying at Fiervilles, then took off at 4.15 pm to return to their aerodrome solo. He describes in the next long letter home what happens next. The letter is written from a convalescence home for officers in Bournemouth.

Mont Dore [Formerly a 'posh' hotel, according to Bert]
Military Hospital
Bournemouth

8-12-1918
My dear Mother and Dad,

One can hardly realize that this ghastly war has at last come to an end – when the news of the armistice came through to the squadron, it left everybody in a stupor, and we could not then realize its significance.

We had been bombing right up to the last, long and tiring shows they seemed to be. On one of the last, the average time of each machine that reached its objective was four and a quarter hours. It all seems so strange now, obliterating all visions of being strafed by the Bosch by his searchlights, his Archie and tracers, like many, many others I am indeed thankful to Almighty God that this business has come to an end.

I had not been feeling up to the mark for some time towards the last, quite a number of the fellows in my flight had been down with influenza or had to be sent to hospital as a result of crashes, and I had a busy time of it flying and looking after the machines. As a result of this, several days after the armistice had been signed, the C.O. asked me to form one of a party of four for a trip down to Paris in his touring car – he thought the change would do me good.

Trip to Paris to celebrate the end of the war.

We left the squadron early the next morning when it was freezing hard, and got in to Paris for luncheon, we did seem wonderful going along some of those long straight roads, so common in France and, I am afraid, exceeded the speed limit a little. It was a bad time of the year for scenery, nevertheless some of the country we passed through was magnificent. France was 'en fete' and the towns and villages we passed through were bedecked with flags and crowded with farmer folk – it was impossible to describe the enthusiasm and joy of the people. We were however to witness bigger things in Paris.

After an enjoyable lunch – we had developed wonderful appetites after our long ride – we set about looking for rooms. We had bought along a French interpreter in another car, who said he knew where we could be fixed up comfortably, but we found he knew next to nothing and proved worse than useless. After spending a few hours chasing up and down boulevards in the car we eventually got two big rooms in a quiet hotel off the Opera House. It was now supper time and after a clean-up, we dined at a Café on the Boulevard de la Paris and then went on to some theatre. 'My hat' the French know how to charge, one has to pay to breathe. We were all feeling very tired, and the theatre besides being hot and stuffy was very crowded, so at half time we beetled back to the hotel for a good rest – we had decided on early rising to go sightseeing in the car.

What little we saw the next day convinced me that Paris was a wonderful place, a beautiful city, its buildings, streets, squares and parks knock London into second place somehow. My one wish at the time was to have you all with me to see its splendours. Major McCrae, a Canadian, took us up to a big French Canadian hospital at St Cloud, where all the doctors entertained us to dinner. I never met a nicer lot of fellows. I had always been slightly prejudiced at the behaviour of these people in Canada, but these fellows gave me quite a different impression.

That day was the official day of celebration for France, and on our way back to our diggings we met a huge procession that you no doubt read about in the papers. In the Place de la Concorde was a wonderful collection of war trophies, guns and captured Bosch machines.

Parisians went mad that day, crowds surging through the streets, held up traffic for hours, we had managed to keep clear for a while, but were eventually caught up, and went through an awful ordeal – we were almost smothered with confetti, people kept jumping on the car and I expected to hear the axle give way at any moment. Major McCrae counted thirty-two people at one period, and we were quite helpless. After a wait of a couple of hours which seemed interminable, we managed to get in to a side street and by a roundabout way reach our hotel.

Collecting our things we started off again on our long ride back to the squadron. After an eventful journey we got back at about three in the morning. I could have written pages more but knowing my incapability with the pen have desisted.

Two days later I was sent over to England on a fortnight's furlough entrusted with important Xmas commissions. I had to spend three days in town and then came on to Bournemouth to see Mrs Rutter, hoping then to go to Aunt Mabel. While stopping at Mrs Rutters, I developed acute pains in my stomach. Dr. Rutter thought I had some internal trouble necessitating an operation, so I came into the convalescence home for officers; after stopping in bed for five days and having nothing but milk I pulled round very quickly. I am now feeling ever so much stronger. I leave tomorrow morning to interview the officials at the Air Board in London. I may be able to get an extension of leave. The Rutters were very good to me but I thought it much better going in to the hospital.

I am very undecided as to what line of engineering I ought to take up. I do not know what schemes of demobilisation for the R.A.F. are going to be brought in. It may be advantageous my remaining in the R.A.F. or something in that line. At any rate I am coming out to South Africa at the first opportunity even if it is only leave. Please write and inform me of your and Uncle Ted's wishes.

When I have the opportunity I shall see Schreiner, the High Commissioner and ask his advice.

I have had no news of Jimmy Yates – large batches of R.A.F. prisoners are coming through daily. When you write give Arthur my love, I do not know where he is stationed at the present… Bert.

Bert is now clearly thinking hard about his future; the family felt very strongly he should stay in the RAF. Indeed his father sent a telegram from SA just saying 'stay in the RAF.' Clearly one option for him was to return to the 'School of Mines' course he was doing before the war but he had done well in the RAF and was highly thought of. However he now returns to the squadron for Christmas.

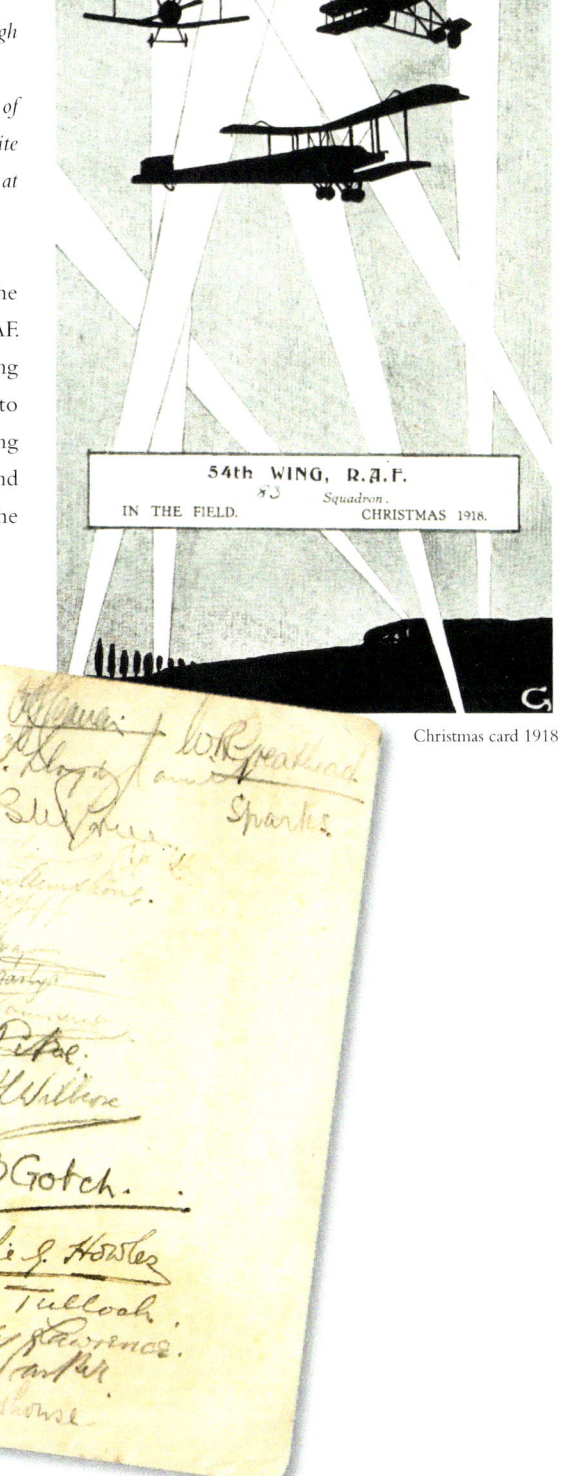

Christmas card 1918

The 83 squadron menu for Christmas Victory Dinner 1918. Signatures of officers on the back of the menu.

83 Squadron
27.12.1918
Dear Aunt Mabel

An awful catastrophe occurred when I reached Paddington. I was so intent on getting a taxi that I left half my belongings in the carriage… I wrote to the lost property office but have heard nothing as yet…

We spent a fairly quiet Xmas at the squadron, but enjoyed ourselves nevertheless. The mess was a fairy palace of its own with holly and mistletoe in abundance we combined our creative powers and quite transformed the place.

The squadron had moved while I was on leave to this place not far from St. Omer, and we are much more comfortably off in the way of Nissen huts and Quarters.

At present I am wonderfully fit and well. Exercise in moderation and fairly wholesome food seems to have done a great deal.

The weather lately has been very damp and chilly, but I have been up several times flying round the country. At ten thousand feet the cold is rather severe, but one does not remain at that altitude for long… Bert

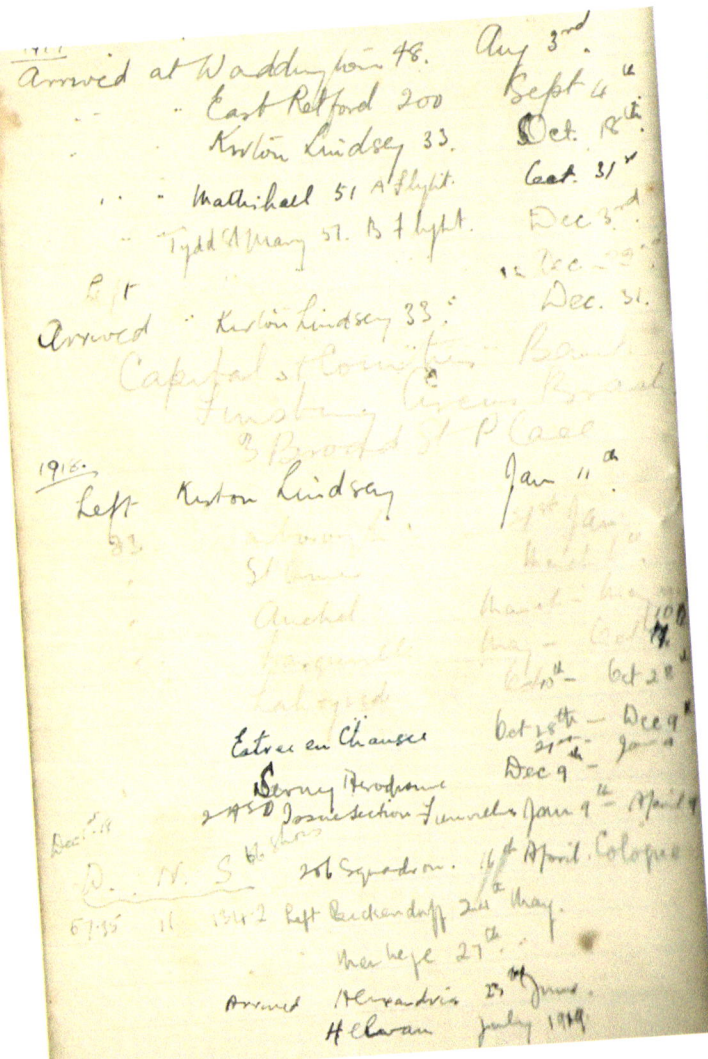

Back page of WW1 flying log book showing where he served.

Bert and fitter working on FE2b, winter 1918.

On the back page of Bert's first flying logbook he kept a rough list setting out the many airfields and squadrons he flew from and with. It is particularly revealing of just how many times the Squadron moved its whole base in response to the tactical position of the front line. The censor did not allow letters to reveal the Squadron whereabouts so this is the only record of where they operated from.

Translated it reads: 1917

Arrived at Waddington, 48 Squadron August 3rd

Arrived at East Retford, 200 Squadron Sept 4th

Arrived at Kiton Lindsey, 33 Squadron Oct. 18th

Arrived at Mattishall, 51 Squadron A Flight Oct 31st

Arrived at Lydd St Mary, 51 Squadron B Flight Dec. 3rd

Arrived at Kirton Lindsey, 33 Squadron Dec 31st 1918

Arrived at Narborough, 83 Squadron Jan 11th

Arrived at St Omer, 83 Squadron March 6th

Arrived at Auchel, 83 Squadron March-May

Arrived at Franqueville, 83 Squadron May- Oct 10th

Arrived at Lahoussoye, 83 Squadron Oct 10th- Oct 28th

Arrived at Estrée en Chaussée, 83 Squadron Oct 28th – Dec 9th

Arrived at Serny, 83 Squadron Dec 9th – Jan 9th 1919

Arrived at Funviels, Issue section Jan 9th – April 9th

Arrived at Cologne, Bickendorf 206 Squadron April 16th – May 24th

Arrived at Merheje, in transit May 27th

Arrived at Alexandria, Egypt June 23rd

Arrived at Helwan, Egypt July

Bert had survived the war without a scratch other than a rugby injury, though he had been struck down with influenza, malaria and dysentery. He had fought in three campaigns on two continents and shown himself to be a reliable and gallant pilot in the newly-formed Royal Air Force. Since learning to fly, his log book shows he had clocked up 284.55 hours of flying, mostly on active service and about a third at night. He had several near misses, at least three crash landings while training and several engine failures over enemy lines necessitating gliding to our side; he always landed safely with minimum damage. He had risen in rank to acting captain in charge of a flight and was still only 22 years old. Nearly all his flying was in the outdated, but reliable, FE2b pusher aeroplane; mostly tactical bombing and ground strafing in support of the army at night when the enemy were trying to conceal troop movements in the dark.

The net result of this intensive period was to cause nervous exhaustion and some sort of stomach ulcer, which necessitated a period in hospital at Bournemouth. He recovered quickly and was soon back at the front, always terrified of losing his place in 83 squadron, with his chums, and being sent to the dreaded pool, for reallocation anywhere. The bonds of friendship were vital to getting through these very stressful operations.

He decided to pursue his engineering career in the post-war RAF and was advised to get into the army of occupation in Germany while the 'powers that be' decided on the future of the Air Force. He was hoping for a permanent commission specialising in the engineering branch; this would take time while the whole future of the RAF became clearer.

Chapter Six

EGYPT AND CAMBRIDGE, 1919-1924

The First World War ended on 11th November 1918 at eleven o'clock and many had a feeling of disbelief that the terrible carnage could have stopped so suddenly. Bert recovered from a stress-related illness quickly and decided he would try and stay in the RAF. This was a difficult time for such men, because they were vulnerable to the cuts required by the new peacetime economy.

The war had started with a mere 60 aircraft and 2073 personnel, and by 1918 this had grown to some 4000 front line aircraft and 114,000 personnel, of whom 5182 were pilots. By March 1920 the RAF had been rapidly demobilised, and only 3280 officers and 25,000 other ranks remained. The Women's RAF was completely disbanded, although the nursing service was retained and in 1923 it became Princess Mary's RAF Nursing Service.

For those who wanted a permanent commission in the RAF, this was a time of limbo while the future was determined. An even bigger danger was that such a small force could not survive independently from the much larger Army and Navy. That it did survive was largely due to the vision of two people, Winston Churchill, Minister for War and Air, and Hugh Trenchard as Chief of Air Staff, who believed very much in a force that had potential for the future to profoundly alter strategy.

Churchill and Trenchard worked hard to lay down the basis of the peacetime RAF, based on the concept of good training to reduce accidents and the development of new concepts, ideas and equipment. From this base the RAF could be effectively expanded in a time of need and cost-effectively 'police the Empire', which Churchill

Bert at no 2 ASD Mess

declared was its first duty. This is precisely where Bert fitted in so well; engineering, flying and colonial war experience were rare in 1919.

Soon after the war, 83 Squadron, like many others, was disbanded and Bert Lewis-Roberts moved to the No. 2 Airplane Supply Depot (ASD) at Funviels in France. He was in the issue section, which involved test-flying many different types of aircraft before delivery to squadrons or to airplane parks for eventual sale.

Between 14.1.19 and 24.3.19 he flew at least eight different types, including the FE2b, DH9, Bristol F Sunbeam, Bristol F Rolls, RE8, A.W., S.E.5 and S.E.5 Viper.

He writes home:

3.2.1919

I have left 83 squadron – On an application from the Wing for a senior flight commander to take over this station, Major Price and the Colonel, unknown to me, put my name in for the job. My posting came through the same day, and I had to leave in a hurry. It grieved me greatly to part from the squadron. I had always managed to stick to it somehow right from the start. It was like living in a big family circle, and what friends one made were true and tried friends.

The fellows gave me a rousing send-off which made me very sore. I managed to get Hooper and Greathead to accompany me in the tender as far as depot headquarters.

What with the rate demobilisation has set in, it was only a question of time before the squadron was broken up. I have heard since that more than three-quarters of the squadron have been posted away, some have blossomed forth as town Majors, and others drafting officers. It is rather comical taking flying officers for these positions.

Instead of caring for six meek and tame FE2b's, I am now responsible for the upkeep of twenty large hangars filled with ferocious winged creatures of all types with a personnel of 200 men and officers. At the time when I first took over I thought it a most formidable job, but have somehow managed to drop in to the swing of things alright.

This place is an issue section where squadrons from all areas collect machines when they are in need of them. There is not anything like the work now as there was during the war, but there seems to be a fair amount of responsibility attached, and I only hope I do not make an unholy mess of things.

Apart from doing a fair amount of office work, checking returns and writing official letters and signing red tape literature, I am expected to fly these types of machines testing occasionally, although I have other pilots whose work it is and it has been almost like doings ones first solo all over again. I found it extremely strange flying a tractor after spending so much of my time on the pusher type of machine…

Whilst on leave, my batman at the squadron had packed away a big bunch of letters in a valise and had forgotten to tell me about it, the result was I had letters many months old… Yates my school friend, who went missing last August while trench strafing on a machine, has arrived safely in England. I had the news from some of his friends, but have up to the present heard nothing from him - his experiences in Boschland could have been none too pleasant. I heard some of the experiences of fellows who had been repatriated whilst on my last leave…
Bert.

A considerable argument develops over his future and staying in the RAF:

23.2.1919

My Dear Mother and Dad

I read through all your letters carefully, including Uncle Ted's, and their contents made me think very hard.

I realize what an inane ass I made of myself while on my last leave in England. I should have liked to have seen Aunt Mabel's letter to Uncle Ted (her brother). I can never forget what she must have written to him, if this letter to you expresses the true facts. To begin with I cannot make out why Aunt Mabel should take upon herself to send in a report on me as suffering from nervous prostration, and decided that I had decided to quit the Air Force for good as a result of this. I know she herself has her own views on the R.A.F., and her information has been supplied by Frank Robertson. I may be wrong, but I imagine she has the idea that my indisposition at the time was due as a result of degenerate living. Perhaps I am too sensitive. I am writing to Uncle Ted and want him to explain matters explicitly.

I sought advice from Uncle Ernest, and talked things over thoroughly. I was looking too far ahead of things and thought at the time that I may be able to qualify in engineering in S.A. I had too much dread of the blind alley occupation.

I realize how stupid and foolish I have been.

My application for a permanent commission went in to Depot Headquarters before your cable arrived, and my repatriation claim has been cancelled. I think it will be sometime ere I hear whether I have been accepted or not.

Demobilization has set in at such a pace, that I think it will not be long before this Issue Section will be closed down. The Colonel came round this morning and had a talk; he wants me to take charge of the aeroplane testing section of the big repair Park depot, when this place has been finished with.

Since coming to this place I have flown quite a number of types of machines, and have now taken to flying scouts (fast single seaters), and it has been splendid experience. When the weather is fine trips have to be made to places, in the Army of Occupation, ferrying machines, and these expeditions are full of interest… The Bristol fighter is a machine I do a fair amount of joy riding in… Demobilisation has set big industrial and labour problems going, and for the present England is a good place to be out of. This last fortnight I have been extremely busy getting machines serviceable with the present number of men, so many have already been demobilized. I was lucky enough in getting a bunch of Bosch prisoners to do the rough aerodrome work, by visiting the O.C. Prisoners of War Camp and inviting him to dinner.

I had a long letter from Mrs Rutter, she is a dear and very kind lady, and I think a great deal of her and the Doctor.

I cannot tell you how grieved I am about all the uncalled for trouble on my part; also Aunt Mabel's missive to Uncle Ted… Bert

Clearly from this letter to Aunt Mabel it is a very trying time for him:

Issue Section
2. A.S.D.
R.A.F.
9-3-1919

This last month I have had an extremely busy and worrying time. What with testing and ferrying machines to places in the Army of Occupation and conducting courts of inquiry, I have not felt like writing, and I only hope you have not been worrying about me.

One of my pilots and another one from the Pilots' Pool had very serious crashes at different intervals, both of them had been severely maimed; they are now out of danger, I am thankful to say.

The Major at Repair Park always in the habit of playing with explosives has finished his career by allowing an improvised bomb to go off in his hands.

My mail seems to tour half round France before it eventually reaches me; it is most aggravating.

Demobilisation has set in at such a pace that I don't think it will be long ere this place closes up, and I shall then be on the move again.

After flying various types of two-seater machines, I have managed to trust myself to fast scouts, although often it is quite a squeeze getting into the cockpits

Mother and Dad in their last letter are very worried about me.

I hope you did not send in an alarming report about me – re suffering from nervous prostration and as a result of this giving up the idea of remaining in the Air Force. Uncle Ted in a letter to Mother did some straight talking.

We had your cake for tea in the mess and it was a great treat……Bert.

Maurice Piercy, one of Bert's single-seater friends, a famous upside down flyer.

55 Maurice Piercy records an inverted flight of 4 mins and 45 secs, written on the wing in the picture upside down! Addressed to Captain Roberts ('Robbo' soon became his nickname)..

11.3.1919

Dear Mum and Dad

These last few weeks we have been having a busy time flying machines away from this section to places in the Army of Occupation. This place is due to close down at the end of the month. These trips are full of interest, and as we are bought back by tender, we can view the sights at our leisure.

On one of these excursions we made an extensive tour of the country round Lille, Donai, Cambrai and Arras. I shall not attempt to picture some of the ungodly tracts of desolation and waste, only those who have seen some of it can realize what it is like. Some of these places were of great interest to me, for example railway stations and Bosch aerodromes where we (the squadron) had dropped bombs and had performed our night reconnaissance. Were it not for occasional spells of dud weather, we would find this ferrying job rather trying, not the flying part of it, but the long tender drives back.

Today the section had a general holiday, the 19th Div. Artillery held a race meeting on the aerodrome, and an enjoyable afternoon was spent… The R.A. commander, Brig-Gen Peel, has promised me several horses for exercising… The Depot Adjutant has told me I am due for leave in another fortnight. I am going to make enquiries and see if I cannot attend one of the investitures at Buckingham Palace. It will be an ordeal I dread, but ought to have comfort that I shall be quite an insignificant recipient amongst so many who usually attend these functions… Bert.

Jan 1919 at Bailleul, seeing the terrible destruction of war.

On the Menin road, same trip.

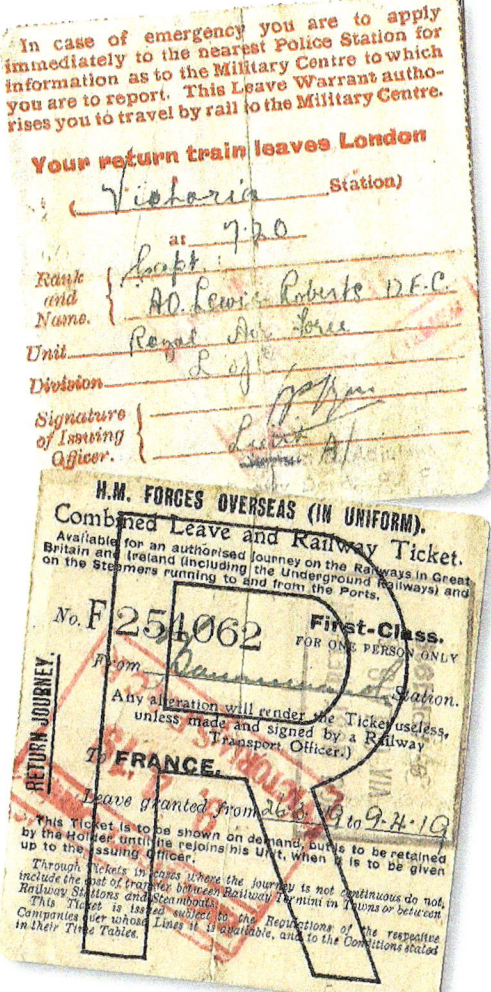

Bert's leave travel document from No. 2 Aeroplane Supply Depot RAF.

While on leave in England he stayed with the Rutters in Bournemouth. He again contemplates his future and gets good advice from a friend in the Air Ministry in London.

22 Poole Road
Bournemouth
7.4.19

I can't tell you how pleased I was to meet Jimmy Yates, Greathead and Hooper in town; we spent a very enjoyable week in town and did not run the pace. I have been spending the rest of my leave with the Rutters. I was very pleased to see Dr. Frank and Mabel Robertson, also Stuart when they came up yesterday afternoon for tea. The Doctor showed us around his rooms containing electrical apparatus and an enjoyable and entertaining afternoon was spent.

I leave tomorrow morning for London to catch the early train for Folkestone on Wednesday. 2 A.S.O. will have been closed up by now, and unless H.Q. want me for a special job, I shall be dumped in to the Pilots Pool. There I shall languish until wanted for some squadron in the Army of Occupation. I should then prefer going to a scout squadron.

While in town I went to see a friend in the Air Ministry, and he advised me to stop out in France for another month or two until the Air Ministry come to definite decisions about the Permanent Commission, and those people nominated for the Army of Occupation… I had my photograph taken here last Saturday in R.A.F. outfit, and will send some photos on as soon as they have been finished.

I will write as soon as I find out what is going to happen to me at the Pool… Bert

206 Squadron R.A.F.
B.E.F.
Germany
16.4.1919

As from my new address, it will be seen that I have pushed into the Army of Occupation.

On my arrival in France, I discovered that the depot 2 A.S.D. was non-existent, so had to report to Pilots' Pool. The Major i/c Postings G.H.Q. scared me by phoning through that he had a special job for me, there is often considerable doubt and perplexity about some of the 'special jobs'. Shortly after my posting came through as Flight Commander for 206 Squadron, and as this squadron is engaged on the aerial post mission the work ought to be rather interesting.

I caught the Cologne Express at Boulogne on Monday night and a very poor express it is. Apart from it being frightfully crowded and uncomfortable, I was reminded of one of our goods trains crawling from one station to another in S.A.

My first reflections of Cologne are rather weird and extraordinary. Coming into personal contact with the Bosch in his home after four years of deadly strife with him, one's curiosity is more than tinged with the feeling of suspicion when he appears so docile, good tempered and anxious for your welfare.

The R.T.O. at the station did not know the whereabouts of this squadron, and this information was only gleaned by an interview at the Town Mayor's Office.

This squadron has its mess in a palatable residence in the Kaiser Wilhelm Ring, and the officers are billeted in houses in the vicinity. I have a very comfortable bedroom, bathroom attached in the house of a German physician, the house is also in the Ring and quite close to the mess, and the Dr. is also one of those anxious for my welfare.

Tea in the Mess at Cologne, Bert on the right.

Officers outside the Mess at Cologne, Bert on the right.

There is not a soul in the squadron I have met before, and the experience of mixing with new people as of old are unpleasant, but I suppose this state of things can't last for long.

Once I find I have been accepted definitely for the Army of Occupation I mean to apply for six months' leave to South Africa. I think there is every opportunity of my being granted it.

Have you received any South African mail lately, mine does not seem to be coming at all regularly.

The squadron at the present, does not seem to be over busy, there is a duty flight each week, so that when one is on, the other two have the afternoon off from 12.o'clock. I hope to now be able to devote some time to study. I spent a lot of my spare time working at maths when at Fienvillers, but it was inconsistent study… Bert

DH9 at Cologne, Bickendorf Airfield.

Bert with DH9 in Germany, 1919.

In his next letter he reports to Uncle Ted a typical mail flight, a job which was not to last very long.

206 Squadron B.E.F.
4.5.1919

My flight was duty flight this week and had to ferry the mail, weather permitting. Four days ago I left with several bags of mail for a place a hundred and sixty miles away, and made a new pilot accompany me on another machine, to show him the route and the country. Just prior to leaving no weather reports had come in from places I had to pass en route, and the weather in our vicinity was none too settled, so I set off trusting to luck that the weather would clear as we went forward. At Duren it started to rain heavily and we had to come down a bit to get clear of the mist and clouds, the further we went the higher rose the ground, and although 2000' was shown on our aneroid we found we were just skimming the ground.

The country between Duren and Liege is bad, thickly wooded and very hilly, and scarcely a square foot to force land in. We struck the Meuse at Liege and started following it down to Namur, flying in the valley and between the hills. Mist, rain and low clouds made observation difficult and we almost ran into a collection of chimney stacks of a factory on the river bank. This got beyond a joke when I thought of the other pilot on my tail, so decided to land at the first opportunity. A nice field fortunately showed itself on the valley cliffs and I turned and landed safely, the other fellow eased my mind when I saw him make a decent landing. Within a few minutes we were surrounded by Belgian peasants, to whom an aeroplane was apparently a rare sight. Without delay we found out the nearest railway station and disposed of our mail to the R.T.O.

About four hours later it cleared up a bit and we decided to push on, but had tremendous difficulty in starting the other machine. It was only after an hour's strenuous work, 'doping', 'sucking in' and twirling the propeller that she eventually started; this done I managed to get mine started very quickly and off we went, to the consternation and surprise of the Belgians, who thought we had been stranded for good. We arrived at our destination, Morville, safely, too late in the afternoon for our return trip to Cologne, so we had to stop the night.

The next morning and for two successive days it did nothing but drizzle, with occasional falls of sleet, and we had to wait until it cleared.

We eventually got away and did the return journey to Cologne without a hitch.

The Wing have about forty horses stabled in the outbuildings of the Bosch racecourse just outside the town, for the use of pilots and observers. My C.O., Major Macfarlane-Reid D.S.O., M.C. & Bar, is acting Wing Commander and is very keen on riding; he and I and sometimes another Flight Commander take the best nags out very frequently in the afternoons, into the country and have great sport…

News has suddenly come to hand from the Brigade that the squadron is to stand by to go to Egypt, and we may leave any day. I do not know how Egypt will appeal to me, but will certainly find it interesting, and the climate a good deal warmer than what I have experienced this last season… Bert.

From this account, it seems that developing a mail service with these rather primitive aeroplanes was very unreliable, however it was deemed important to maintain the morale of the 'forgotten' troops of the Army of Occupation. The other exercise he did, recorded in his log book, was flying a German Fokker DVii in mock combat against fellow pilots in British makes such as the DH9, to compare performance. No comment was recorded. Bert and his squadron set off for Egypt.

206 Squadron

B.E.F.

19.5.1919

My Dear Aunt Mabel

In my last letter I mentioned that the squadron had been ordered to Egypt; but nothing has materialised as to the exact date we leave, rumour hath it on the 23rd inst. At any rate we have disposed of our machines. I handed over my flight machines at Marquise which is just outside Boulogne; I led the formation of machines from Bickendorf (Cologne) to Marquise, and did the through trip in two and a quarter hours, catching the Cologne express back that same night.

I should be very pleased if Uncle Earnest could recommend and send out to me a fairly advanced book on Electrical Engineering or Electrotechnics(?) …Bert

P.S. Will you please send me Miss Bennett's address and give her my love when you write.

206 Squadron

RAF

29.5.1919

My Dear Mother and Dad

This last week I have had a very busy time… We had been given two days' notice to pack up and the Squadron left Cologne on the 24th inst. I was put in charge of the convoy consisting of nineteen Lorries and five tenders with the personnel of the squadron.

The convoy covered eighty miles up to Ververs on the Belgian frontier, on the first day, and another sixty miles to Ardennes on the Meuse on the second day; we finished the biggest part of the journey to this place, Maubeuge, on the third day. Although the trip was somewhat tiring and we were continually being smothered in white dust, we passed through some wonderful country and saw some very interesting towns, places like Aix-la-Chapelle, Liege and Namur. Although held up rather frequently on the road with running repairs, I managed to bring the convoy to this place, our destination, intact, much to my relief and joy.

We had been given a big house in the town for our mess and quarters, but the place was so indescribably filthy and impregnated with pungent odours, which would not disappear even when the rooms had been washed and smothered in disinfectant, that I persuaded the C.O. and a few others to camp out with me in an orchard adjoining the aerodrome. We pitched seven tents and have an ideal camp free from smells; being without our machines now, we do a fair amount of Physical Training and Drill in the mornings and enjoy it.

Camping in France during Squadron move to Egypt.

The canals and rivers surrounding this place are unfit for bathing and after consulting some large scale maps of the district we found a sheet of water some six miles south of the town. The C.O. took me out in his car and we found the dam to be an ideal spot for swimming, and this is where we spend afternoons now, swimming or bathing in the sun.

We expect to entrain any day now for Marseilles. Mrs Rutter is not keen on my going to Egypt, but as I am fit and having signed on for the Army of Occupation, I cannot see how I can back out; it also helps me to retain my say and rank as the Air Ministry are reducing so many temporary Captains now…
Bert

Moving in French railway horse trucks.

206 Squadron staff car being loaded on transport in Marseilles.

After another week or ten days they entrained for Marseilles, where they boarded the boat for Alexandria in Egypt and to Cairo, the Headquarters of RAF Middle East. The peacetime drive to reduce the costs of the military actually gave a boost to the RAF, as it was seen as a cheap way of 'policing the Empire'. Although later it was to become a controversial strategy, this was a very good posting for Bert to land in as a young RAF officer, although from his letters he could not see it at the time!

Cairo was the hub of many air and sea routes of the Empire, and thus of vital strategic importance. It was also the centre of British power in the Middle East and North and Central Africa. Air routes first to Baghdad, then India and Africa were soon to be pioneered by the RAF from bases in Egypt, which led to the formation of Imperial Airways in 1924. Many of the senior commanders in the Second World War cut their teeth in the Middle East, such as Bert's Squadron Commander, Arthur 'Bomber' Harris, and Air-Vice Marshall Sir Geoffrey Salmond. Bert was in at the beginning of all this in 1919, giving him a wonderful opportunity to show his worth and develop his future in the peacetime RAF; as we shall see, it shaped his career in many ways and he returned later to serve with the Air Staff in Cairo.

He writes on arrival:

12.7.1919

My Dear Mum and Dad

After five weeks of moving about from place to place, we at least seem to have found permanent quarters in this spot Helwan, which is fifteen miles south of Cairo.

On our arrival at Alexandria we were sent to a base or rest camp outside Aboukir for four days. Early in the morning and in the afternoons bathing in the sea and tennis were the main attractions, but at night our slumbers would have been much disturbed by every conceivable variety of vermin were it not for liberal quantities of Keeting's Powder in and around our beds.

From Aboukir we were sent to Heliopolis, a suburb of Cairo, and remained there for a short time until HQ made up their minds and posted us to this place.

Naturally there is a distinct change in the climate and country here, hotter than what we had been accustomed to in France and Germany, even though we thought it rather warm there at times.

The heat is far from being oppressive, a clean dry heat, good breezes, and although one perspires freely it is not uncomfortable – the nights are wonderfully cool and exhilarating.

Outside the Nile valley is a land of waste and desolation, and so tremendous is the control of the fertility and intensive cultivation in this valley that one marvels that there is sufficient water left in the Nile when one considers how small the rainfall is throughout the year.

Our machines have not arrived yet, but we have been given three Avroes (training machines) to keep our hands in. All our flying is done in the morning and afternoons in the cool of the day; it would not be impossible to fly when the sun is in the middle of the heavens, but the extreme heat (it is an average of 102 in the shade) and air bumps tend to make flying uncomfortable.

Avro 504 landing at Helwan, Egypt.

Our camp is on a bit of a rise away from the village of Helwan and consists entirely of stone buildings, our sleeping quarters in stone buildings are admirably built, cool and with plenty of fresh air to circulate in and about the rooms.

As all fresh fruit and vegetables are only obtainable in the native market, and as these natives are all so keen on getting and making contracts for supplies to the camp, we had to insist on nominal rent being paid in to the regimental fund; the same thing applied to the camp tailor, barber and fancy goods merchant. The CO made me responsible for this regimental fund which entails the supervision of the men's messing and a host of other things. This regimental fund is known as the P.R.F.

I am responsible for all grants paid out for supplies etc. for the welfare of the men, so it is almost like running a small business concern, and most of my time each day is taken up with it.

This moving about has paid havoc with all my mail…

Last Sunday we made an extensive tour of the pyramids, starting from Memphis to Sakana and from there to the Giza pyramids and Sphinx by camels, a distance of seventeen miles.

Our guide, one of Cook's dragomen, was quite an expert at his job and with the aid of a history book on the Ancient Egyptians gave a most interesting discourse. To take this subject seriously one could spend weeks and weeks on these ancient relics in the tombs and temples without any fear of becoming bored. The visit has encouraged me to study the ancient history of this country, and I am finding it very enthralling. I took a number of snaps and will send prints of those that have come out successfully.

My expenses for the month have been a little above normal. I have had to practically re-equip my kit as regards clothing, all light khaki from Army Ordinance, and this had to be altered to fit me.

You may have read in the papers weeks go of the discussions and regulations arrived at by the Air Ministry and the Army Council about relinquishment of acting rank to substantive rank: this for some time past has been a bad bone of contention, my present substantive rank is Lieut. acting Captain in the capacity as Flt. Commander. It is quite possible that I shall have to drop the Acting Rank through not being recommended by the late CO of 83 Squadron, Major Price; up to the present I have not been notified, but in any event like this happening, I shall still retain my position as Flt. Commander.

Cairo, although a city of perplexing nationalities and a certain insidious charm does not worry me in the slightest. Bert

206 Squadron
R.A.F.
Egypt
13.8.1919

My Dear Mother and Dad

All this week and last I have been having a really busy time of it, what with attending courts of enquiry and supervising the assembling of the flights machines, and have had very little time to myself.

This sudden 'rush' has abated somewhat and things ought a normal course for some time.

Last week I had been detailed to preside at a court of enquiry at a place El Rimal, quite close to Ismalia. I flew over in a machine and did the trip of over a hundred miles in good time only to find that the other members had not put in an appearance and so was obliged to postpone it. On attempting to get away in the afternoon, I had an awful job starting the engine, and it was only after about two hours' strenuous labour going over the ignition circuits and carburettors that the engine took it in to its head to behave properly. The sun was just sinking, but I was determined to get away after once starting the 'blamed engine'. In no time it was dark and there was no prospect of a moon, but I had little difficulty in following the Ismalia Canal to Cairo and then on to Helwan. I surprised the camp by dumping the machine on the aerodrome safely without flares.

Two days after I paid another visit to El Rimal, and took the precaution of bringing a good fitter in the observer's cockpit; we finished off the inquiry satisfactorily and got back home in good time.

Most of my time at present has been taken up in flight sheds, where our machines are being assembled. What with superintending the construction there are so many modifications to be carried out that special care has to be exercised.

I am awfully sorry to hear that Uncle Ted and Aunty Margaret have lost their little son – it seems so unfortunate… Please do not take some of the yarns re 'flying' as gospel truth from some of the fellows who have returned; a certain type are inclined to 'stretch the longbow' and you must not take them to seriously.

No definite news has come to hand about permanent commissions. I could not draw my gratuity straight away, but was given the opportunity of investing it in Victory Bonds. In the event of my being granted a permanent commission, the major part of the gratuity would have to be refunded, so thought it best to make use of it while in my possession.

I have cabled Cox and Co transferring part of my account to the branch in Cairo, and am waiting to see how much I have in hand and will then forward a draft on to you.

I had a letter from Miss Bennett; she is still in the W.R.N.S. but talks of going to East Africa farming. I think she should stop in the W.R.N.S., she has done wonderfully well in it and is the work I imagine she would prefer…Bert

23.8.1919

I was very sorry to hear Alice and Art had been laid up so bad, and what with the servant problem you must have had a very wearying and anxious time. This servant problem seems to be very acute all over England – the Bolshevistic element coming to the fore. I do not know how many Auntie Rutter has had to sack. (!!!)

One of the pilots in my flight, while buying mess supplies in Cairo the day before yesterday, saw in the Times Gazette of Aug 1st or 2nd that I had been granted a permanent commission in the R.A.F., with substantive rank of a full Lieut. This, I suppose, is a distinction in a way, as we have been led to understand that very few permanent commissions have been granted in the force. The scale of pay for permanent Rank is lower than the Army of Occupation pay, but of no great material difference, and instead of a gratuity of about £200 now being paid to my agents, only fifty will be given. This may seem strange but the Army has its own way of doing things, and I think everything will pan out alright for the future.

In this new profession I have taken up, there are wonderful facilities for study of motor engines, photography, wireless telegraphy or telephony, and aerial navigation. This would have been a totally different aspect if I had joined the infantry or cavalry and I do not want you or Dad to ever worry again as to what profession or occupation might have suited me; I am a materialist in this respect that I am making the best of what opportunity has been given me, without pining for 'what might have beens'.

Now that we have hopes of settling down for some time, I ought to be able to send out regular amounts. I am sending out a draft in the next day or two a soon as Cox's inform me of my balance.

Once Dad is successful I should make tracks for a house towards the upper end of town, the atmosphere of the houses around cannot now be of the pleasantest. [They had moved to Dundee in Natal to try and improve the dentist business, without success, sadly.] Our machines are fast nearing completion, and I expect we shall be busy shortly on some job or other… Bert

17.9.1919

Now that most of our machines have been completed we have been doing a fair amount of flying, formation principally and alternated frequently with squadron formation. These stunts are interesting and at times very amusing, especially when 'contour chasing', i.e. hedge hopping when there are any hedges.

'A' Flt. My little command has been rather unfortunate this

'A' Flight 206Sq Helwan. Bert, Flight Commander, 3rd from left front row.

past week, what with several forced landings (I had one myself but managed to get into an aerodrome safely while over Cairo), and rubber tyre and rubber petrol connections. The rubber in this climate lasts no time and we are continuously busy changing perished stuff. One must expect these little trials and setbacks, but they are annoying and help to disturb one's equanimity, when keen on bringing the flight to a state of efficiency and smartness.

This last fortnight I have been accompanying the C.O. on trips to various places in the country; we flew over to Alexandria last fortnight for a weekend, and spent the Sunday morning surf bathing. We had a wonderful time, and although fairly tanned at the time, we found we had been caught badly by the sun, especially on the legs and shoulders.

We did the trip back to Helwan that afternoon in an hour exactly, a distance of a hundred and thirty miles – the wind helped us along considerably.

On our return to the squadron we found that we were going to suffer somewhat for our bathing entertainment. I remembered your recipe for sunburn backs at Oudtshoorn, and got the M.O. to make up a mixture of glycerine and methylated spirits. This proved great relief…

I see the Times Gazette has confirmed my acting rank from the end of April, when I thought I might have to relinquish it.

This weekend I accompanied the Major to Ismalia on the Suez Canal. After he had completed his duty we spent the day on the smaller Bitter Lake, sailing in a small boat. I took the precaution of shielding my skin from the all too scorching rays of the sun by wearing a light suit of pyjamas. The water in the lake is frightfully salt and as you can imagine very buoyant – it was almost impossible to sink. We spent an interesting time navigating the shoals and creeks and inspecting the canal itself. I took some photos and as soon as the prints are ready will send them along.

Please send me Arthurs address in B.E.A. (Kenya)… Bert

Bert sailing in his pyjamas, to protect him from sunburn, on the Great Bitter Lake, Egypt, with his squadron CO, 1919.

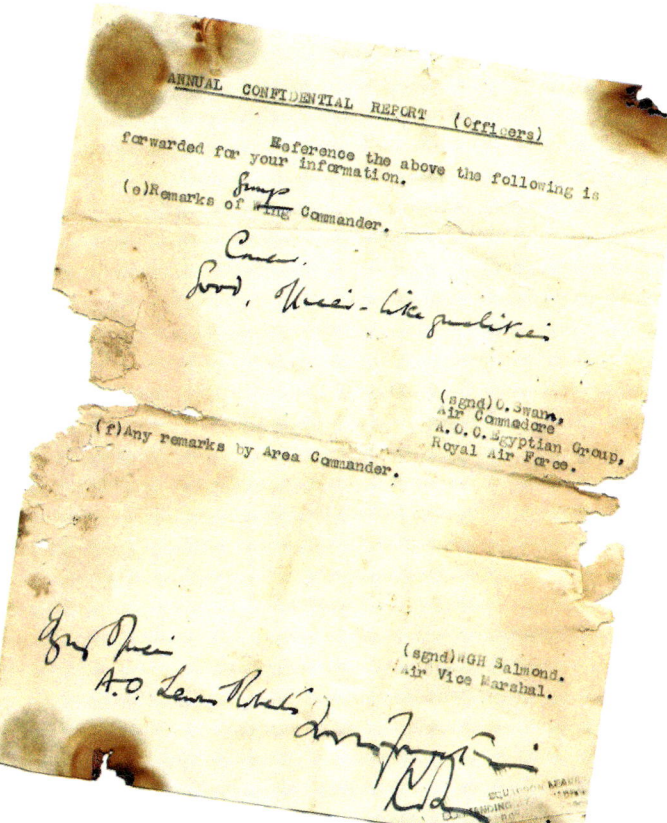

During this period an annual confidential report was started on each officer's character and performance; normally a copy was sent to the officer concerned. I have found two of them for Bert and copy one above (rather tatty!) This dates to about 1920 while he was with 47 Squadron.

The other one, of unknown date, I transcribe here:

Annual confidential report.
A hard and very conscientious worker. Slow but thorough thinker. Quiet and reserved in manner. Extremely reliable. An exceptionally keen and very good pilot.

Another annual report:

During the two and a half months I have known this officer I have formed a high opinion of his ability and character. He is, I should say, an exceptionally dependable and level-headed officer with a gift for leadership. The spirit and work of his recently formed squadron, are a fine tribute to his capability as a unit commander.

I think these comments are very important in describing this young, developing officer who was making his way in the post-war RAF, and they entirely reveal why he was as valued as an officer.

Bert in desert kit, about 1920

15.11.1919

My Dear Mother and Dad

These last few weeks have been a somewhat trying time for me; in my previous letters I stated we had been extremely busy erecting machines, these have been finished, but we were very unfortunate in having a couple of 'write offs', machines rather badly damaged whilst landing.

In consequence we were hard put to it to make these machines 'good' as well as keeping the others serviceable. Everybody has worked hard and uncomplainingly, and the 'esprit de corps' of the flight has been wonderful.

Last week we had a visit from the G.O.C. R.A.F. Middle East and the Sirdar of Egypt, G.O.C. Egyptian troops. Two other fellows and I flew over to Heliopolis to fly them over to our aerodrome. The G.O.C. RAF Air Commodore, Groves, piloted one of the machines himself and I flew the Sirdar over. I had been ordered to lead the way and the three machines 'formatted' perfectly until over the aerodrome when we all landed safely. The inspection went off very well and I think the G.O.C. was very pleased with the work and efficiency of the squadron…

The squadron held a dance in Helwan about a fortnight ago and it was a great success. The squadron, considering its short stay in Egypt, has made many friends with a number of charming English folk. The Gezira Club, HQ Middle East and the Golf Course at Helwan have been the sponsors in this respect.

I did a fair amount of dancing, had to in fact, rather than allow a number of fair damsels to appear preoccupied twiddling their fingers; a number of English fellows from a Sikh Regiment had failed to put in an appearance and every fellow had to do his share of dancing.

I am by no means a brilliant exponent of the art of jazzing, but had to do my best as I was one of the hosts.

Two days ago I led the squadron formation over Cairo as a parade celebrating the event of FM Allenby's arrival. The formation on the whole was good and we received a note of congratulations from the G.O.C

Your loving son Bert.

29.11.1919

My Dear Mother

Last week I had a very interesting trip into Upper Egypt by air. A pilot in another machine accompanied me; we left our aerodrome early one morning just at dawn to reach Luxor a well-known place four hundred miles up the Nile.

Half way down we landed at Assuit for a report on the aerodrome there, and filled up with petrol and oil. The Colonel of an Indian regiment there took us in to breakfast, and we found him to be a charming fellow; we could not stop any time and were on the way to Luxor.

The country between Assuit and Luxor is full of interest, at the former place a sight unfamiliar to most people is the barrage; this consists of a tremendous concrete wall stretching across the Nile, in this wall are a number of large openings spaced at equal intervals, steel doors let in on top of the wall cover these entrances. In this way the water of the Nile can be dammed, led away through canals and cuttings to irrigate all arable land, or the flow regulated for the lower reaches of the Nile Delta.

It is by this system of barrages, locks and canals that all Egypt is irrigated. Were it not so, every inch of land would be flooded during the heavy rain season in the region of Upper Egypt.

We reached Luxor safely and had a busy time filling the machines, ourselves, with petrol and oil. Indian troops were there to carry supplies, but were useless as regards being entrusted with the filling of the tanks. Luxor is world famed for its temples and tombs of the Ancient Egyptians; it was there I think, that Rider Haggard gained his material for the plots of some of his stories. We had no time to visit the ancient relics of a bygone race and could only see them from the air as we crossed the river on the way back to Assuit.

Oxland on landing at Assuit was extremely unfortunate in wiping the undercarriage off his machine. While the oil pressure on my machine was being attended to, and tanks being filled John Lowe, my observer, Oxland and I had time to slip over to the Colonel's launch on the river for tea and bread and butter.

On the way back to Helwan there was a slight wind against us, nevertheless we made good time and reached the aerodrome just after dusk. We had covered the distance of eight hundred miles in seven hours forty minutes flying time which was not too bad

I found a letter from you awaiting me at the mess and was filled with joy, dated 15th October, it had six weeks to reach me... I shall cable you fifty pounds this week for Xmas.

I spent a busy day shopping in Cairo with Gray, the other flight commander, several days ago. I did not buy much as I could not find anything really suitable that was not frightfully expensive. The best bargains are to be had in the native quarters of Cairo but these have been placed out of bounds to all troops since this latest unrest. I bought some Maltese lace which I thought you might like, a scarf each for Alice and Josephine and a black silk shawl for Grannie, I want you please to get a small present each for Dad and Uncle Ted. I had a wonderful letter from Arthur, he says he is in with a good firm which means a great deal. I have replied and am sending him some silk handkerchiefs... This letter will reach you in time for Xmas... my thoughts will be with you... Bert.

As we move into 1920, Bert's flying logbook gives a very detailed record of his flying service. 206 Squadron is disbanded and renumbered 47 squadron on 1st Feb 1920. He appears to fly most days; flights lasting 20 minutes to 2.5 hours. The shorter flights are nearly all test flights and frequent trips to 58 Squadron at Heliopolis on duty. While he undertakes some aerial photography he also does quite a lot of mail delivery and pioneering new air routes, exploring the equipment and techniques needed. The Cairo to Baghdad air route carrying mail was developed at this time, forming the basis for developing longer distance air routes to the east and south in to Africa. Frequent flights are to Aswan, Wadi Halfa and Khartoum. Much of this work was to support the strategy of policing large areas particularly in the Sudan and Iraq.

To quote the official history of the RAF:

The arteries of the British Empire gave the RAF the opportunity to pioneer new air routes – to Egypt initially, and then on to India, Singapore and Australia as well as southward to the tip of Africa. Frequently, of course, such flying was done as part of the normal operational routine by individual Squadrons. From such unsung work, however, British civil aviation established itself throughout the Empire as Imperial Airways, formed in 1924 as the chosen instrument of the Government to develop British commercial air transport on an economic basis.

The RAF had cut its teeth for this work by operating the airmail and passenger service to Paris for government officials attending the Peace Conference in Paris in 1919, as well as an air mail service to British troops of the Army of Occupation in Germany, which did much to restore the morale of men who appeared to have been forgotten so quickly after the war had ended. (As we have seen from Bert's earlier letters).

The first major route, Cairo-Baghdad, officially began in 1921. It was pioneered by a convoy of cars from Amman accompanied by 47 Squadrons DH9as and Handley Page 0/400s of 70 Squadron meeting another convoy which had set out at the same time from Baghdad escorted by DH9as from 30 Squadron as to act as guides. The two convoys met roughly

Off duty – an unusually relaxed picture of Bert in Egypt.

half way across the desert; the tracks provided visible navigation aids until a permanent track was ploughed★ and a route had been established. Later, landing grounds were marked along the route, underground fuel tanks were installed and mail reached the British troops in Iraq only 5 days after posting in London. This Cairo-Baghdad route became so important it was the first overseas sector and basis for routes of *Imperial Airways* in 1927.

★ Reputedly ploughed by a Fordson Tractor!

12.2.1920

My Dear Mother and Dad

I sent you a p.c. from Suez on 23rd Dec; I had flown over there with another fellow, Giles, with mail for some of our pilots and men, who were off on a special stunt; they were very pleased to see us when we boarded the boat. Our stay on the boat was of short duration… we were ordered to get into a motor boat which took us ashore with a wonderful dash of speed.

On the morning of the 24th the sand storm which had been raging the previous day was as bad as ever, and sea mist had started to come in, so Giles and How, my observer, and I wasted no time in getting back to the aerodrome and starting up our machines, as we had no intention of spending Xmas away from the squadron.

The weather was very bad at the time, misty and very bumpy, so we climbed right above it and steered a compass course for home. We had been flying into a strong head wind and only reached the aerodrome after two hours whereas the previous morning we had done the trip to Suez in forty-five minutes.

Xmas morning Lowe and I and a few others attended early communion service in the English church in Helwan. All that day I had a busy time as President of the Regimental Institute, PRI. I had my hands full supervising the men's Xmas dinner, and what a dinner they did have; starting off with excellent soup, they had as much roast turkey, beef, potatoes, green peas, cauliflower, and sauce as they wanted. Then came the final effort with the Xmas pudding and brandy sauce. Fruit followed and cigarettes and matches were distributed to every man.

Altogether it was a wonderful success and everyone enjoyed himself to the full.

We had our Xmas dinner at seven that night, and a very jolly affair it was, nevertheless I developed a 'hump' and went to bed early after an impromptu concert in the men's recreation hall. Metcalf our PMC and I had managed to get a cinema show going and were very fortunate in procuring a Charles Chaplin film – this was appreciated greatly.

I only hope you had a cheery Christmas; all my thoughts were with you that day.

I have met some cheery English folk in Helwan. Mr Quinell, who is one of the world's leading experts on Egyptian antiques and OC of the Cairo museum, and his wife are a most charming old couple. I have been invited to their house for dinner on several occasions… With the Air Commodore's permission I took Mr Quinell up in the air on an interesting trip to the Fayoum, a large district south of the Nile Delta and flew over all the Pyramids… Low, Carter and I played for the R.A.F. against Gazira Club Cairo at Rugger. The Gezira club Cairo represent the Army in Egypt. I played as a forward and the game was a very fast and hard one. We did all our scoring in the first half, and in the second half maintained our lead despite their most determined onslaught. The game finished 11 points to 3 in our favour. The air commodore and several other R.A.F. notables were watching the game and were pretty delighted by our win.

There was a big Boxing Tournament on the 8th, 9th and 10th. The squadron had only been notified a week in advance and we were asked to send in an officers' team and as many other competitors as possible. We raised an officers' team with difficulty; there were four competitors needed and I volunteered to make it up, rather against my better judgment. Our event came off on the 10th and there was great excitement. The other fellows did well in their bouts and then it was my turn. I was against an officer, Meecham by name, renowned throughout Egypt and India as a wonderful fighter and boxer. Meecham, though a little shorter than I was, was half a stone heavier and beautifully built.

It was quite a novelty for me to be boxing with an eager audience a thousand strong, including a lot of 'Brass Hats' from the Air Force and the Army, watching with super critical eyes. I knew my nerves and senses were in a state of 'high tension'.

The canvas floor of the ring, although covered in resin, was inclined to be slippery, so I discarded my tennis shoes with leather soles and boxed in socks.

The start of the first round was fast and furious; my only hope lay in making short rushes using my 'left' and 'right' as much as possible and then retiring to prevent any 'in fighting'. It was in one of these onslaughts that one of the boards of the ring gave way and as I was backing a wood splinter under the canvas penetrated my right foot and tore away all the skin. In the heat of the contest I had not noticed anything much, until after the referee had stopped the fight. I noticed that I was padding the ring with crimson spots. The pain became rather intense, and while the ring was being repaired I had the wound dressed with iodine and lint which made me jump. I found I could not do anything with the right foot and had to retire, which was rather unsatisfactory in a way even though the other fellow might have given me a good 'pasting.'

Our officer's team proved the winning team and after the show the Commodore presented us each with a miniature cup.

I simply long to get home on leave… but things are in such an unsettled state in the R.A.F. and even in the squadron that I have been advised to hang on for several months until the atmosphere quietens down a bit. I am the only flight commander left at present in the squadron. You may have read in the papers of the new R.A.F. programme in the way of future developments. Egypt and the East are going to be the big centres of flying, instruction and navigation… Your loving son Bert

Bert records in a letter of early 1920 the arrival of the 'Silver Queen', a pioneering flight from Cairo to Cape Town piloted by Col van Ryneveldt and Capt. Brand. Bert knew Brand from the war years and asked him to take a letter with them, to his mother and father, and post it in Johannesburg, which he duly did. That cover, which is in our possession, must be one of the first airmail deliveries ever undertaken on this route.

First air mail cover, carried from Cairo to Johannesburg in the 'Silver Queen'. Below – first air mail from Karachi to Cairo.

47 Squadron (late 206 Squadron)

R.A.F. Egypt

14-3-1920

My dear Mother and Dad

I hope by now you will have received my letter wishing you the very best and lots of love for your silver wedding day. I met Col van Ryneveldt and Captain Brand at Heliopolis after their wonderful flight across the Mediterranean and gave them the letter to be carried in Silver Queen no 1.

I knew Capt. Brand when he was a squadron commander in France; his squadron of night flying scouts did wonderful work against the Hun long distance bombing machines which were at one time a frightful menace to all hospitals in northern France.

I saw the Silver Queen take off that night from Heliopolis and prayed hard that it might make the Cape without mishap. It was at this time that the C.O., Sqdn. Leader Reid, had arranged a trip to Luxor. Johnny Lowe and Major Glynn from H.Q. Middle East were of the party; I was to have joined them if my leave came through… At the very last minute after all the arrangements had been made and rooms booked at the Winter Palace Luxor, my leave came through… here was no other course open but to join the Major's Party for local leave, which does not in any way interfere with home leave and free railway vouchers are given to the place you intend to visit, so no heavy travelling expenses were incurred.

We spent a most wonderful week at Luxor visiting the temples of Thebes, Karnak and others as well as the tombs of the Kings, Queens and Nobles… The temples were some miles from the hotel and it cost a fortune to hire out donkeys. It was always a great source of amusement riding these animals as not infrequently many spills were encountered. The art of keeping on was balancing and not gripping the saddle as if riding a horse…

It was at Luxor that I heard of the Silver Queen's crash at Korosko; it seemed frightful luck after the wonderful performance she had put up. Undaunted, the Colonel and Captain Brand salvaged the engines, had them reinstated in a new machine at Heliopolis and had left before I got back to the squadron. Last news of the new Silver Queen was that they had landed at Livingstone…

About a week ago, our Padre introduced me to the Bishop of Jerusalem. After permission had been granted by the Air Commodore, I took him up for a flight in my machine 'A', over Cairo and the surrounding country; we went up to 10,000ft, flying amongst the clouds and above them. The Bishop enjoyed himself immensely and whenever I looked round he was busy taking photographs… When we landed he told me that he had an overwhelming inclination, when in the air, to take off his flying helmet and shout, so exhilarating had he found it.

Four days ago after having been up in the 'limpid blue', the C.O. came up and told me that I had to leave at dawn the following morning in a machine, accompanied by McGregor in another, for Wadi Halfa, where a Handley Page had force landed and was awaiting spares. Halfa is about 800 miles up the river and quite a fair distance for a machine of our type, with a single engine. After going over my machine and engine carefully with my mechanics, and McGregor with his machine, we loaded up with spares.

Mac and I left at dawn the following morning, landing at Assiut and Assuan for supplies of petrol and oil… However after eight hours flying we arrived safely at Halfa and then off to the place where the H P had force landed, delivered our spares, interviewed the Colonel who was in charge and then back to Halfa again for the night.

The Governor of the Province, a Mr Tibbets and his wife, were on the aerodrome to meet us; they were very nice to us and put Mac and me under the charge of an aide-de-camp. Their home was full of visitors and they regretted not being able to have us for dinner that night, for which I was rather thankful in a way being rather tired after the day's work.

Major Jervis took us to his home, where after a steaming hot bath an excellent dinner made new men of us.

The next morning we were away again to the H.P.; we did not forget to thank our hosts for their kind hospitality. At Ballana where the H.P. lay picketed, I had to leave my trusty mechanic Paley and pick up Colonel Drew. After stowing him safely away with his kit in the back seat, we took off again. We passed over Korosko, the scene of the Silver Queen mishap, and the ground there was far from inviting… landing at Assouan in the early afternoon and filling the machines with petrol and oil, we left them in charge of a Sikh detachment and put up at the Cataract Hotel. The next morning we were away at dawn and after two and a half hours flying landed at Assiut for petrol. Here I punctured a wheel landing but soon fitted on a spare one which I had carried on the bomb rack.

Both machines landed safely at Helwan at two in the afternoon; our engines had behaved wonderfully well.

Today being Sunday I took the Church Parade, and after that was able to sit and write a few letters… Your loving son Bert.

The British Government had funded, starting in 1918, the construction of landing fields (about 150) on the Cape to Cairo route at suitable intervals, and it was declared open at the end of December 1919. Several expeditions declared their intentions to take up the challenge for a substantial prize offered for the first to complete the flight. The Vickers Vimy 'Silver Queen' was sponsored by the Government of South Africa and was flown by two of Bert's wartime friends, Lieut. Col. Pierre van Rynveld, D.S.O., M.C., and Capt. Quinton Brand. With them were two maintenance engineers, Mr Burton, an airframe fitter, and Mr F W Sherratt, of Rolls Royce. They took off from Brooklands aerodrome on 4th February 1920 and flew to Cairo, where they met Bert, who gave them a letter to deliver to his mother in South Africa. A forced landing, in the dark, at Korosko wrote off Silver Queen No 1. They were undaunted, and another airframe was made available and the engines transferred.

Silver Queen No 2 set off from Cairo on February 22nd and arrived safely at Bulawayo a week later. The Vimy was found to be overloaded for the altitude of the airfield and crashed on take-off after a mile or so. No one was hurt, but the machine was a write-off. A DH9 named 'Voortrekker', belonging to the fledgling South African Air Force, was flown up to Bulawayo and the flight to Cape Town was completed on 20th March, leaving the mechanics to continue by sea. Captain Brand duly delivered the letter for Bert's Mother on 17th March in Johannesburg. Both pilots were knighted by the King and Col. Van Ryneveld became the first head of the Union Air Force.

47 Squadron

12-4-1920

My Dear Mother and Dad

We spent a quiet Easter in camp, and although the R.A.F. had been given a couple of day's general holiday, I was busy on an urgent photographic job of an island in the Nile off Cairo. I attended the early morning communion service at the C of E church at Helwan, our padre officiated and enjoyed the service. It bought back to me memories of other happy Easter mornings.

I am at present the only member of 'A' flight… Giles, the other officer, has just accomplished a wonderful flight to a place eighteen hundred miles up the River Nile; we had been busy getting the machine ready for the flight some days past, and although I had tested his engine and had found it to be a good one, I was more than relieved when I heard that he had reached his destination safely; he had several nasty tracts of country to cover for a single engine machine.

I have been taking lessons in Arabic for the last three weeks with an Egyptian school teacher, the C.O. and two other fellows are in the class… I have been on a big stock taking board as president, this particular one was held at the squadron and I had quite a busy time of it. Tomorrow I am on a Court of Inquiry, and what with my flight duties, and the Regimental Institute, the Arabic lessons have been in abeyance… I am by no means a budding Carpentier, and have been persuaded again to enter for the Officer Bouts which take place in the Big R.A.F. Boxing tournament at the end of the month. I shall not be let off so lightly this time and will deserve a drubbing for my audacity… Bert.

Accidents were not uncommon.

Not usually fatal – Bert had several!

In accordance with the written orders copied above, Bert undertook an interesting flight to Sollum on June 2nd 1920; he describes it in the next letter, but just who or what were 'the 4 S Russian Officers' he does not relate. As can be seen, the orders were scribbled in haste by his squadron leader. Perhaps it was intelligence gathering?

19.6.1920
47 Squadron
R.A.F. Egypt

Dear Mother and Dad

I told you I was about to fly to Sollum on the North African coast. I started off early that next morning with my trusty mechanic Corporal Paley and reached Aboukir in time for breakfast, I knew several fellows in the squadron stationed there, and was fixed up very comfortably.

The day turned out wonderfully bright and clear and I have never seen the Mediterranean appear so beautiful and inviting. The contrast of colour of the various shades of vivid blue, the white sand of the coastline, and the dull opaque mass of brown of the receding desert with the skyline was startling. The sea was as calm and peaceful as you could possibly wish it to be and so transparent that you could see the coastline shelving in to plateaus and ravines to unknown depth.

About two hundred miles from Alexandria I landed at a little settlement on the coast and picked up the pilot of a crashed machine who had force landed due to engine failure. Edelston and I had lunch with the Governor of the province and left the ground at three in the afternoon for Sollum. I left Paley with Edelston's mechanic to salvage what stuff he could from the damaged machine and flew off with Edelston in the back seat.

The country west of Alexandria is desert devoid of all cultivation, with the exceptions of oases stationed at long intervals. After an uneventful flight of two hours we landed at Sollum and I handed over the machine to O.C. of the R.A.F. detachment there.

They had no accommodation in their mess for Edelston and me, so Colonel Davenport of the Egyptian Army kindly took us in to his quarters. I had met him before as a guest in our mess and was very pleased to see him. The only means of travelling between Sollum and Alexandria is by boat and as one was not expected for several days we had a perfectly wonderful time bathing and sailing out into the bay in the Colonel's yacht.

After I had been there a week a small steam boat of about four hundred tons put into the Bay and I left the following morning having had a really pleasant change, luckily the weather was very calm, otherwise with a heavy swell, the 'Imogen' would have rolled and tossed about like a cork.

I spent a day at Alexandria arranging for aeroplane spares to be sent to Sollum and returned to the squadron the next day by train… Bert.

The workhorse of 47 Squadron was the rather unreliable DH9, which was replaced by the redesigned and much improved DH9a in the latter half of 1920. The main problem with the DH9 was its lack of power; Bert also reported, in his letters, problems with rubber hosing and tyres perishing quickly in the heat. As well as lengthened wings and stronger fuselage, a new 400 HP American Liberty engine was fitted. The first of these modified DH9s were delivered in March 1918 and at the end of the war it was decided that the DH9a would be the standard light bomber for the post-war RAF.

Five squadrons were deployed to the Middle East, one

of which was Bert's 47 Squadron. He often reported engine overheating in his log book, so for the hotter climate, a larger radiator and extra water containers was fitted and frequently spares were carried. Sometimes even spare wheels were strapped to the outside in case of damage in the remote, harsh and arid conditions. It proved a successful and popular machine and it went on in Squadron service till 1931.

The DH9a was armed with a fixed synchronised Vickers machine gun firing through the propeller and a Scarff ring mounted Lewis gun handled by the Observer/gunner in the rear cockpit. Bert records regular testing on the ranges along with bombing practice as well as engineering courses.

1.8.1920
47 Squadron R.A.F.
Egypt
Dear Mother and Dad

Last fortnight I and two others were sent to A.E.R.D., a huge engine repair depot in Cairo, for a course on a new engine; the squadron is being re-equipped with a new type of machine [DH9a which is very much faster and higher powered than the type we are using now [DH9].

The course seemed to be an absolute farce in as much that no tuition or technical help was offered by the 'technical experts' there; we were given an engine to dismantle and with a handbook on the engine itself, we had to fend for ourselves.

Our time there was by no means wasted however and what with running up, testing and experimenting with 'gadgets'; we picked up a great deal of useful information… For the past ten days the men have worked like Trojans erecting new machines; they were given a time limit to erect a number of machines, and so quickly and efficiently was the work carried out that the Air Vice Marshal himself sent a letter of congratulation.

I forgot to mention in my last letter our C.O. Squadron Leader Reid went home to England on two months' leave; he had to pay his own passage there and back. A senior Flight Lieutenant was posted to the squadron two days before he left

DH9a over the desert, typical of the type that Bert flew (Wikipedia)

Mid-air picture of a DH9 taken by Bert while flying in the Middle East.

and took over the Squadron. On my return from the engine course, I found that Bailey had put another officer in charge of 'A' Flt., this fellow is slightly senior to me on the Air Force list and I had to hand over to him, having had command of it for over a year. I was then detailed to take over the QM stores, so now behold in me a Quarter Master to the Station. I am responsible for all men's clothing, kit, equipment, rations and petrol and oil supplies… I was called away suddenly to fly a machine to Alexandria. Since then I have been busy flying our new machines from Alexandria, as soon as I had brought back one machine to the squadron I would have to leave the same night by train for Alexandria for another, and what with a fair amount of office work in the Q.M. stores I have had little time to myself.

I met a Major Sancroft Baker at Middle East H.Q., he is an elderly man and holds a permanent commission in the R.A.F. I had to see him on duty one morning and in conversation I learnt that he had been through the Boer War, was present at the Relief of Kimberley, and after the war had settled down on a farm at Standerton. I had gone to see him about a special engineering course which will start at Cambridge University next October. I had put in an application and wanted to know further particulars. I explained that I had put in two years work at the School of Mines at Johannesburg and was very keen on taking up this course at Cambridge; he appeared greatly surprised at me being a South African… well after this Baker dropped South African conversation rather abruptly and made me feel rather uncomfortable; he was too much of a gentleman to appear rude and discourteous, but he never the less made me feel uncomfortable.

I was wondering if you or Dad had ever come across him in the old Kimberley days, it seems strange but I have a premonition that Baker has heard of us before…

I have not heard anything more about my application to fly to the Cape. Our late Commodore Greaves was very keen on it, but since he was killed in a flying accident a little while ago, nothing more seems to have been done about it, that was why I put in an application for the Cambridge course.

Your loving son Bert

From the next letter it appears Bert's plan to go up to Cambridge in the autumn of 1920 has as he says been 'squashed', the reason is not clear. It could have been because of trouble brewing in Mesopotamia or just because Cambridge was not ready for the course. Nevertheless, to his delight, he goes up in the autumn of 1921. He writes a rather disconsolate letter home:

23.9.1920
47 Squadron, R.A.F.
Egypt
My dear mother and Dad

My application for the Cambridge course has evidently been squashed; no news has come through from headquarters, and as the course starts October 1st, it is pretty definite I shall not go. All this trouble in Mesopotamia may be partially responsible, as everybody is on the alert and waiting…

My Q.M. duties keep me fully occupied these days, nevertheless this last week I have been playing a great deal of cricket. I was picked for the R.A.F. Cricket Trials but did not do anything very extraordinary. I was very surprised when I found I was chosen for the R.A.F. xi versus Army xi of Egypt and Palestine; we had a two day match at Gezira Sporting Ground. Although we were beaten rather badly by the Army folk we had a good game and I enjoyed myself. In the second innings I was in for fifty-five minutes and only scored seventeen runs… I was complimented for my fielding but it was an absolute pleasure to be fielding on good green turf again.

Things do not seem to be very bright these days at home what with the impending coal strike and the ghastly trouble in Ireland… Tomorrow morning I leave by air for Palestine to play in a cricket match against the Lahore Division. The C.O. very kindly gave me permission to fly my own machine.

The warm season is drawing to a close, and the weather at present is ideal. Flying in the early mornings is a sheer delight, it acts as a wonderful tonic, clears cobwebs from the brain and prepares one for the somewhat exacting work in the Q.M.'s office… Bert

In the summer of 1920 Bert was planning his future in the RAF. Having been granted a regular commission, he was keen to finish his university education in engineering. He applied for 'Officer Training' on Form 361 in August

1920; he aimed high and applied for the first BA course in Aeronautical Engineering at Cambridge University. The application went in with the letter shown on the next page, to his squadron commander, who fully supported him and helped promote his cause in every way; as we have seen, the course was delayed a year but Bert was due for home leave.

In January 1921 he returned to the home establishment; from March to October he was posted to the Central Flying School and Royal Aircraft Establishment at Farnborough on engineering courses. While on this course he was hospitalised again. This time he was operated on at Tidworth Military Hospital for appendicitis by surgeon E Huntley Cape Rowe. He noted: 'The appendix was found to have had a previous attack of trouble and was much swollen and matted.' Bert was highly commended by his tutor at the Central Flying School for keeping up his studies while in hospital: 'This officer has shown great keenness on the work and promises well, during his spell in hospital he has not fallen behind… in any way. - Flt. Lt. F. Sailey, Instructor in Theory of Engineering CFS, 6th May 1921'.

The CFS engineering course prepared him for Cambridge, and to his great delight he was awarded a place at Christ's College on the very first aeronautical degree course there. He went up to Cambridge in November 1921.

On returning from Egypt he took leave with the Rutters in Bournemouth. One of the most significant events of Bert's life happened during this stay; he met his future wife, Marjorie Gresham. The Greshams were a well to-do family living at Branksome Manor in west Bournemouth. Col. Gresham had been a great Victorian engineering entrepreneur whose Manchester company, Gresham and Craven Ltd., amongst other things, owned the patent for the vacuum brake system fitted to most railway trains worldwide. However, having commanded the 7th Manchester territorial regiment at Gallipoli, Gresham was invalided home; on medical advice he was advised to retire to the south coast, and moved to Branksome. They had two daughters, Marjorie and Nancy.

Bert relates how, when returning from a shopping trip to Bournemouth on a tram, Mrs Rutter found Mrs Gresham and Marjorie travelling on the upper deck. They were acquainted, so Mrs Rutter introduced Bert to them. Bert says 'my Lady Marjorie gave me a pert little nod' and then 'ignored me completely'! No encouragement yet! It was to be a very slow courtship and another ten years before they were married. The strange thing was seeing Mrs Gresham on a tram, when they had a chauffeur-driven car. Nevertheless it was an encounter of great significance in Bert's life story and led to tennis parties, balls and social encounters while he was in England for the next few years.

His course at Christ's College started in the autumn of 1921, and he clearly went up full of excitement and determination to succeed. He embraced college life with joy after being on active service for seven years

Application for Cambridge course, 1920.

almost continuously; he had not been home to South Africa since 1917. However he was granted leave to return home from 8th February to 31st May 1922. The authority was, strangely, granted by the RAF School of Photography at Farnborough.

I have found little about this trip, but it must have been a great joy for his family to see him after so long. It appears Bert must have gone by sea, as there were no scheduled flights yet and nothing is noted in his flight logbook. However he did keep up his flying even at university in an Avro 504, for about five hours a year, with 100 Squadron.

Permission for leave in South Africa, 1922.

Miss Marjory Gresham at about 21 years old

Tea on the Cam. Bert is second from left on the boat, next to the lady.

His absences made his first-class degree even more creditable. On June 19th 1924 his engineering lecturer, R. Lubbock, wrote to him:

Peterhouse
Cambridge
Dear Lewis-Roberts
Just a line of hearty congratulations on a well-deserved first! You certainly worked for it! The whole examination result is very satisfactory – no failures… I hope to see you before you go down – if I am not in college I shall generally be at my house.
Yours ever
R. Lubbock.

A kind and rewarding letter kept by Bert as a memento of his happy time at Cambridge.

Promotion came slowly in the interwar years. However in 1923 Bert was promoted Flight Lieutenant, duly noted by his former Egypt C.O. at Heliopolis.

His time at Cambridge ended with the graduation ceremony recorded in 1924 in the photograph below.

Christ's College Graduation. Bert on the left, the most suntanned man there!

Congratulations on promotion from Air Commodore B.C.H. Drew, A.O.C. Egypt Group

Chapter Seven

TEST PILOT, STAFF COLLEGE AND MARRIAGE, 1924-1931

From Cambridge Bert was posted to become a test pilot at the newly formed Aircraft and Armament Experimental Establishment.

The RFC experimental establishment had moved from Upavon to the bleak and windswept Martlesham Heath in Suffolk on 16th January 1917. In 1924 the airfield was enlarged, and on the 20th of March became the RAF's Aeroplane and Armament Experimental Establishment (A&AEE). At this time, as well as Military, Civil Aviation came under the Air Ministry, and it was the Air Ministry that issued Certificates of Airworthiness; thus all new civilian types were tested at the A&AEE. Under the far-sighted leadership of Air Marshal Sir Hugh Trenchard, the post-war RAF, whilst small, was determined to be of high quality in both men and machines. Aircraft manufacturers, desperate to get their new marques adopted by the slowly-evolving and much smaller RAF, now had the A&AEE to test them for service suitability as well as armaments.

The test pilots were drawn from serving officers, all of whom had seen war service and were widely seen as the cream of those available. They were formed into two Squadrons, No. 15 and No. 22, both re-formed for the purpose of experimental flying with planes supplied by A&AEE. Bert served with both squadrons. He first served with No.15 Squadron, from May 17th 1924. The squadron was set up to test such weapons as bombs, bomb sights, release mechanisms, guns, gun sights, flares and so on. Testing of live ordinance was carried out on the ranges acquired at Orford Ness, where there was also an aerodrome.

He started with 558 hrs flying in his log book and ended on August 4th 1927. More remarkable is the vast number of different types of machines which he flew and helped evaluate in just under three years.

His logbook shows he started in No. 15 Squadron on his old familiar workhorse, the DH9a, as an instructor or testing instruments, bomb sights, flares and so on at Orford Ness. While rigging seems to have still been an issue, with the DH9a forced landings still seem to have been caused, mainly by fog or bad weather.

While he had as many trips testing new features on the DH9a and for communication purposes mainly to Northolt, Bert still appears to be doing a lot of engine testing and flying instruction. In January 1925 he starts an intensive period of test bombing with the DH9a as a light bomber, and the twin engine Vickers Vimy heavy bomber. The tests were done at Orford Ness and were from the relatively low heights of 200ft, 500ft or 1000ft. While Orford was only ten minutes' flying time from Martlesham, planes were stored and landed for adjustment at Orford airfield. Flares of several types, including parachute flares, were tested and reported on.

While with No. 15 Squadron, Bert flew predominantly the DH9a and Vimy bombers, but also the following types (taken from his flying log book): Bristol Fighter, Parnall Plover, Avro Aldershot, Avro Lynx, Fairey Flycatcher, Armstrong Whitworth Siskin, Gloucester Grebe, Blackburn Cubaroo, Vickers Vimy, F2B, Bristol Bloodhound.

He moved to No. 22 Squadron from April 2nd 1925. This squadron was reformed to test and report on all new civil and military prototypes as well as substantially remodelled older types. To do this the squadron was split into three flights:

A Flight – for testing fighters and light civil aircraft
B Flight – tested bombers and larger civil aircraft.
C Flight – tested all aircraft that did not fit in to the above categories such as, Army co-operation or naval aircraft.

Bert was O.C. of C Flight. Testing included every characteristic of the aircraft; rate of climb, maximum ceiling, maximum loads, maximum speed, stalling speed, general handling and the most hair-raising, maximum speed test in a dive. That is, he would take a plane to a great height and then put it into a dive at maximum speed. Speeds of 240 mph are on record and he recorded such alarming comments as 'wing flutter'. This is an amazing speed when one realises the maximum speed in level flight was, typically, 120 mph. Spinning was another alarming test recorded; from 11,000ft to 4000ft he records 13 turns before pulling out, in a Beaver in 1927. Just '*stick and unstick*' was often noted in his log book against a new type under test. Again a critical performance issue; unstick speed is the minimum speed at which a plane will take off into safe flight and stick is the minimum steady flight speed at which the plane is still controllable.

It is worth noting that parachutes were not mandatory in the RAF until 1925, by which time Bert had recorded several test jumps out of his machines. Exiting a DH9a, for instance, must have been very difficult, as they were not designed for jumping out of in flight and there seems every chance they could get entangled in the rigging wires. However all these tests were managed without damage to himself, although several machines are recorded in his log book as crashed or failed in flight.

On June 3rd 1927 he records a flight to Bournemouth for a stay of three days in a Napier Vixen. Of course Marjorie Gresham lived in Bournemouth, and one cannot think of a more exciting way of advancing the relationship than arriving at speed in a Napier Vixen! His log book makes no comment of any testing, except that it took 70 minutes to return to Martlesham. He did record, in a later letter to Marjorie, his delight and the freedom enjoyed while flying with his chums in No. 22 Squadron. Although it must have been very hair raising at times, at least no one was shooting at him!

As time went by performance improved, and he notes ceilings of 23,500ft in tests of a Boarhound in 1926 and 23,000ft in a Hound, followed by the small note, '*no oxygen -30C*'. He recorded temperatures as low as -40C at 27,000ft! It is truly amazing to think of him flying at these altitudes in an open cockpit. There were also many 'climb and speed' tests, often with different types of propeller, including the first metal one he recorded in 1926 followed by the note 'nuts broken'. In the same year he experimented with picking up messages in two different types, Vespa and Hyena, entailing some very accurate low-level flying. His log book does not often record speeds attained, but in 1927 he recorded the speed of 156mph in level flight in a Condor Vixen, clearly a memorable speed for him.

Having tested the Avro Aldershot heavy bomber, his log book noted 'Qualified first pilot of the following machine in accordance with A.M.W.O. 462/25 ALDERSHOT'. Quite what the significance of this entry is I don't understand, as the prototype first flew in 1921, piloted by Bert Hinkler.

While with No. 22 Squadron Bert flew a remarkable number of different types, listed in chronological order as first flown from 3.4.25 to 17.9.27: Aldershot, Bison, Fairey Fawn, Hancross, Blackburn, Bristol Fighter, Bristol Brandon, Avro Andover, Avro Bison, Springbok, Blood Hound, Bristol Brownie, Hawker Horsley, Berkeley, Gamecock, Wolf, Siskin, Ferret, Possum, Brandon, Hedgehog, Grebe, Breguet, Flycatcher, Vernon, Virginia, Vixen, Atlas, Boar Hound, Woodcock, Bristol P.T.M., DH56 Hyena, DH54, Vespa, Avro, Airedale,

Navro, Avro Lucifer, Vendace, Fairey 111F, Pixie, Sprat, DH Moth, Westland Widgeon, Avro Avion, DH9A, Heron, Wapiti, Beaver, Goral, Valiant, D H Hound, Stagg, Hawfinch, Venture, Metal Virginia, Goring. (Please see appendix A for more detail).

This adds up to 57 different types, and on top of this major variations were also tested; modifications included engine type, move to metal construction from wood and so on. While he did record several forced landings, he did not appear to have any crashes, which seems very lucky considering the number of planes tested and what they were put through. He was also a remarkable pilot! It is worth noting also that it was not just performance that was taken into account; serviceability and ease of maintenance sometimes won the order.

He wrote one last poignant letter to Marjorie Gresham from Martlesham, reflecting on his next posting to the Staff College:

15.5.1927
Dear Marjorie,
I was greatly delighted to get your letter.

I sent the book [Jock of the Bushveld by Sir Percy FitzPatrick] in the hope that you might find it interesting. Years ago I thought it a wonderful dog 'tale'. The author's son was with me in S.W. Africa.

I caught my connection at Liverpool St for Ipswich and was in time to meet the new C.O., Ted Hilton. Our other flight commander was also recalled from leave; he unfortunately had to come up from Cornwall, Lands' End to be precise…

I have come to the conclusion that I am a dreamer, often on some of my shows I commune with the fairies. When aloft one takes a very detached view of life and I am much afraid that I have taken life's responsibilities in a very light-hearted manner, and the Andover business is going to give me a rude awakening. In less than two months' time I shall have to hand over my flight to somebody and it will be a terrible wrench. Martlesham has been a home to me for three years, I love the place, the work and the good fellows one usually finds at a station like ours.

I wrote to Mrs Gresham and tried hard to explain what a wonderful weekend I had enjoyed. I had not forgotten the organiser, hostess and O.C. party to the 'Majestic' and to you again I express my grateful thanks.

From Bert

P.S. Am practising hard at the golf game, but it is a sorry business, terrific expenditure of energy with but poor results. Will persist however. B

He was selected for the sixth course of the RAF Staff College at Andover and started in September 1927. The college was first officially proposed in Command Paper 467, dated 25th November 1919. It was based at Andover for economic reasons, as surplus accommodation existed there. The first Commandant, Air Commodore H.R.M. Brook-Popham, C.B., C.M.G., D.S.O., A.F.C., arrived on 14th November 1921 and the first course started on 3rd April 1922. For Bert it was a hugely prestigious course to take part in and many future leaders of the RAF appear on the list of members, such as Leigh-Mallory and Saundby and the first member of the South African Air force to attend a staff course, Captain C.W. Meredith. The course is recorded in detail in 'The Hawk', the Annual Journal of the RAF Staff College.

The first visit was to Kidbrooke, for what purpose it is not quite clear, except that it mentions Anodic Treatment. Then the 29 students went to the Hawker and Vickers Works and the Oxford Air Squadron. Morris Motors at Cowley was next followed by a visit to see the training of RAF apprentices at Halton. A more familiar visit for Bert was the one to the top secret testing establishment at Martlesham Heath and Felixstowe. The visit to Farnborough was followed by a visit to HQ Fighting Area and the Fairey Aviation Co. The aircraft carrier HMS *Courageous* at sea was next visited, with the opportunity to study aircraft deck landing when weather permitted. An editorial comment was, 'somehow gin does seem to suit a salty atmosphere'.

Weeks were spent at various naval establishments, with a lot of liaison work done including work in submarines. Cardington was the next visit to the Royal Airship works and inspecting the construction of the R101. Combined operations were held with the Navy at Greenwich and the Army at Larkhill, the Royal Tank Corps Centre at Lulworth and the Army Staff College at Camberley. The RAF depot at Ascot, which packed planes for transport, was an interesting and unusual visit. Interspersed with these trips were lectures and many exercises, including a one-hour lecture given by each student on a subject of their choice. Bert's paper was entitled 'Service Experience'. Students were expected to undertake a travel experience and Bert and his friend McGregor went to Norway and Denmark to visit military establishments.

Flying was not neglected while attending the staff course. Bert frequently flew to visits in a Bristol Fighter based at Andover and indeed acted as an 'Air Raid Umpire' flying a DH9A while 7 other DH9As attacked the Air Ministry. Another exercise was attacking Hornchurch from Lympne. He flew to Stokes Bay for a submarine exercise in the College DH Moth. Poole Harbour, Wimborne and Devizes are recorded in his log book; could he possibly have met up with Marjorie Gresham? I hope so! Incidentally all flying was signed off by Sq/Ldr. R. Graham on behalf of the Commandant, and a selection of planes were retained at Andover for the use of students. His log book shows he flew a total of 83 hours in nine different types while attending the staff course.

As before we get a very charming insight into Bert's doings from his letters; however, now most of the missives are to Miss Marjorie Gresham. This also gives us a delightful record of how the romance developed through 1927 and 1928.

To start with, a rather cool letter lamenting the lack of correspondence.

18.11.1927
R.A.F. Staff College,
Andover.

Dear Marjorie,

I have been at this place for two months and am still in the land of the living.
The change from Martlesham to this place is a big one. No longer do I have the happy carefree existence of former days when I played about and tested aeroplanes. I now have to sit at a desk, listen to lectures, and write very bad appreciations, staff papers and exercises. I do not excel at the writing game, consequently my efforts are very laboured.

The course is a very interesting one; it covers a multitude of subjects and we are kept very busy.

I am afraid I have been neglecting the golf game, but play a great deal of squash racquets in the late afternoon and evenings.

Please write me a line sometime. Kind regards to you, the Colonel, Mrs Gresham and Nancy.

From Bert.

18.2.1928
R.A.F. Staff College,
Andover.

Dear Marjorie,

I am the world's worst letter writer, I have been hard at work and somewhat worried, but these excuses do not absolve me from not having written earlier. Very many thanks for your letter which I was so pleased to receive. Don't call your letter a rigmarole, otherwise I shall have to call mine something stronger.

I survived Christmas despite an unpleasant attack of influenza, and after a short visit to Dr. and Mrs Rutter at Eastbourne, spent the remainder of my leave at Dawlish with my aunt…

Just before the last vacation started, the Commandant informed me that I would have to give my students a lecture at the beginning of this term. This news was a great surprise to me as I had previously been informed that my subject would not be dealt with till near the end of the course. Since then I have been busy collecting material and making slides, and to make a long story short I am for the 'high jump' on Friday morning when the Directing Staff and the other fellows will have to listen to me for an hour.

Lecturing is about the last amusement under the sun I would think of playing with. As a small boy my attempt at infusing a tract of 'Macbeth' with spirit, was rewarded by the master remarking, 'Word perfect Roberts, but given like a dying duck in a thunderstorm'.

So now you may appreciate my state of mind on this coming Friday morning.

My foreign trip has been postponed until the beginning of April. McGregor and I may not go as far afield as Romania. I think there is every indication that we may visit one of the Baltic States.

Most of my flying is confined to the weekends. Unfortunately I do not do anything like the amount of flying I did at Martlesham. The weather for the last few months has not been ideal and cross-country flying with boisterous winds and low cloud, although exciting has not been pleasant…

I occasionally travel up to London on visits to the Air Ministry. But if you and Nancy spend two nights alone in London again, I shall have to come and enlist the aid of Scotland Yard to provide a strong escort for you both.

How is the rock garden progressing?

Kind remembrances to you, Colonel and Mrs Gresham and Nancy.

From Bert.
24.5.1928
R.A.F. Staff College

Dear Marjorie,

I am sorry I have been such a time replying to your long letter. I returned from tour at the beginning of May and then had to spend several days in London. The new term commenced shortly afterwards and this last fortnight we have been away on visits to Portsmouth and Devizes. At the former place we spent some time on the new aircraft carrier 'Courageous', and this last week we have been engaged in a big military exercise at Devizes, in reality a big paper war. We worked in syndicates representing different staff formations and were kept rather busy.

McGregor and I spent a most interesting and enjoyable tour in Norway and Denmark. I will tell you all about it when next we meet, if you are interested.

I shall be delighted to come to the wedding [Nancy and Sam Walker] on Saturday June 16th and officiate as one of the ushers. I may be arriving rather late on Friday evening and so unable to attend the 'meeting of the ushers'; never-the-less I shall endeavour to carry out my duties as efficiently as possible at the Church.

We are having an 'At Home' on June 22nd and all the squadrons of the bombing area are giving a flying display, preparatory to the Hendon Display. The mess is sending an invitation to you all. I could give you all details and arrangements when I visit Bournemouth.

Kindest wishes from Bert.

8.6.1928
R.A.F. Staff College,
Dear Marjorie,

We have been on the move again for the past week and only returned this evening. I sent off a hurried wire this morning from Gosport on receipt of your letter. If it is not too late I shall be delighted to accept Mr and Mrs Berry's kind invitation to put me up for the weekend. Please write me a little note if it is the least inconvenient as I can easily put up at some hotel in Bournemouth.

The course this last week has been visiting naval units and ships at Portsmouth and the fleet air arm station at Gosport, Lee-on-Solent, and Calshot, altogether a strenuous but most interesting time. Apart from the visits to Whale Island and the ships in Portsmouth Dockyard we spent two most interesting days with the submarine folk at Fort Blockhouse. Half the course on the first day went out with the submarines on some diving experiences while the other half watched the manoeuvres from the air in their machines, and on the second day the people who were in the air took their turn in the submarines. While at Calshot we took several trips in flying boats…

All being well I hope to be present at the ushers' meeting at 8-30 on Friday evening. I have sent off a little present to the bridal pair, a hand pierced dish or bowl. I am a terrible duffer at shopping but I hope the bowl may be of some little use.

Yours Bert.

28.6.1928
R.A.F. Staff College
Dear Marjorie,

I was greatly pleased to get your letter. I was so sorry that I was unable to meet you when you arrived at the aerodrome. I had waited until 2-30 pm but had to hurry off to start and warm up the engine of old A-E-R-O-PLANE; he needs this little attention before I take him up.

I am glad you, Mrs Gresham, the Colonel and the Berrys

enjoyed the Friday afternoon. The afternoon passed away very quickly and I wanted to show you my quarters and the staff college rooms.

Unfortunately I am not flying at Hendon this year. The members of the Naval and Army Staff Colleges, Greenwich and Camberley respectively are our guests at the Display. Many weeks ago I was asked if I would assist in looking after them and consented, otherwise I would have loved to have taken you to the Display and shown you the aircraft, at the same time introducing you to some of my wild friends who fly them.

I was so glad to have been some little assistance at Nancy's wedding. The D.S. have been keeping us very busy working fairly late at night and I feel as if I could sleep solidly for a forty-eight hours. Kindest remembrances to you, Mrs Gresham and the Colonel.

Yours Bert.

18.7.1928
Dear Marjorie,

Quite by accident I discovered that one of the station photographers had taken a couple of photographs from the air on the day of the 'At Home'.

The enclosed might interest you. This is what you would have seen had you accompanied me in a trip with old R-E-O-PLANE.

We returned this weekend from Greenwich having spent an interesting week in a war game with the sailors at the Naval College. Although we were all kept very busy in the mornings and part of the afternoon we found time to play the sailors at squash, tennis and cricket. This warm spell of weather has been delightful but I do wish Andover was a little nearer to the sea.

Early next month I shall be detailed as an umpire for the air exercises over London for a week and then go in a cruiser or battle-cruiser for Lord knows how long.

My final term commences in October but I do hope I shall be able to spend a week in S. Devon bathing before the cold weather comes on again.

Have you had your trip on the motor boat yet!!! Yours aye. Bert

19.11.1928
R.A.F. Staff College
Dear Marjorie,

The telephone lines are all down, I tried to phone you on Sunday evening and again this evening.

At Camberley the Commandant informed me on the Saturday morning that I was being posted to HQ Middle East (Air Staff). No definite date, but I presume I shall leave in January. If this does not meet with your approval, dear lady, I shall apply to go to Timbuktu.

Our week at Camberley was interesting. I did not ride in the Drag but went out riding on the following afternoon and came off at one of the jumps, my animal, a good jumper, 'baulked' at the last second and I went sailing over his head.

You are a terrible correspondent. Bestir yourself, young lady, and write.

Yours aye, Bert

The Staff College Course is over and Bert, being posted to the Middle East, takes embarkation leave. He and Marjorie are getting closer, as can be seen from the tone of the correspondence!

4.1.1929
20 Southfields Road,
Eastbourne.

Dear Marjorie,

You are an angel to write and enclose that hanky. Please forgive me for not writing earlier.

On the afternoon just before I left I had the wind knocked out of me completely as the result of hitting Mother Earth a nasty bump! I may recover, in time.

Improvident harem scarum lads like me should not be allowed to dream; they should be jumped on when they are very young.

I wanted to tell you, when I said goodbye, that you were the kindest and dearest little lady I knew, but like the clumsy blockhead I am when near <u>you</u>, I could not voice anything!

That was all, I had no appointment with **Her –** Terrible tease, you knew that quite well. I just felt a wee bit miserable; the after effects of inoculations, I imagine, so thought I had better wander off fairly quickly.

You were a naughty girl to send that hanky. I shall use it as a flying 'neck-kerchief'; and will treasure it.

I have spent a week here with Auntie and Dr. Rutter and will be moving on to Devon in a few days' time.

I hope to hear something definite very shortly about my date of sailing.

I do hope you spent a cheery Xmas and New Year.
Bert

11.1.1929
Dear Marjorie,
I am still at Eastbourne. Your letter dated 8th reached me this afternoon… I shall be in London on Tuesday to see Leverson-Gower, one of my COs in France, and several other lads of the village. I should be staying at the R.A.F. Club, and will keep Wednesday afternoon and evening free for you. Send me a line c/o R.A.F. Club what the arrangements are to be. I must be back at Andover to pack up my heavy trunks for Liverpool on Thursday.

I do not believe a single word of your letter. I always thought you were a stickler for the truth! You have issued some terribly stringent instructions – However, as you have always mastered me I shall have to obey them! I have always managed to hold my own in the Ring with most fellows despite bad punishment, but you leave me beaten at the outset always. A hefty Light Heavy Weight laid low by a Feather Weight!!

I must not say any more otherwise I shall contravene Regulations.
Yours Bert

From this moment on Bert and Marjorie grow closer and closer until they wed in January 1931, ten years after they met! Their severest test is about to come, as they are to be separated for two years before they can marry. Their meeting in London evoked the following reply.

19.1.1929
Royal Air Force Club, London.
My Darling,
I was an utter brute to you. Forgive me.
You were an angel to forbear with me so long.
Please don't let the letter be a trial to you. Just be very brief and I will understand.
Bert

Bert reported to H.Q. Middle East Command, Villa Victoria, Cairo on 11.2.1929. He is now a staff officer in the Command and describes his duties in a letter to Marjorie:

The Middle East Command is in reality a big one; it takes in Egypt, the Sudan, Palestine and Transjordan so that there is plenty of air space. My work at HQ is interesting and keeps me well occupied. I am responsible for 'Flying' and 'Operations'. I keep an eye on all flying, civil and service, and various chains of landing grounds throughout the area. In 'operations' I deal with all defence schemes etc. Since I have been out here I have been fortunate with my Wing Commander 'Air'; Peirse was my boss until a few months ago when he was promoted and posted station commander at Heliopolis; Sholto Douglas took his place and now keeps me up to scratch.

Although I am kept busy in the office I always manage to get away by air to visit units and stations. I love these trips immensely. I am always happy when I am piloting my own aircraft.

In the summer of 1929 trouble was brewing, with an outbreak of serious interracial strife between the Jewish and Arab elements, later known as the 'Palestine Disturbances of 1929'. British troops were moved in by Vickers Victoria troop carriers of No. 216 Squadron and aircraft of Nos. 208 and 45 Squadrons were brought in to help; aircraft from the Carrier *Courageous* arrived at Jaffa from Malta. While Army units were put in place to support the police, RAF armoured cars were moved into Palestine from Transjordan, augmented by armoured cars from the Egyptian Command.

In a letter home to his mother and father, Bert describes how the 'emergency' affected him at HQ and vividly describes a trip to Jerusalem by air:

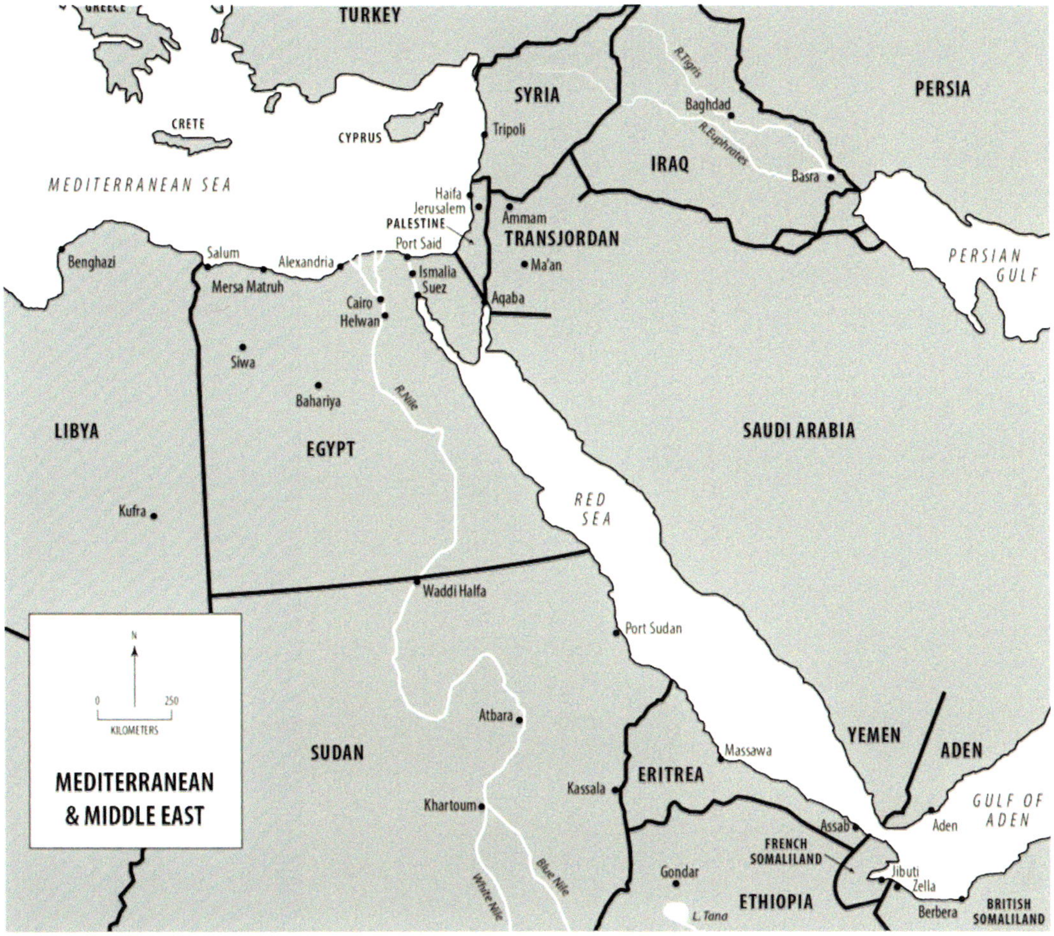

Map of RAF Middle East Command area

Fairey III F over Egypt. The 'workhorse' of the RAF. In the lead a float plane for use on the Nile.

14.9.1929

My farther stay at Heliopolis sick quarters was cut short, much to my relief. This Palestine trouble broke [on the 23rd August] rather suddenly and for the first fortnight we were rather busy at headquarters. A number of folk were still away on leave and it meant the fellows left behind had an abnormally busy time. My knee had improved rapidly and although not quite strong I asked to be allowed to get away to help the others. Things have slackened off considerably these last few days but prior to this I was kept at Middle East practically all the time, afternoons and evenings with a break for meals, a tub and a change.

Last Sunday I flew to Jerusalem. I left Heliopolis at 5.30am and landed at Abu Sueir, Gaza and Ramleh to see how the units there were faring and then took off again, and headed for Jerusalem. From the plains I had to cross the Judean Hills which rise above 3000 feet and then landed at Kolundia, a small landing ground north of Jerusalem on the Nablus Road. A car was awaiting me at Kolundia and motored direct to Air Headquarters, which is now in one of the Government buildings of Jerusalem. On reporting and interviewing the folk there Lawson took me off to lunch in one of the hotels.

Jerusalem appeared abnormally quiet, troops and gendarmerie piquetted all crossroads and the streets bordering the Jewish and Arab quarters. Jews and Arabs were subdued and more frequently proffered expressions. I think the Jews were as much to blame as the Arabs over the recent riots, the seriousness of the whole show was much exaggerated and there was no national concerted movement on the part of the Arabs to extinguish the Jewish colonies. The Zionist organisations report to the world contributed largely to this idea.

It is an awful tragedy that there should be all this trouble and constant friction over the holy places of Palestine; it will continue, I am afraid, until either one party or the other holds supreme sway.

After lunch I went back to Air Headquarters and finished off the business which I had come up for. I renewed acquaintance with Group Captain Playfor, OC RAF Palestine and Transjordan; he was OC Netheravon when I was at Upavon. The fellows on his staff were a very nice lot; they do their work well without any fuss.

I motored back to Kolundia at 4.30pm, helped Dickinson, my fitter, with the bus and we were soon off again. Jerusalem from the air has a most picturesque setting, the temples, churches and other buildings on the tops of the hills show up very well. As I circled above the city all these edifices were caught in the rays of the setting sun and warmed with golden splendour. Away farther to the East the enormous gloom of the Jordan valley and the Dead Sea showed up in marked contrast. With the surrounding hills rising to between two and three thousand feet _above_ sea level the depth of the Dead Sea valley is greatly accentuated when one realises the Dead Sea is 1300 feet _below_ sea level.

Heading right into the setting sun I soon reached Ramleh and landed before dark. I spent the night at Ramleh, the fellows of 45 Squadron fixed me up comfortably. The dawn patrols from 45 Squadron and the flight from 208 Squadron were off the ground by 5.15am. As soon as they were off and away I followed suit and made for Gaza, where the Fleet Air Arm units of HMS Courageous were stationed. I had visited them the previous morning and they were then busy preparing to move at short notice to fly on their craft. The aircraft carrier Courageous was off Jaffa. I knew their Wing Commander Collishaw; while he gave me breakfast, the last of the flights took off in formation and were soon lost in the direction of their ship.

I continued my journey to Abusueir; the country between Gaza and Kantara on the Canal is a dreary and awful waste of rolling sand dunes interspersed with occasional salt pans and little clumps of scrub and shrivelled up looking date palms. Here and there one passed over a small group of Bedouin tents, the only evidence of living creatures. The air route follows the railway line and there is a chain of landing grounds.

I refuelled at Abusueir and flew to Heliopolis, and was back at work at Middle East by 11am.

I only wish I could get away more frequently for several days at a stretch. I enjoy the journeys tremendously, they are a real tonic after having been cooped up in the office. But I must not grumble, experience on a headquarters staff is all useful experience…

I am much relieved the Schneider Trophy show went off so well. Squadron Leader Orlebar had the single seater flight at Martlesham when I took over the two seater experimental flight; he has done very well. [He raised the speed record to 357.7mph]

Air Commodore Board, our chief staff officer, always keeps an eye on me. I like him very much, and often join some of his small dinner parties. I always arrange the tennis fours for him and hope to do so again as soon as my knee is strong enough to play.

This journey is recorded in detail in his Flying Log Book and shows he flew an Avro Lynx No. 8992 accompanied by his fitter, LAC Dixon.

In letters from Marjorie before Christmas 1929, their relationship takes a new turn as she declares her love for Bert and he reciprocates with many delightful and loving responses.

23.12.1929

Your letter telling me you loved me took me by storm and cleared those misunderstandings which you wrote of when we first parted.

You know that I am in the Kings Service, still a junior officer living on my pay and helping my Mother as much as I can, with still a period of oversees service still to complete. This will not be an obstacle to our happiness… I seek your hand in wedlock - I want you to be my wife… Sweetheart, tell your father how we stand in this matter… I must be straight with him; he is true steel, so let me know when I can write to him.

I do not know what I shall do for Christmas – I have had several invitations to join parties at Shepherds and the Continental, but I have kindly declined them. If you were with me I would have gone.

Cairo is not crowded out with tourists, the political situation and the American Wall-Street Smash has kept many away this year.

South African flight leaving Heliopolis.

Victorias and Fairey IIIFs ready to leave Heliopolis.

Bert awaited with considerable apprehension for a letter from Col. Gresham after Marjorie informed her father of their feelings for one another soon after Christmas 1929. Meanwhile he organised, with others, the traditional Christmas Day celebrations for the men at headquarters, put on by the officers. On Boxing Day he and Mr and Mrs Ted Hilton motored out to the Sphinx to see the new excavations on the north side.

PROPOSED ITINERARY FOR ROYAL AIR FORCE CAIRO - CAPE - CAIRO FLIGHT IN 1930.

DATE	STAGE	MILES	REMARKS
January 1930.			
11th.	Cairo - Wadi Halfa.	670	Refuel Aswan.
12th.	Wadi Halfa - Khartoum.	521	Refuel Atbara.
13th.	Remain Khartoum.	–	
14th.	Khartoum - Mongalla.	751	Refuel Malakal.
15th.	Mongalla - Entebbe.	355	Refuel Nimule.
16th.	Remain Entebbe.	–	Co-op. with 4th K.A.R's.
17th.	Entebbe - Nairobi.	330	Call at Kisumu.
18th.) 19th.)	Remain Nairobi.	–	Co-op. with 3rd K.A.R's.
20th.	Nairobi - Tabora.	381	
21st.	Remain Tabora.	–	Co-op. with 2nd K.A.R's.
22nd.	Tabora - Abercorn.	280	
23rd.	Abercorn - Broken Hill.	445.	Refuel N'Dola.
24th.	Broken Hill - Livingstone.	290	
25th.	Livingstone - Bulawayo.	237	
26th.	Remain Bulawayo.	–	
27th.	Bulawayo - Pretoria.	426	Refuel Palapye Rd. and fly over Serowe.
28th.) 29th.)	Remain Pretoria.	–	
30th.	Pretoria - Bloemfontein.	272	
31st.	Bloemfontein - Beaufort West.	306	
February.			
1st.	Beaufort West - Cape Town.	272	
2nd.) 3rd.)	Remain Cape Town.	–	
4th.	Cape Town - Port Elizabeth.	407	Refuel Mossel Bay.
5th.	Port Elizabeth - Durban.	422	Refuel East London.
6th.	Remain Durban.	–	

Page 1 of Cape to Cairo Itinerary 1930.

Page 2, return flight.

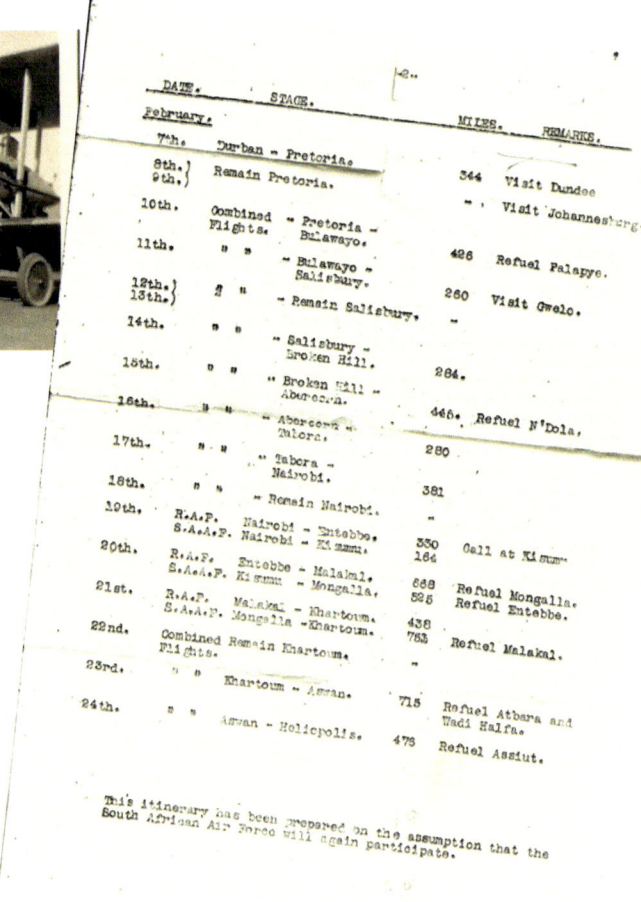

SA flight return inspected by AVM Scarlet.

Early in the new year of 1930 the RAF Middle East Command were involved with the Cairo to Cape flight, still pioneering the route for commercial development by Imperial Airways. Bert very much wanted to be one of the pilots, but as we see in his letters to Marjorie, this was not to be.

3.1.1930

The Cape Flight moves off on the 12th, Air Commodore Board will accompany it. I had hoped to be one of the pilots, but it is entirely a unit show (14 Sqdn.) and the Air Ministry regard it as part of the unit training programme.

Sholto Douglas goes off by air early next week to Khartoum and I may have to fly to Ramleh and Amman on the following day. This month is our busy period, AOC's annual inspections of units and long reports have to be written… I was duty staff officer on New Year's Eve and busy all the forenoon of New Year's Day. The A.V.M. had returned from Khartoum the previous day and had several important things to attend to…

I was up in the air the other morning in an old Avro and looped spun and rolled for sheer joy of living.

11.1.1930

I was going off to Palestine last Monday, but Group Captain Pearse kept me behind, from the Air Staff, as there were only two left behind to keep the show going. Pearse is taking Air Commodore Board's place while the latter is away on the Cape Flight. The Cape Flight leaves tomorrow morning at 6.30, and I must be at the aerodrome to see them off. This last week has been a busy one for me, arranging last-minute details in regard to this flight and the A.V.M.'s inspection of units in Palestine, and I have had to be in the office after hours to finish off the routine letters.

7.2.1930

The Cape Flight are on their homeward journey now; they were due to visit Dundee today or tomorrow. I told the Air Commodore he was to make a point of seeing the Mater and my Dad. I gave Gibbons, the navigator, a bunch of letters and there ought to have been plenty of time for Arthur at Nairobi, and the Mater and my Dad to meet the Cape Flight in Dundee.

As can be seen from the original schedule for the flight it included stopping at Dundee in Natal, presumably only to see Bert's mother and father. There was also an overnight scheduled stop at Nairobi, where they met Bert's brother, Arthur. The four Fairey 3F's of 14 Squadron performed well, but sadly Air Commodore Board was injured in a car crash in Bulawayo. This was one of several proving flights at this time, being precursors of a scheduled service which we will hear more of later.

His new boss at this time is Wing Commander Harris ('Bomber Harris') who joins the Air Staff in Cairo.

Another unusual event is related in a letter dated 24.1.1930:

You will have read the news by now, Padre Warner, a great friend of mine and Somerset Thomas had to jump for it yesterday afternoon. They were on their way to Heliopolis when their propeller went 'west', it may have hit a bird or hawk, the engine disintegrated and moved out bodily from its bearers; they jumped clear of the machine and landed OK. Padre Warner told me this morning over the telephone that the angels were looking after him so he did not worry.

This is the first mention Bert has made of exiting a plane by parachute since the tests he did at Martlesham Heath. Parachute wearing became mandatory for the RAF in 1925.

In the meantime Bert has written to Colonel Gresham, Marjorie's father, declaring his love for her and asking his permission for her hand in marriage. He asks that nothing be made public until he comes home on leave in about June 1930. Colonel Gresham replies, dated 28.1.1930 from Branksome Manor, Bournemouth West.

Dear Bert,
I received your letter of 7th & have naturally been giving it a great deal of thought because both her mother and I are so very anxious about Marjorie's future happiness and want her to realise that in accepting you she will, owing to the nature of your profession, have to live an entirely different life from what she has hitherto been accustomed to. If she is willing to do this and you can make her a suitable home we cannot stand in the way. We want you both to make quite sure of each other's love, & advise you both to wait until you come home before deciding anything definite; it will give you the opportunity of seeing more of each other & also of my having a talk with you.

Marjorie is a dear girl, but she wants the help and advice of a good man to complete her happiness; she has up to now, naturally, relied on us, and has not taken too seriously any responsibility.

I was very interested to hear what you were doing, I have always been fascinated by the wonders of Africa and shall never forget my seven months in Khartoum [CO 7th Manchester Regiment before going in to Gallipoli]. *Of course it is a country one doesn't want to be in for ever.*

Mary will have no doubt told you most of what is going on here. I have just finished another shooting season I am sorry to say, we have had quite good sport especially in Norfolk. Our shooting here has been spoilt by the recent gales as our best coverts have had so many trees blown down & this makes it impossible either for beaters or dogs to get the game out… With kind regards in which my wife joins and hoping you are keeping very fit.

Yours sincerely,
H.E. Gresham.

After this kindly and sensible response from Col Gresham, Bert, in a "fever of excitement", as he put it, sent off by registered post a small and secret engagement ring, for Marjorie to wear discreetly round her neck. At HQ, meanwhile, things are going apace for the annual RAF Cairo Air Display.

1.2.1930

We have our display on Monday afternoon; and after a hurried lunch today Wing Commander Harris and I accompanied the Air Vice Marshall to Heliopolis for the final rehearsal. Our show is a miniature Hendon Display, our numbers and types of aircraft are of course limited but the standard of flying is very high. The rehearsal went off fairly satisfactorily; if anything there was too much time lost between events; broadcasting details and minor matters in the flying of the events needed a little attention.

The Royal enclosure to my mind is receiving undue attention, I have in mind The Royal Box at Hendon as comparison; we have erected a special awning sumptuously fitted with carpets and special chairs for King Fuad and his suite. What with our own guard of airmen and N.C.O.s, the Egyptian Govt. have supplied a further quota of twenty detectives in plain clothes. I am supposed to be in charge of the whole outfit which will include H.E.'s suite and the enclosure for the foreign diplomats and other distinguished visitors… I do not like the grand jobs; while am young and feel the life blood coursing through my veins I would be infinitely happier doing something in the air with the other fellows… Bert.

Bert was also keeping an eye on the Cape Flight and developments in East Africa and the Sudan. In a letter dated 16.2.1930 he writes:

At the time I was very worried about Air Commodore Board; we sent a signal to Pretoria and he sent a reassuring reply that the press reports were exaggerated and that he was proceeding with the flight to the Cape. About 18 months ago he had a hard shaking in an aircraft smash at Khartoum and took some time to recover.

While busy with 'staff' matters, Bert found time to greet 'The Doctor' Auntie Rutter's husband on his way to New Zealand. A letter dated 20.2.1930 relates the story.

Group Captain Peirse allowed me the morning off to fly to Port Said. Rowe and I left in two Avros, with mechanics, just as it was getting light; we had a following wind and did the journey in an hour and ten minutes. The weather was a bit misty and we careered across the desert at a height of about 200 feet, passing Tel-el-Kebir on our left, then on to Kan Tara following the Canal until the little sandy landing ground on the East Bank hove in sight. We have no housing facilities or airmen at Port Said, so leaving the mechanics to keep an eye on our aircraft we hurried to the landing stage, where the Embarkation Staff Officer (E.S.O.) launch awaited us. I had previously wired the Doctor overnight that I was coming to meet him.

The P&O S.S. Narkunda *was within easy range and once aboard we soon found the Doctor, who was dressed and waiting. The Doctor was looking fairly fit and well. He had enjoyed the voyage out, although it had been rough he had not been inconvenienced. I suggested breakfast at the Eastern Exchange. Rowe and I had ravenous appetites after the early morning fresh air. I made the Doctor put on a light coat because the weather was still fresh and we then wandered ashore. After breakfast we felt new men and then accompanied the Doctor to the P&O where he bought quantities of stamps. A pleasant walk to the sea wall and back, and it was time for me and Rowe to get back to the landing ground, also the* Narkunda *was sailing at 11.00am. Rowe and I took off and made a turn to fly past the ship in close formation. Before bidding the old Doctor farewell I impressed on him that he was to take things quietly, otherwise the trip would not do him any good. We refuelled at Abu Sueir and then carried on to Heliopolis, where we landed about 12.30am.*

Another trip related in the same letter gives a good insight in to the type of 'staff' work Bert undertakes in these interwar years:

Harris and Peirse have allowed me an outing of several days. I am flying Jolly of stores staff and a fitter to Wadi Halfa early tomorrow morning, we are investigating rail and steamer transport facilities for rushing stores in an emergency along the Cairo-Khartoum route. Our present programme is more or less as follows. Leave Heliopolis 0700hr, refuel Assiut which is 219 miles south, and then complete the hop of 400 miles to Wadi Halfa if the wind is favourable. Should we encounter a strong head wind we can land at Aswan to refuel. At any rate we should make Halfa by 3.00pm at the latest, and meet the Sudan railway authorities. The rest house at Halfa is on one of the Nile river boats and from past experience accommodation and food is quite fair. We intend leaving early on the Saturday morning for Aswan to meet the other folk at Shellal on the Dam, just above the Cataract. All being well we hope to arrive back at Heliopolis sometime on the Saturday afternoon.

This was the plan. What actually happened came in the next letter 23.2.1930, which describes in detail peace time flying in the desert:

I packed in Jolly and Corporal Lake with the usual quota of spares and kit into the back cockpit of the Fairey 111F and we were off the ground at 7.00am yesterday morning. We made Asiut in two hours, refuelled and headed for Aswan. There was very little wind, what little we had was in our favour and we approached Aswan with time in hand, so I decided not to land and refuel at this place, instead I dived down and flew low over the landing ground and skimmed across the dam, gained height and headed onwards. The Ghaffir in charge of the petrol dump would then know that I was not landing. Between Aswan and Wadi Halfa the air was very hot and bumpy and poor Jolly had an uncomfortable time; he had quite made up his mind to be thoroughly ill when Wadi Halfa came into view and that cheered him up; we landed about 3.00pm. The sun had caught my face and what with the exhaust fumes, it was almost a brick and feeling somewhat tender. After refuelling and picketing the Fairey down for the night, Jolly and I interviewed the Governor and railway officials on the job we had come down for; we obtained the information we wanted and then made for the river steamer for a cold bath, change and tea.

We were up early this morning and on our way back to Aswan at 9.00am where we landed. Here again we interviewed the railway and steamer authorities at Shillal. It took us some time to get out to Shillal and we did not get back to the landing ground till 12.00. We had time for a hurried sandwich and cup of tea and were in the air again for Assiut. On the trip to Assiut we encountered a head wind and a thick sand and heat haze and visibility was poor. Again the air was bumpy and Jolly was none too happy.

However I gave him a respite by landing to refuel at Assiut. On the last stage visibility improved and the head wind did not impede our progress very much. We landed at Heliopolis at just after 5.00pm, helped to park the Fairey in the hangar and then made for the mess where after a wash-up Jolly and I did justice to a splendid tea and buttered toast.

The Cape to Cairo Flight, accompanied by four South African Air Force planes, arrived back safely, recorded in Bert's letter of 27.2.1930. This was preparation for the first commercial Imperial Airways Flights in 1932, of which we shall hear more later.

Both flights arrived punctually to time on Monday… A large party including the A.O.C. and the G.O.C., Sir Peter Strickland, welcomed the flights when they landed. I saw Air Commodore Board and the other fellows however during the evening; they had met the Mater and my Dad at Dundee Natal on the return journey to Pretoria; my parents were well and enjoyed to meet the fellows who bought up mail for me; similarly my brother, Arthur, and his wife Mabel met the flight at Nairobi and gave them mail for me…

I had a busy morning today arranging for the return trip to Pretoria with Col. Sir P. van Ryneveld for the South African Flight; they intend leaving on the 3rd and I had numerous signals to send off warning the Governors of the various areas and colonies over which they intend flying; also other details in regard to supplies of petrol and oil. Whilst I was in 'the thick of everything', Air Commodore Board sent for me to arrange a court and four for tennis at Gazira, he and Gen. Brink, the South African Chief of Staff, were most anxious to have a game… I had to accompany van Ryneveld in one of our tourers to Helwan for a big luncheon party which the squadron were giving in his honour; van Ryneveld had commanded this squadron in France during 1916 when they had a very fine record. After lunch Squadron Leader Vincent, who is OC 45 Squadron, and I took van Ryneveld around the aerodrome.

Bert breathed a sigh of relief when the Air Display passed off very successfully. The formation and stunt flying were really very good despite very bumpy conditions. He was kept busy meeting VIPs, the King's Chamberlain assisted in looking after Egyptian Ministers and other guests in King Fuad's enclosure. The whole event raised considerable funds for the RAF Memorial Fund.

5.3.1930

The Sudan and Transjordan are keeping us busy with odd things. An Italian aviator, Count Calabiano, en route to Nairobi, came down in the Sudd area between Malakal and Mongalla; the Sudd is a great swamp of hundreds of square miles in area. The squadron at Khartoum had a busy time conducting a search over this very inhospitable district; two of their aircraft came to grief, forced landings, fortunately nobody was hurt. Calabiano and his passenger eventually succeeded in making Juba, a village about 25 miles south of Mongalla; his aircraft was crashed at Yombio. Again there is odd raiding in Transjordan which keep the squadron at Amman on the 'qui vive'.

Another dignitary passing through, referred to only as 'H.R.H.', was probably the Duke of Windsor on his way back by air from East Africa. In a letter dated 24.4.1930, Bert describes how H.R.H. came in to his airspace.

I was given a message that the Duty Officer at HQ wanted me back there to clear up a lot of aircraft movements. H.R.H. and his party with luggage and escort aircraft were due to reach Khartoum for Aswan in two flights of five aircraft each early the next morning the 16th… H.R.H. and his party left Khartoum this morning and I had a busy morning and afternoon keeping an eye on the arrival and departure signals also position reports of the two flights 'x' and 'y' each of five Faireys until they reached Aswan safely. A Fairey of 'x' flight came down between Wadi Halfa and Aswan, a sergeant pilot with w/t, and I soon wired out assistance to him; fortunately there was nothing seriously wrong and he was able to take off early the next morning and join up with the other flights.

17.4. H.R.H. and party arrived O.K. at Heliopolis at 13.50 hrs. and were whisked away to the Residency. I had to remain at the office and could not join the A.V.M. & C.S.O., who went to meet him. There was only a small gathering as H.R.H. wanted no fuss or formalities. I understand the Residency had prepared a formal luncheon party. Poor H.R.H. after a long air trip and arriving clad in shorts and open neck shirt would not, I feel certain, welcome rushing off to attend a big luncheon party at 2-3pm!! I have met some of the Residency people and with a few exceptions, the fellows there are not particularly bright, the epithet 'wet' would not be unduly harsh if applied to them…

Bowen-Buscarlet (?), H.R.H.'s pilot, and Steel, both flight commanders of 47 Squadron, insisted on my meeting them at the Turf Club that evening; they are both good lads and I have known them for some time.

The Air Commodore informed me that I was to stand by to fly H.R.H. to Port Said, where he would embark on a P&O for England… I have my three Avros standing by and the luggage can go by train. I am very excited at the prospect of flying H.R.H. on Easter Sunday.

Later - the Residency have just informed us that H.R.H. and party will travel by train to Port Said… we are rather disappointed but it can't be helped.

Two weeks after this letter Bert was off again on an inspection tour; interesting background to the RAF's role in the Middle East at this time:

30.4.1930

I left Heliopolis with Wing Commander Anker as passenger and Dixon my fitter at 09.20hrs last Friday in the Fairey. Weather reports were not too favourable but I decided we could make Ramlah without much difficulty. We had a boisterous following wind and we covered the ground at a rare speed, the clouds were low and the weather bumpy and after passing El Arish we ran into heavy rain squalls; visibility was not too good but I managed to keep the railway line to Ludd in view without much difficulty. I landed at Ramlah at 11.30 having taken two hours to cover 266 miles. Ramlah was rain sodden, Amman unserviceable and the Judaen hills enveloped in cloud so we decided to finish off the Sarafand and Ramlah inspections first while waiting for more favourable conditions.

Sarafand covers quite a big encampment made up of Army W/T Coy, the RAF Palestine General Hospital, RAF Supply Depot and other quarters. My main duty concerned the defences of the camp and I spent a busy afternoon with Major Elsdale, who as senior combatant officer was OC Camp and W/T station. I know Elsdale fairly well, he is a sapper and we were at Cambridge together on the Mech. Science Tripos Course. The Tripos Course was a nightmare to me, but Elsdale as one of the brightest lads found little difficulty in keeping pace with the work.

Elsdale and his Missis very kindly put Anker and me up for the night in their comfortable bungalow. Otherwise we would have had to put up in a Hotel in Jaffa.

As there was no improvement the next day in the weather, Anker decided we should travel to Jerusalem by car. The journey along the good road took about an hour and a half; heavy rain and low cloud marred the visibility but the trip was most interesting never the less; ... Anker and I reported ourselves at RAF HQ Jerusalem and spent a busy two hours with the folk there. I saw Group Captain Peirse for a moment, he and his wife are returning to England about June 15th.

Anker and I put up at the Allenby Hotel and after a late lunch changed in to mufti and went sightseeing; we were out for about five hours and visited all the more interesting places, such as the Wailing Wall, the Mt. of Olives, the Mosque of Omar and a number of religious sights and churches... Jerusalem is a tragedy, this is my general impression: all these religious creeds and sects appear to be warring and squabbling over their respective rights to the holy and reputed holy places. The traffic in religion also came as a shock, one must pay to see a number of the places. From the air Jerusalem spread over the hill tops has a beautiful aspect, but when one wanders afoot through the streets an atmosphere of sordidness and shallowness pervades. The Jews and Arabs are as poles apart and I can never foresee a reconciliation taking place...

The car was round at the Hotel early the next morning, the weather had improved greatly and during our ride and during our ride back to Ramlah we had bursts of sunshine although the hill tops were just touching the clouds. Amman was serviceable and I got the Fairey started up and we were soon up and heading for our next station. The clouds were still low and we skimmed across the Judaean Hills at just over 3000ft... Amman lies on an escarpment above a big wadi at 2500ft. above sea level...

John Russell, the Wing Commander, and Soden, the OC of 14 Squadron, were very good to us and we were comfortably billeted. I know both of these fellows of old. Aircraft and armoured cars are having a busy time just at present in Transjordan trying to stop the Bedouin raiding between the Nyd and Transjordan tribes; cars and aircraft are out in the blue about 120 miles due east of Maan and the fellows there lead a strenuous existence.

A patrol of Transjordan Frontier Force liaising with an RAF Officer.

AVM Dan Scarlet in conference with local leader 'The Mamon of Solum'. Typical of 'staff' work of the time.

We left Amman for Maan by air the following morning, more or less following the railway due south, and arrived at the latter place after an hour and a half. The air was bumpy and poor Anker was not too well. Maan landing ground is 3500ft above sea level and the air here was keen and exhilarating, a wonderful tonic after the heavy Cairo atmosphere.

Anker had previously arranged for our visit to Petra, which was going to be a very hurried one. After an hour's journey by car we reached the head of the Wadi Musa and then continued our journey on horseback for an hour and a half through the gorge. The gorge narrows down to a mere cutting or defile only 12ft wide and with cliffs towering to 3-400ft for about 3 miles.

I took many photos... The ruins of Petra were a tremendous revelation to me and I would not have missed this visit. It was decidedly chilly motoring back and we got into Maan just after dark.

We spent the night in the comfortable quarters of the S.S.O. Strange was a most interesting fellow, he is responsible for intelligence in this part of the world and often has to disappear into the blue for days at a stretch.

The following morning Strange took us out in his big Buick tourer; 50 miles out on the Akaba road towards the Wadi Araba to a range of hills 5000ft above sea level in the direction of the Rum. We passed over stretches of country Lawrence wrote about in his book. Having reached the high ground, the vista of the valley below came as a surprise, one had a very impressive view for many miles around. We managed to get back to Maan for lunch and in the afternoon visited the Transjordan Frontier Police and our own camp where the aircraft and armoured cars were quartered. All the cars were of course out in the blue. On the return trip to Amman we made a detour east of the Maan-Amman railway to see what the country was like and reached Amman just before dark.

Next day we completed the last stage from Amman to Heliopolis in 2 hrs. And 50 mins, arriving back at 1.00. Bert made other trips to Jerusalem and Haifa at this time of heightened tension in the region. As he had been promised, at last, in early June 1930 he was given three months' home leave. He telegraphed Marjorie: 'Sailing P&O. Ballarat arriving Tilbury about twelfth – Bert'.

He had a hectic leave getting to know Marjorie and her parents better and with the full approval of Col. And Mrs Gresham they announced their engagement on June 19th 1930. Marjorie could now wear publicly, with great pride, the little engagement ring Bert had sent home to her from Cairo some months before.

Engagement announcement.

FLIGHT-LIEUTENANT A. O. LEWIS-ROBERTS AND MISS GRESHAM

The engagement is announced between Flight-Lieutenant A. O. Lewis-Roberts, D.F.C., Royal Air Force, elder son of Mr. and Mrs. Lewis-Roberts, Dundee, Natal, and Marjorie, elder daughter of Lieutenant-Colonel and Mrs. H. E. Gresham, Branksome Manor, Bournemouth, W.

Engagement photograph of Bert and Marjory, taken at Branksome Manor, Bournemouth 19.6.1930.

Much of his leave was taken up with the arrangements for their wedding, which was booked for 17th January 1931 at St. Ambrose's Church, Bournemouth West. Banns were to be read at Dawlish and at the Anglican Church in Cairo. In the meantime Bert returned to duty HQ, RAF Cairo, in early September, full of sadness at being parted once again but with much to do to get their new home ready for January 1931.

The return journey was interesting in that he went to Trieste from London, by train, and then by sea to Alexandria. He travelled with his old friend Lloyd Williams from Victoria station to Paris, where they caught the Milan express. In Italy he noticed particularly the Fascist regime.

The Fascist regime makes its presence felt, black shirts military and civil guards vied with each other in their eagerness to marshal, control and direct passengers, goods and baggage… All Italians wore little badges in their button holes signifying membership to Fascista or one or more military organisations. As a result foreigners could be distinguished with consummate ease.

At Trieste we were put through the usual customs formalities. The Lloyd Trestino agent collected 5 lire per packet which was handed to the customs official who marked our kit without examination. Queer procedure but as we were keen to get on board the SS 'Helouan' we put up with it.

On arrival at Venice, the following morning, great was my surprise when I met Padre Warner. He told me if I flew to his station he would arrange banns to be read in Egypt and Dawlish… After leaving Brindisi the ship headed a direct course for Crete, passing within one mile of the island of Gardo and then to Alexandria. I was very glad I had written to Jolly to have the Embarkation Staff Officer meet our ship; he was not there in person but a Sergeant assisted by an Airman got us through customs in double quick time. We cleared the customs by 5.30 pm in ample time to catch the Cairo train at 7.00. We had arranged for a tender to meet the train at Cairo about 11.00pm and take us to the Heliopolis House Hotel. I shall stay here for a couple of days until I can fix up a more permanent abode.

The Air Commodore, Wing Commander Harris and the other fellows were very pleased to see me back and they waxed very enthusiastically in their congratulations and good wishes.

Bert wasted no time in catching up with what had been going on in his absence but he also started searching for a suitable flat to live in when married. In October he secured the lease on a first floor two bedroom flat in a modern building, most importantly, facing north, to be cool in summer and with a fireplace for the cold winter months. Rent for flat and garage was £14 per month.

In the frequent exchanges of letters many things are settled, including ushers for the wedding, guest list, shipping of household goods to Egypt after the marriage and so on. Bert also relates buying carpets, rugs and Jordanian china in Jerusalem, shipped back in his aeroplane; many of these are still in use by us!

Again in a letter to Marjorie in November 1930 he relates more of his staff work. When he is Duty Officer out of hours he becomes OC of HQ and holds a watching brief for all branches. Excellent experience, to stand him in good stead in the future.

Another pioneering flight coming under the RAF Middle East Command is to West Africa, from Cairo via Khartoum to Nigeria and Gambia. He had a signal to say 'One of the West African flight has force landed about 100 miles East of Kano in Nigeria; nobody hurt; but it tends rather to spoil Howard Williams effort and I feel sorry for him. I enclose The Itinerary for your interest'. This route proved to be very useful during the Second World War to move aeroplanes in to North Africa without going through the Mediterranean.

ITINERARY.
ROYAL AIR FORCE WEST AFRICAN FLIGHT 1930.
NIGERIA - GAMBIA.

Map Reference:- Stanfords Library Map of AFRICA, 1928 Edition.

DATE.	STAGE.			MILES.	REMARKS.
Oct: 19th.	KHARTOUM	-	EL FASHER.	560	Refuel EL OBEID.
" 20th.	EL FASHER	-	GENEINA.	210	
" 21st.	GENEINA	-	FORT LAMY.	520	Refuel ATI.
" 22nd.	FORT LAMY	-	KANO.	440	Refuel MAIDUGARI.
" 23rd.} " 24th.} " 25th.}	Remain KANO.				Army Co-operation and Overhaul.
" 26th.	KANO	-	SOKOTO.	250	
" 27th.	Remain SOKOTO.				Army Co-operation.
" 28th.	SOKOTO	-	NAIMEY.	220	
" 29th.	NAIMEY	-	OUAGADOUGOU	275	
" 30th.	OUAGADOUGOU	-	BAMAKO.	460	Refuel SEGOU.
" 31st.} Nov. 1st.}	Remain BAMAKO.				Overhaul.
" 2nd.	BAMAKO	-	TAMBACOUNDA.	410	Refuel KAYES.
" 3rd.	TAMBACOUNDA	-	BATHURST.	250	
" 4th.} " 5th.} " 6th.} " 7th.}	Remain BATHURST.				Army Co-operation.
" 8th.	BATHURST	-	KAYES.	410	Refuel TAMBACOUNDA.
" 9th.	KAYES	-	BAMAKO.	270	
" 10th.	Remain BAMAKO.				Overhaul.
" 11th.	BAMAKO	-	OUAGADOUGOU	460	Refuel SEGOU.
" 12th.	OUAGADOUGOU	-	NAIMEY.	275	
" 13th.	NAIMEY	-	SOKOTO.	220	
" 14th.	Remain SOKOTO.				

West African Flight Itinerary page 1.

West African Flight leaving Heliopolis.

- 2 -

DATE.	STAGE.			MILES.	REMARKS.
Nov: 15th.	SOKOTO	-	KANO.	250	
" 16th.} " 17th.}	Remain KANO.				Overhaul.
" 18th.	KANO	-	FORT LAMY.	440	Refuel MAIDUGARI.
" 19th.	FORT LAMY	-	GENEINA	520	Refuel ATI.
" 20th.	GENEINA	-	EL FASHER.	210	
" 21st.	EL FASHER	-	KHARTOUM.	360	Refuel EL OBEID.

Landing grounds occur at frequent intervals from OUAGADOUGOU to BATHURST and return.

Itinerary page 2

At last on December 19th 1930 Bert could tell Marjorie his itinerary for coming home via Lloyd Trestino Co:

Depart from Alexandria mid-day 27th Dec. On S.S.'Helouan' arrive Trieste 30th: Depart Trieste 15-10hrs. 30/12 via Milan, Paris, Boulogne, Folkestone, arrive Victoria 22-47hrs. On the 31/12.

So my darling I hope to arrive in London at about 11-00pm on New Year's Eve, about the most awkward day and hour of the year... I pray and hope that I may be by your side to herald in our Big New Year.

They met as planned at the Hotel Rubens to travel down to Bournemouth by train the following day, full of excitement about their forthcoming wedding. The remarkable thing was the amazingly long courtship of ten years, including many years of separation by overseas service. Return journeys of five days were considered quick compared with today, when the journey can be done in as many hours!

The scene for this fashionable wedding was St Ambrose's Church, Bournemouth West on Saturday 17th January. The Rev. Pat McCormick, vicar of St Martins in the Field officiated, helped by Rev. Chas Bostock, vicar of St Ambrose's. A reception at Branksome Manor followed. With many hearty congratulations and good wishes the couple left for their honeymoon at Hotel Grosvenor, Swanage. They decided to cut the honeymoon short, as Bert had to be back on duty before the end of February and they decided to make the boat trip back part of the holiday by using the P&O Liner *Orford*, sailing from Tilbury. Sadly Bert went down with an attack of malaria and spent most of the journey in his cabin.

Wedding day, January 1931.

Marjorie was very pleased with Bert's choice of flat in Cairo. Facing the cooler north and with tall airy rooms, it came complete with male Egyptian cleaner and cook. It was within walking distance of the Gezira Club and close to RAF HQ. Their next duty was to sign in at the Residency and for them both to meet the Air Vice Marshall. Bert was promoted to Squadron Leader. His Air Staff and Engineering duties increased, but they found time for various trips. In March Marjorie went to Jerusalem by train on her own, while Bert flew on official duties and they met up in the evening. She felt very brave making her first solo foreign journey!

Bert's log book is an interesting record of many visits, conferences and inspections all over Middle East command area; some were particularly adventurous and involved the saving of crashed planes and their crew, for example:

4.9.1931

Flying Avro No. 8679

Pilot – self. Passenger S.M. Donaldson.

From Heliopolis en route Mosfig refuelled Abu-Sueir from No 4. FTS to Mosefig L.G. where I ascertained exact position of force landed Victoria 9762 from Festing-Smith on standby Victoria at L.G.

To force landed Victoria 9762 position 8 miles due south of Bir-el-Abd railway station. Landed in sand dune depression close to damaged Victoria, sand very soft and fine sand up to axle of the Avro. Saw Flt/lt Chichester and examined Victoria. Decided airframe and engines could be salvaged and signalled HQ to that effect. Avro manhandled by Bedos to hard ground on edge of depression. Take off OK and returned to Mosfig L.G., refuelled from Victoria there. Returned to Heliopolis and interviewed S/l Penderell on salvage arrangements.

The Victoria was a large twin engine transport aeroplane and was duly salvaged. All in a day's work!

In June they took local leave for an idyllic holiday at the Castelis (sea-view) Hotel at Kyrenia in Cyprus. There was lots of walking and swimming from very quiet beaches. Soon after they returned to Cairo they were struck by a great sadness – Bert's father died suddenly of pneumonia in Johannesburg on 28th August 1931. He was ill for only three days but at that time antibiotics had not been invented and the disease was often fatal. There was no chance of going quickly to the funeral so they resolved to use their next long leave to fly by the new Imperial Airways service, due to open in 1932, and turn it into a long-awaited visit to Uganda and South Africa.

216 Sq. Vickers Victoria of the West African Flight.

Chapter Eight

FLYING ACROSS AFRICA, 1932

In February 1931 a weekly service via Cairo, between London and Mwanza in Tanganyika, was instigated by Imperial Airways as part of a proposed route to Cape Town. On the 9th of December 1931 the route was extended experimentally to Cape Town. Bert had been part of the pioneering work done to make these routes possible, so he was very keen to show his new bride their exciting potential.

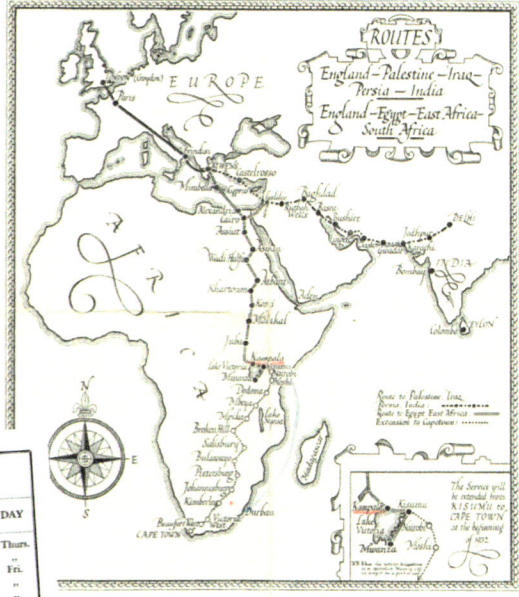

Imperial Airways Map showing route to Mwanza and proposed extension to Cape Town.

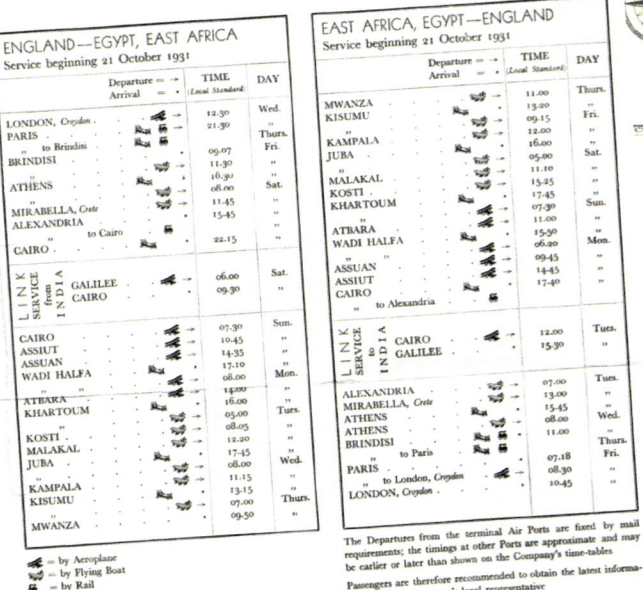

Imperial Airways Schedule, October 1931. London to East Africa.

They planned to fly from Cairo to Kampala, where they would be met by his brother Arthur, then go by road to Nairobi and rail to Mombasa, where they would board a cargo/passenger boat for the voyage to Durban. From there they could reach his mother in Dundee, Natal, by train. Quite an adventure in the very early days of long distance commercial passenger flight!

Marjorie was very excited, but realised the risks and made a will! She kept a wonderful diary, a charming account of the trip and a very early record of passenger flying; its narrative cannot be bettered, so I quote from it:

CAIRO. May 1932

For weeks we had been making plans and preparations for this momentous holiday, but there was much that could not be done until almost the last moment, so that the last few days were more than fully occupied. We made a most exhaustive search round the Cairo shops trying to find suitable cases for the luggage. They had to be extremely light in weight, as Imperial Airways only allowed one 220lbs including your own weight! …We eventually found two suitcases weighing two and a half kilos and I was eleven pounds to the good and Bert five.

*We were fortunate in letting our flat to Sq Ldr and Mrs Cottle… at last came 28*th *May and the hour for handing over the keys of our home. The car was jacked up on blocks so Sq Ldr Cottle kindly drove us out to Heliopolis where we were spending the night with Sq Ldr Hilton.*

WADI-HALFA 29.5.1932 Flying time 7 hours 20mins. We were called at six o'clock this morning, and breakfast was soon after as the machine was timed to leave the ground at seven thirty. Those awful "quaking" feelings came over me as I was dressing and I could hardly eat my breakfast, and they increased much more when we reached the aerodrome and I saw the great machine waiting. Our luggage and ourselves were all checked and weighed and the last formalities gone through. Ted Hilton came to see us off and was surprised to find the machine was an [Armstrong-Whitworth] Argosy type "The City of Arundel" with registration marks G-EBOZ and about six or seven years old – it was the very one he had tested at Martlesham Heath. But even more surprising it was the first Air Liner I had ever looked into at Hendon when Bert showed me over, years before we were even engaged. So I felt it was an old and trusty friend and was consequently cheered.

We had not long to wait before the steps were put out for passengers to ascend… I had time to take stock of our fellow passengers… two men and a Belgian lady and her five month old son for the Congo. Just before we left an official came up to me with a lovely bunch of red carnations saying they were from Mr Cross, the Imperial Airways Manager, and his wife, I felt just like a film star! Almost immediately the cabin door was closed and bolted, the wireless officer scrambled along into his little cubby hole and we began to slowly taxi out over the sand… we turned and quickly gathered speed and then very

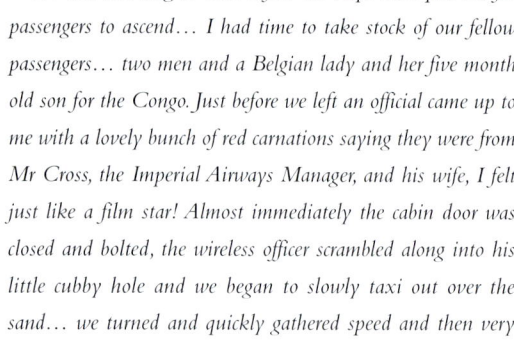

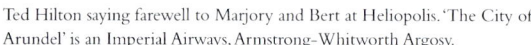

Ted Hilton saying farewell to Marjory and Bert at Heliopolis. 'The City of Arundel' is an Imperial Airways, Armstrong-Whitworth Argosy.

G-EBOZ at Heliopolis. loading 29.5.1932

gently the wheels left the ground, it was almost imperceptible, AND WE WERE IN THE AIR!

I was so thrilled and excited and twisted and turned in my chair as we flew low over the roofs of Heliopolis till we had gained height a bit... We rose quickly to 3000ft and cruised steadily at that, sometimes reaching 5000ft, our airspeed was between 70 and 75 miles per hour...

After we had been flying for 2 hours and 5 mins I noticed we were losing height and the engine was throttled down... we were flying over a very arid waste of desert with no sign of habitation... and then far below, as we circled round, I could discern a couple of tents and a tiny group of men. Bert told me we had reached Assuit, our first stop. Then we were skimming along close to the ground and all at once we felt the wheels give a little bump as we touched the earth and we taxied slowly into position. It was my first experience of landing. We came to rest alongside a very small square tent made of the special kind of ornate canvas beloved of the Egyptians... Inside were chairs and a little table on which was a pot of tea and some biscuits. The heat was intense and the glare, but we were quite glad to get out of the machine and stretch our legs. What came as such a blessed relief was the absolute quiet when the engines had stopped.

Whilst we were trying to get the hot tea down the machine was refuelled for the next leg of our journey to Aswan. So after a stay of some twenty minutes we climbed back into the machine and set off again. The machine could hold 20 passengers, we had quite comfy wicker seats arranged in two rows of ten in the cabin with a rack overhead for odds and ends. Cotton wool in sealed envelopes was provided for our ears and it certainly helped to deaden the noise. Above each chair was a thermos of water. There was a lavatory in the aft of the cabin with the baggage room. Forward of the cabin was the tiny space for the wireless operator. Shut off by a door beyond him the pilot's (open) cockpit. The windows of the machine were large and of talk with royal blue curtains to match the chair cushions...

We still followed the course of the Nile, with odd stretches of stony desert intercepted by deep wadis, the whole country looked as if it had been the bed of a large river, long since disappeared, and you could easily see the water tracts. I began to feel queer due to the noise and heat which was pretty bad, but the machine was pretty steady and the movement did not worry me. I was very glad to see we were approaching Aswan on the lovely palm fringed banks of the Nile. The landing ground is to the southerly end of the town, and we landed at 1.10pm. The heat absolutely smote us on getting off the machine, it registered 117 in the shade.

We sat under the veranda of the little wooden rest house and had lunch; sandwiches, biscuits and oranges, but it was far too hot to eat and the drinks were quite warm, so our pilot, Capt. Foy, very kindly offered us cool, delicious lemonade out of a large thermos he had bought. Hot though it was in the air I was really quite glad to be off again after half an hour's boiling!

We flew over the Great Dam and so was able to get a very

Departing Wadi Halfa.

Arriving at Wadi Halfa.

good view and saw the Temple of Philae... actually I was feeling rather miserable and was indeed glad to see the landing ground at Wadi-Halfa. As soon as the machine touched the ground at 4.15pm my spirits revived and beyond a yellow face I felt all right. Rather more officials to welcome us here, passports and identity papers had to be produced as we are now entering the Sudan, and are to spend a night in the town. We all climbed in to an open sort of bus and what luggage we required came along too. The pilot and the passport officer got in and we set off, bumping over the sandy road. The landing ground is quite close to the very small town...

We drove in through the gate set in the white wall surrounding the hotel garden, and our first thought on getting into the hotel was a long cool drink! I flopped into the nearest chair and wallowed in a long cool lemonade! Our passports were checked and we followed the white robed and turbaned soffraghi up to our room and what a delightful one it was, most artistically furnished in soft blues and pinks, with modern furniture and leading out of it the loveliest of little bathrooms... By the time we had finished dressing the sun was setting. What held my breath was the marvellous and vivid orange hues of the sunset and the one solitary evening star, and over all the penetrating stillness that for me was the most wonderful thing about the Sudan...

Dinner was served on little tables on a wide terrace overlooking the Nile. It was not long before we retired to bed as we were tired after 7hrs and 20mins of flying in so much heat too. The fan was turned on and the mosquito net safely tucked in and so ended the first day of our most wonderful leave, and the very first time I had been up in the air.

KHARTOUM 30.5.1932 *Flying time 7 hours 15 mins*
We spent an awfully hot night and were called at 6.00 am. After breakfast there was some little delay as Mde. Wiser, the Belgian lady, had her baby ill all night with a high temperature and had to get the local M.O. I went up to help her; the child seemed better but fretful and anyhow she had to resume the journey. I was sorry to leave Wadi-Halfa which we did at 8.00am. Almost immediately after taking off we left the course of the Nile and headed inland and followed the railway line over a desolate stretch of sand before we joined the Nile again at Abu Hamed. Our course was S.E.

After we had been flying for one and a half hours we began the descent into what I thought was a totally deserted spot until, on a turn, I saw a tent or two and a shed beside the toy railway line. But it did prove to be a most Godforsaken spot which went by the name of Station Six, and was one of the refuelling places. The heat was intense, but the pilot thought it would be a little cooler for us two women and the baby under the shade of one of the wings, so he had a couple of chairs put there for us, and we mopped and were grateful! After about twenty minutes we resumed our journey still over the desolate desert with never a sight of life, this stretch between Wadi-Halfa and Khartoum was the least interesting of the whole flight.

Rest house at Atbara.

After a time we joined the Nile again... And soon we saw the little town of Atbara lying below... We landed at 1.20pm and had lunch and a wash in the little wooden hut on the landing ground. All these rest houses are on much the same lines throughout the journey with a small veranda and one main

47 Sq. Fairey IIIFs, Khartoum.

room with a table down the centre laid out for lunch. We all had it together, the pilot usually taking the head of the table. It was at Atbara that I descended from the machine holding Mde. Wiser's large and attractive baby… I did my best to amuse him while she mixed his bottle.

We had a cold luncheon and then off again at 2.00pm with the broad ribbon of the Nile shimmering in the noon day sun below us… I was getting tremendously excited at the prospect of seeing Khartoum although the heat in the machine was very bad, the pilot went up to 5000ft to try and find cooler air.

At last the fringes of Khartoum North and one of my dreams about to be realized, the place I had heard so much about, I wanted to see it because of Dad being in command of the British Troops there in the winter of 1914-1915… Finally we made a perfect landing and came to rest close to the hangars at 4.30pm. I think we were just a tiny bit disappointed that none of our RAF friends were there to welcome us as we scanned the faces of the few spectators. Once again we climbed into a funny little bus and set out for the Grand Hotel. We drew up at the hotel, which overlooks the Nile and is a long two-storey building with a veranda and balcony running the whole length. Rather an old fashioned hotel…we bathed and changed and Bert took me to see the sights before dark… to the British

Imperial Airways Plane over Khartoum.

Grand Hotel Khartoum

Barracks and the CO's house that Dad once had… arriving back at the Hotel we wrote letters home and Andrew McGregor and S/Ldr Howard-Williams came breezing in. McGregor asked us to dine at the Club, so we did and spent a pleasant evening… We dined on the terrace in the beautiful gardens, it was awfully hot but dry heat that did not exhaust us. We did not stay long as we had an early start in the morning.

JUBA S.SUDAN 31.5.1932 Flying time 10 hours 5 mins

Today was so exciting and interesting I cannot describe it adequately. We were called at 3.30am after a very hot night and came down to a light breakfast in the deserted hotel. It was not yet light and was all very mysterious, the handful of passengers grouped on the veranda watching their luggage being put into the bus which went on first and came back for us. We had a car to ourselves and drove over the Omdurman Bridge, rousing the sleeping native tollkeeper and down the slipway to the White Nile, as this time we were to board a flying boat for the rest of our journey. There she lay dimly and gracefully on the water with her cabin lights reflected in the still Nile and the ruby and emerald of her port and starboard lights. It was thrilling!

Imperial Airways 'City of Khartoum' on the White Nile near Khartoum.

Nile Sud passing 47Sq Fairey IIIF and 'City of Khartoum'.

We bundled into a launch and went out to the machine and climbed up the steep side to drop down into the wonderful little cabin like a large motor launch, with seats arranged one behind each other on one side and two together on the other, in all seating about twelve. In the rear of the plane was accommodation for freight, etc., like the land plane. Cotton wool was in little containers on the back of each seat; on the wall dividing us from the wireless operator and the pilot was a picture showing how to put the life jacket on! The machine was called the "City of Khartoum", three engine Calcutta Class piloted by Capt. Prendergast, a very nice fellow. We had to wait a little as we heard there was a lady racing from Suez to try and catch the machine, on her way to her husband in Southern Sudan… Presently our missing passenger arrived breathlessly, the engines were started up and the hatchway closed and then the noise was rather terrific. We taxied for the take-off point, turned, and came tearing back at 60mph with the spray flying up, obliterating the view from the windows. Very gently we left the water and flew over the Omdurman Bridge and above the White Nile at about 2000ft. The country was much more interesting and very much greener than North of Khartoum…

After a time the wireless operator came along distributing little cardboard boxes containing rolls and sandwiches and fruit; as we had had such an early breakfast I was quite hungry! After two hours and ten minutes of flying (we left Khartoum at 5.00am) we began descending and it really was a lovely sensation coming gradually down on to water, finally touching with a little splash and the waves shooting out each side, we taxied slowly along the water and tied up to a buoy in mid-stream, for we had reached Kosti. A raft came alongside with petrol and our tanks were filled. Oh how lovely when the hatch was lifted and fresh air came in, though it was hot air… at 7.40 we left Kosti and the nature of the country quite changed, it was like a huge dried up prairie with scattered thorn bushes and the occasional native huts. For as far as one could see in all directions was nothing but this dried up grass and one realized the vastness of the Sudan… At 11.00 am we saw below us the small village of Malakal… we came down on to the water and tied up to a buoy in mid-stream, but this time it needed a little manoeuvring as the northbound machine had not left and was occupying the best position. The drifting Sudd, little floating islands of grass and reeds, made landing a difficult and precarious job, as the Nile here was full of it.

'City of Khartoum' at Malakal.

At last it was safely accomplished and we went ashore in a launch and up the bank to the low wooden rest house. The passengers of the other machine had just finished their lunch and were about to go on board the "City of Swanage", so we watched her take off amongst the Sudd before going in for lunch… Presently Capt. Prendergast said it was time to be off and we got into the little launch, but the current was so strong and we were nearly decapitated by the lower wing as we came alongside.

Taking off took quite a while to avoid the Sudd. We took off at 12.45pm, and now came four and three quarter hours of continuous flying, our longest flight so far without a break. After a short while we left the Nile and cut across country to the tributary of the White Nile called the Baler el Jebel, which we followed all the way to Juba.

We had now started to fly over miles and miles of Sudd country, beginning to get green again; I've never seen such a vast swamp… I heard the engine throttle back and we began to descend and I knew what that meant – ELEPHANT!

The Bor herd of elephants.

Our pilot had told us at Makatal that we stood a good chance of seeing the famous Bor herd of elephants as the northbound machine had sighted them and he said that when we got near the place he would dip his wings twice as a signal to be on the lookout. Of course tremendous excitement reigned in the cabin, all of us craning our necks and getting out cameras.

"There they are!" yelled Bert, violently grabbing my arm and I am sure the machine heeled over as we all rushed to one side! Gradually as we came down to 1000ft I saw this huge herd almost hidden in this long swampy grass and wallowing in a pool. What an experience, what excitement! As we circled over them we could see them quite distinctly. The cows and young elephants took fright and began to flounder off, but not so the magnificent old bull, he stood his ground with his huge pointed ears well out and his trunk raised in defiance at us. It was really a sight of a lifetime to see this old fellow defending his herd from he knew not what terror dripping upon them from the skies. Some of the cows remained with him circling around him to gain what protection they might no doubt…

We soon left them alone and carried on south. We saw game all the way… hippos in ones and twos; a large herd of giraffe with their long necks up above the trees, various forms of buck and even a crocodile in the Nile. Nearing Juba the country got very pretty with hills in the distance, quite often we could see the gravel road running through the forest, even the Cape to Cairo road! Once again the thrill of landing, this time the Nile was the narrowest it had been. Gently we touched the water and came alongside our moorings where there was a raft with petrol pumps on board and a couple of black native boys with a white topied Englishman. A little stiff, we clambered into the launch and made for the bank, where willing hands hauled us up, and great was the reunion between Mde. Wiser and her young husband, who had motored up from the Congo to meet her after several months of separation. The poor baby was nearly dropped in the water, such was the excitement.

We climbed into a wagonette-shaped motor bus and drove in the failing light to the hotel. We quickly washed and had tea on a wide terrace overlooking the gardens with an enchanting view across to the hills we saw before landing……. Night came quickly and ere long we were driven indoors to seek refuge behind mosquito wire. Especially in this district prone to malaria. After dinner Mde. Wiser's young husband came up and bowed to me, and thanked me in French most profusely for helping his wife en route…………I was most touched and thought it extremely nice of him. The other Belgian passengers also came and wished me bon voyage……. Soon we were tucked in under the net, very tired and happy after our longest day, 10hrs and 5mins. in the air, we had landed at 5.30pm having departed at 5.00am.

KAMPALA, UGANDA. 1.6.1932. Flying time 4hrs 10mins

We were called about 3.30 this morning.. The stars were still shining as we walked across for our bacon and eggs, and the luggage was being collected and taken on in advance. Soon we were all seated in the bus and jogging and swaying down the lane, the headlights never showing up a sole at that early hour… As we drew up on the bank at the edge of the water we could faintly make out the machine lying in midstream, her lights ablaze and looking very ghostly and unreal. When we got on board the cabin seemed cosy with her little electric lights, we were able to have the same seats as before.

No time was wasted, the engines were started up almost at once and they seemed to gib a little at the early hour and the cool morning air! They made a great splutter and backfired and the flames from the exhausts looked most terrifying in the dark as if the whole thing was going to catch alight and blow up. At last they were running smoothly with the occasional backfire as we taxied along the river for the take-off, being intensified a little as we gathered speed. Bert thought it dangerous on the ill lit water to go at that speed, an odd log might have been in our path even a crocodile.

We left the water at 5.30, it coming light later than in Egypt… I had always wanted to fly in the dark and I got my wish and saw the fairy lights of the odd huts far below, but dawn soon began to break. I saw the sun rise in all his golden glory, a never to be forgotten experience.

We climbed up to over 6000ft, and were now flying over very green country with thickly wooded hills and valleys. A totally different type of scenery to the preceding days. We went up to over 9000ft to clear a long grass covered escarpment… Soon we saw again our friend the Bahr el Jebel, broad and shining in the distance as she swept in a wide curve over the green lands. Odd little habitations were here near the river, which we crossed on a broad plain and we were over the border into Uganda. We flew now over the sleeping sickness area… Since leaving Juba we seemed to have passed out of the game country. We passed over a river which eventually ended in Lake Albert, a glimpse of whose broad shining waters we were lucky to catch away on the right. A short while later we crossed the same river, called the Victoria Nile, more of which we were to see another day. To the left seemed now to be a series of lakes and much papyrus grass as we proceeded nearer to Kampala… The country was undulating and I began to get very excited straining my eyes for the first glimpse of Kampala.

I had read in the "S and E African Year Book", a volume that was both interesting and helpful to us, that Kampala was built on the tops of seven hills, low and flat topped… At last I saw the seven green hills with the buildings showing above the trees, all clearly defined against the background of the vast bright expanse of the lake. Bert and I darted from side to side of the machine, eager to miss nothing. Lower and lower we came till we were skimming over the papyrus fringed edges of the great lake, which was like a sea it was so immense, with little grass fringed islands and peninsulas. We saw the jetty and sheds and the little groups of spectators and wondered if we could pick out Arthur and Mabel.

Hardly before we knew it we were at rest on the water and the hatchway was thrown open, letting in the fresh morning air, Bert was standing in the opening looking for Arthur, with me equally keen to see at his elbow. A little motor launch came alongside with the Imperial Airways Superintendent, who came on board and was handed the official documents etc. before we were allowed to get into the launch. There was only one young man beside ourselves, the rest of the passengers left the machine at Juba.

It was a beautiful morning with a cool breeze and light clouds, and we were soon speeding over the water towards the little group on the bank, and saw Arthur and Mabel waving to us, and the next thing we were alongside being warmly kissed and welcomed. It was such a momentous meeting, we were all rather overcome for the moment. Bert had not seen his brother for over sixteen years, and of course I had never seen either of them, so I felt a little strange. What a magnificent specimen of manhood Arthur was, over six foot of strength and gentleness and infinite kindness, looking so fresh in his white linen suit and topie and Mabel in her beautifully ironed cotton frock. It made us feel and realize how crumpled we were after our four days in the air.

Port Belle, Kampala on Lake Victoria.

We walked up the path to the rest house, Mabel who was very slight and dark asking me questions in a pretty, soft voice. The rest house was just a small bungalow with a veranda enclosed with mosquito mesh… We had customs papers to sign and our passports inspected and then on into an inner room where a most delicious breakfast was served… They were anxious to get us home, so we bid goodbye to our pilot and climbed into Arthur's big Buick, which was quite the strangest car I had ever been in. The back was sloped like a lorry and the seat could be removed for luggage or game. There were no doors, you had to be agile and climb over the deep tool boxes on the running boards to get in to the back; there was a permanent wooden hood with rolled up canvas sides. Arthur had the car for going on safari over the many hundreds of miles during his tours of inspection as manager of the Texas Oil Co for the whole of Uganda.

Off we set, swiftly traversing the seven miles between Port Bell and Kampala. The road was winding and countrified… We drove up the long wide red gravel main street of Kampala… finally we turned into a very steep drive on the side of the hill and we were at Arthur's place with the puppy tearing to meet us. The house was a most attractive stucco bungalow. Our room was pretty and cool, we were glad to get in and bathe and unpack our belongings… We were on the slope of a hill with the gardens stretching down to the road. Below the road were the little round whitewashed huts of the native police barracks, they seemed to keep up a steady drill all day with the commands in English. Over fields and more low hills glittered lake Victoria… The streets were all red earth and had no proper pavements and were tree lined and wide. The native police were very fine well set up fellows and smart in their khaki uniforms and puttees.

We woke early the next morning to the sound of the police bugles. Arthur and Mabel called a greeting on the way to the office, so we had a leisurely breakfast. In the afternoon we went a drive to Entebbe twenty-five miles away to take tea with Miss Jones. Entebbe was a most delightfully pretty place, like a huge private park… Here is the administrative centre of the Ugandan Protectorate. There is no town at Entebbe, it's all just like one big garden. Our hostess lived in an attractive house in the grounds of the Secretariat… On our way home we signed our names in the book at Government House and were held up at the gate by the changing of the guard. And also it was sunset and the flag was being hauled down.

Our third day in Kampala we went on a wonderful all day picnic. Arthur and Mabel had a holiday from work and Mabel was up early seeing to the food… We left at 9.00am for Lake Nabugabu 86 miles off. For the most part the road had wide grass border on each side, there was nearly no traffic and we travelled very quickly… We turned off the main road and went along a narrow track with the trees and creepers nearly meeting overhead, and scraping the sides of the car. We saw the most beautiful butterflies and very big ones… We left the car under the trees and walked down a steep little path to a perfectly enchanting picnic spot…

Here they spent the rest of the day swimming and enjoying the picnic lunch. Amazingly this lake is free of crocodiles, which are plentiful in Lake Victoria only a few miles away. They spent another two happy days with Arthur and Mabel before being driven on the next leg of their journey south to Nairobi. Mabel stayed behind and the three of them set off in the Buick laden with luggage and safari kit, including Arthur's guns and fishing tackle. First stop was the Ibis Hotel in Jinja by the Ripon Falls. After a cup of tea they travelled on the 96 miles to Tororo, where they had lunch in a little hotel in the shadow of the towering rock.

Leaving Kampala in the Buick.

Bert and Marjory on the Equator.

Filling the Buick at Naivasha.

Kilindini harbour near Mombasa, last visited by Bert in 1916.

They travelled on, and although the weather turned wet and made the road extremely slippery, they crossed the border into Kenya and arrived at the little town of Eldoret, having covered 265 miles and climbed about 2000ft in the day. After supper they tumbled into bed early, tired but happy after their wonderful drive. Covering the rest of the journey in a long day, they arrived at Nairobi and booked into a hotel on the Tuesday. Arthur arranged visits to the Caltex head office and dinner with his boss as well as visiting farming friends the Tarltons and the Cowies. They were most struck by the fact that although the farms were within seven or eight miles of the centre of Nairobi they were very well stocked with all types of wild game, including lions and giraffe.

Arriving at Durban harbour.

Sadly their visit came to an end on the Friday and with fond farewells they left Arthur in Nairobi by the night train to Mombasa, arriving at 8am the following morning. Their ship for the journey to Durban was the SS *Khandalla* of the BI line, carrying general cargo and only six passengers. They stowed their luggage and then Bert took Marjorie for a trip round the town, which he had first been to in 1916 during the East African Campaign.

Having sailed late, the next stops were Zanzibar, Dar-es-Salaam, Mozambique, Beira, with a top for coal at Lorenzo Marques before reaching Durban, in all about a week at sea. After customs and health clearance they caught the 5.40pm sleeper train to Dundee. At Glencoe junction, about six miles from Dundee, they saw Alice on the platform and decided to leave the train and drive the last six miles with her. It was dark and very cold just as dawn was breaking. Marjorie records the arrival: 'Lights were streaming out from the house when we arrived and Auntie Lal came to the door and greeted us and at once I felt happy and at home, I've never felt anywhere so settled so soon.'

Bert and his mother.

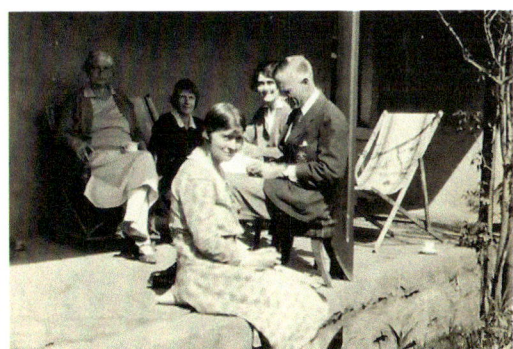

Tea on the stoep at Ann Street.

Dundee, Natal, 127 Ann Street.

The picnic wagon drawn by four mules.

AEG and Family at Rose Bank, Johannesburg.

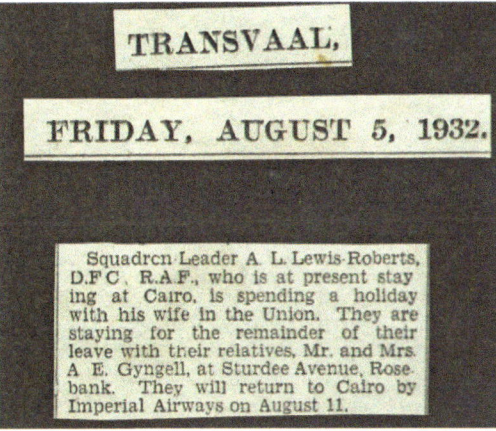

'The Star' recorded their visit!

They found Bert's mother and his two sisters, Joe and Alice, full of 'flu, so they put them all to bed and called the doctor. They had worked hard to prepare their house in Ann Street for Bert's visit, with new curtains and wallpaper. However Bert was very shocked to see how badly off they were, particularly as he had been supporting them financially for years.

They all soon recovered, although Alice remained sickly; the visit settled into a very jolly reunion. Marjorie recounted: 'His mother is a darling, and is a fine looking woman… It makes me so happy seeing Bert at home amongst his dear ones, and seeing them has only strengthened my feelings for him'. Many picnics were planned and walks to Talana Hill, as well as frequent visits to friends and neighbours. One very amusing trip was a picnic on a wagon drawn by four mules. They joined the local tennis and golf clubs and had many happy games for the month while they were there.

When their stay came to an end on August 1st they bade farewell to all their many new friends and along with Joe, Alice and Mother, caught the 3.20pm sleeper train to Johannesburg and arrived at 6.14am, to be met by Uncle Ted (AEG). Using Dr Jean Don's car, they drove out to their house at Rose Bank. Betty, who was still at school, and Tony, who was at Wits University, came home to greet Bert and Marjorie. They visited AEG's studio and much admired his portraits, and he presented a charcoal portrait of Bert and a small landscape to them. Again another very memorable visit, renewing old friendships and making new ones. Most people had not seen Bert for at least 16 years, so there was a lot of catching up to do.

Their return journey, by air, to Cairo started at 6am, when they were picked up by the Imperial Airways bus at a hotel in central Johannesburg. Marjorie tells the story in a letter to her mother:

All the family were already on the Aerodrome at Germiston when we arrived. Tony and Betty were so excited but poor Auntie Lal and the girls were being very brave. I don't think they slept at all last night. We had only 6/8 to pay on excess luggage and were only a kilo over. Don't you think it noble of me not to have collected souvenirs? I can tell you I am bitterly disappointed. We left the ground at 7.00am but came down immediately and wasted 20 minutes, as something had come adrift on one of the wings. It was a bigger machine than the other and we were full up. Two other women and three men.

Departing by Imperial Airways at dawn from Germiston. A de Havilland DH66 Hercules. All the family have come to see them off. This service had only just started and was pioneered by the R.A.F.

The plane was a three engine De Havilland DH66 Hercules which carried seven passengers and mail. The registration was G-ABMT and it was called the "City of Cape Town". Cruising speed was 80mph at 8000ft.

We breakfasted at Pietersburg at 9.30am and lunch at Bulawayo and arrived at Salisbury (Rhodesia) at 4.25 pm. The country was rather dull on the whole. We both felt pretty rotten after breaky and only just lasted out till lunch when we took some of our dope and survived the rest of the way! This is a big hotel (Meikle's Hotel) and we have just had a very good dinner. We went for a walk after dinner and found the place very attractive and clean with very wide roads like most of the towns out here – wish we had not to leave at dawn tomorrow but we have a long stretch ahead.

Her next long letter home describing the flight was written in the air over the Sudan on 16th August 1932 so she could send it off on arrival:

Breakfast at Dodoma. Bert and the pilot heading for the rest house.

Refuelling at Moshi.

A wonderful flight of seven days averaging about 9hrs flying time a day with two or three stops during the day of about 30mins duration. After our stop at Salisbury we left the ground at 5.00am, just as dawn was breaking. We flew over the great Zambezi at 8000ft., a wonderful wide river with flat country on either side but high broken mountains behind… We passed several quite wide rivers absolutely dried up, just a sandy ribbon in Northern Rhodesia, they looked so strange. We had breakfast at Broken Hill, a very small place on the edge of beyond and then lunch at Mpika, a still smaller place. Next we flew over some terrible country as regards flying, just mountains with deep ravines and scrubby trees, not a hope had we been forced down.

Just as the sun was setting we landed in a paradise of a place, Mbeya. Just a handful of houses in a glorious valley backed by high mountains, for all the world like the country near Snowdon. We were introduced to mine host as soon as we landed, a charming gentleman, who drove us in his car to the loveliest of little hotels at the foot of the mountains. Just a long low bungalow with a wide veranda and an adjoining building to sleep in surrounded by beds of sweet smelling petunias. We went up the steps on to the veranda and so into the hotel lounge, a long low room with a huge open fireplace with burning logs, big easy chairs and orange shaded lights; the walls were covered in animal skins and trophies. By the fire where a table was laid with tea were three dogs. A gramophone was playing

Arriving at Mbeya.

that haunting music from Bitter Sweet, just like the room of country houses.

The other guests were most interesting, only about six or eight and they were gold diggers from the adjoining mine in the mountains. Oh! It was just like a book, these brown bare kneed open shirted men of varying ages. The general factotum of the place was a rugged bearded Scotsman, always with a pipe and untidy attire, our pilot in his smart blue uniform and just me and another girl on the machine as the women. We all sat in a circle round the fire with the dogs at our feet and the cat on my lap! We went to bed early as we do, being up before dawn each day.

The centre of Nairobi.

Arriving at Kisumu to change in to a flying boat.

As I crossed the garden to our sleeping quarters the moon was shining on the mountains, a forest fire was burning on a far off hill and somewhere in the hollow a native drum was playing. Quite the most beautiful place we stayed in and we must go back some day. We slept the next night in a modern hotel in Nairobi with a dance keeping us awake until almost 3am, such a contrast! That day we flew over tropical country on the foothills of Mt Kilimanjaro and we got the most wonderful peep of the snow crested summit, but only for a second, then it was lost in the clouds, we were lucky to catch it. After that we flew over the great Masai plain which lies in front of Nairobi and is a game reserve. We saw zebra, wildebeest, ostriches and many kinds of buck, all terrified of the machine as the pilot came rather low…

We saw what we thought at first was smoke but was a cloud of locusts and we saw the same thing in the Southern Sudan. We left Nairobi again at 7.00am this time. (The night before we had rung up Miss Bennett to wish her our remembrances and she was delighted. Such a nice woman.) [She served in the WRNS during the First World War, was at school with Bert and corresponded with him often during the war. She always declared she would like to farm in E.

Arriving at Kisumu to change in to a flying boat.

'City of Alexandria' at Juba.

Africa. It looks as though she might have made it – on her own?] *We breakfasted at Kisumu on the shores of Lake Victoria and after flying above the clouds for quite a while a most beautiful sight like snow fields in the sun… At Kisumu we changed into a flying boat and had the same nice ex-naval officer as pilot who brought us down from Khartoum. We flew over Lake Victoria and its beautiful wooded and island dotted coast line. Bert kissed me on the equator! We were the only passengers until Kampala from Nairobi, it was lovely like our own machine. Prendergast, the pilot, felt unwell, so sent a chit to ask Bert to take over for a while. So I have been flown by him at last! He was in the cockpit for two hours, then came back to me and returned for the landing at Kampala, although he did not do the actual landing.*

We were pleased to see at Kisumu a sugar planter we had met on the boat and had come to see us again as he lived nearby; this was nice of him and quite a surprise. Arthur and Mabel were on the landing stage at Kampala and bought letters from home, a great joy and surprise, which had been forwarded from Johannesburg. They went with us to the rest house for lunch and we were nearly an hour on shore chatting hard all the time……… That night we slept in Juba after landing about tea time, and went for a walk in the twilight, it was so green and humid after S. Africa. A car stopped by us and a couple asked us if we were off the machine and if we would like to join them as their house was nearby. So we accepted their kind hospitality, a Mr and Mrs Richardson, they had a charming place. We went to bed at 9.00pm that night.

We took off before the sun was up the next day… Lunch at 9.00am at Malakal! Such queer hours! We'd had breakfast at 4.15am that morning. At Malakal we met McGregor, who was on his way to Juba with another machine as he had had a crash a few days before. Flying a Fairey Float plane, on take-off from the Nile somehow caused a native canoe to overturn and drown 2 or three of the occupants. The canoe had shot in front of the plane amongst a lot of sudd. We heard the compensation asked for by the tribe was a bull to feast on, and all would be well! We got to Khartoum about 2.30pm, delightful there, not too hot… Prendergast came along for a drink later and W/c. Cunningham and Sq/Ldr. Howard-Williams had dinner with us on the lawn. The W/c was very delighted I had met his new wife who comes out in October…

That night our beds were put on the veranda and I slept under the stars for the first time. I could see the full width of the Nile from my bed – it was lovely! We are now flying over the desert, soon to land at Aswan. We are in a twelve seater machine now and Bert has taken the controls again. [Argosy G-EBLF. Pilot Capt. Taylor] *Since Kampala we have had three other passengers, all Belgians… We have just left Assiut and I am going to see if I am not too late to catch the air-mail on arrival. Landed safely at Cairo at 15.50 hrs.*

It took from 11th August 1932 to 17th August; seven days from Johannesburg to Cairo. The flying time was 58 hrs 20 mins and the total travelling time 88 hrs 10 mins. What a wonderful, exciting and romantic journey, contrasting with today when it is completed in one day easily in one 10-hour flight. When it was done in 1932, all the territories were British or under British control and mainly at peace. I think this was an extraordinary first-hand record of early commercial passenger flying, which has taken over 75 years to evolve into what we have today, clean and efficient, but giving the passenger no idea of distance or what is being flown over, and devoid of romance. Then at 1000-10,000ft in an open unpressurised cockpit, now in excess of 30,000ft in a pressurised and heated cabin, often on autopilot.

It is clear that Bert and Marjorie had the most wonderful three-month trip to meet his South African family after so long an absence. They all got on very well and left a lasting legacy of warm kinship surviving to this day.

Imperial Airways map of return route to Cairo

RIDING THE WIND - THE LIFE OF A. O. LEWIS-ROBERTS, 1896-1966

Showing development of world routes by 1936

Some first day air mail covers

Bert and Marjorie found their flat in Cairo in good order, and having unpacked their belongings he returned to staff duties at RAF HQ Middle East. Their social life was busy, revolving round dinner and drinks parties and frequent sporting fixtures. Bert won the officers' tennis tournament, doubles, partnered by F/O. A.W. Rule in 1932. They also indulged in cricket, golf, swimming and squash, often played at interservice level.

Meanwhile his staff duties involved much flying all over the Middle East command area, frequently to Khartoum and other stations in the south and to Palestine in the east.

Sadly, in the autumn of 1933, Col Gresham fell seriously ill, and Marjorie returned home by sea to be with her mother and father. Following a serious operation Marjorie's father died in late November 1933, leaving the family, in particular her mother, desolate. She returned to Cairo with Marjorie, where they entertained her to help her recover from the tragic loss of her husband.

Flight to the Cape, 23.04.1933. Flt Lt Nicholletts and Sq Ldr Gayford.

Departure of Fairey long-range monoplane returning from world record flight.

In July 1934 a major expansion of the RAF was announced, with the number of Home Defence squadrons increased from 52 to 75 and bringing the total front-line strength to 128 squadrons within five years. This was the time of the rise of the fascist dictators Hitler and Mussolini, both of whom were prepared to ignore treaty obligations, the former in the Rhineland and Mussolini in Abyssinia. The year before, Winston Churchill had had the amazing foresight to warn the House of Commons of this coming danger.

Bert's log book shows that he made his last flight in Egypt on 17th April. A summary of his flying indicates that he had flown seven different types, but most hours in the Fairey 111F. The total was 1615.25 hours. He was rated as an above average pilot, with no special faults to correct, and signed off from HQME on 25th April 1934.

Bert and Marjory outside their Cairo flat while he was on 'Staff' duties.

Farewell to Egypt at Alexandria harbour 28.04.1934

Transit by sea still demanded fairly rigid dress standards!

Drawing of Bert by AEG, used by the Johannesburg Star to announce his promotion to command 142 Sq.

Met at Southampton by Marjory's Mother, Sam and Nancy and daughter Jane.

Royal review at Mildenhall, July 1935. 142Sq Hawker Harts flying.

On his return to England in June 1934, Bert was appointed the first commanding officer of the reformed 142 (bomber) Squadron, equipped with Hawker Harts and based at Netheravon in Wiltshire. The original First World War 142 Squadron had been disbanded in April 1920. Bert always said that of the many different types he flew, the Hart was his favourite. It was a two-seater biplane light bomber designed by Sydney Camm in the late 1920s. Powered by a Rolls-Royce FX1 water cooled V12 engine, it was very fast for its time; at a level flight speed of 184 mph, it was faster than many fighters. The crew of two sat in individual tandem cockpits, the pilot operating a forward firing .303in Vickers machine gun. The observer sat behind, armed with a single ring-mounted Lewis gun, while for bomb aiming, he lay prone under the pilot's seat! Up to 520lbs of bombs could be carried under the aircraft's wings.

Early in June 1934 Bert began to build up his new squadron and started taking delivery of new Harts from Armstrong Whitworth at Coventry. This company was building them for Hawker, as over 1000 were eventually built and one manufacturer alone did not have the capacity. Bert, with F/Lt Carey, collected all the new aircraft over the next month and started the process of working up the squadron to operational readiness. This included map reading for air gunners and a blind flying course at the Central Flying School, Wittering. Blind flying was done in an Avro Tutor before going on to the dual control Hart. The pilot was trained to fly blind under a hood over the cockpit in a dual control aircraft; the course lasted a month till the end of August 1934.

In the autumn of 1934 Bert's work was mainly instructing young pilots in the dual control Hart basic landing etc, followed by formation flying, bombing practice, aerial photography and recovering from spins. Bombing practice was at Porton Down on Salisbury Plain and became intensive in the spring of 1935; a court of enquiry was held when a bomb overshot into the gas range! The average error recorded was 107 yards when bombing from 6000ft altitude. High altitude flying was undertaken at 17,500ft, without oxygen. Intensive front and rear gunnery was practised, with good accuracy recorded.

In May plans were made for the Royal Review at Mildenhall, with many rehearsals of formation flying and landing by flights. On the 6th July HM the King inspected the RAF on the ground, followed by a take-off and flypast by the squadron in fine weather and ideal conditions.

142 (LB) squadron became operational in the summer of 1935 and went into a period of intensive squadron exercises. As international tensions rose, their deployment oversees seemed more and more certain. Bert's Commanding Officer's staff assessment related his early success as the new Squadron Commander:

During the two and a half months I have known this officer I have formed a high opinion of his ability and character. He is I should say an exceptionally dependable and level headed officer with a gift for leadership. The spirit and work of his recently formed squadron are a fine tribute to his capability as a unit commander.

On October 3rd 1935 Mussolini ordered his armed forces to invade Abyssinia. He had not disguised his plans to increase his African Empire. Although the League of Nations objected, there was little they could do in practice; however Britain thought it wise to strengthen its air force in the region. Light bombers and fighter aircraft were ordered to the region in a group called Truforce. Some of these aircraft were dismantled and crated and departed Liverpool on the 4th October 1935, the day after the Italian invasion, and mobilization had been anticipated. Bert's 142(LB) Squadron was one of those leaving on the 4th; he went by train to Liverpool with his men and boarded the Anchor Line transport SS *Cameronia*. It was very crowded, as there were several squadrons on the ship including 12, 33 and 142 Hart squadrons.

Sadly, on the home front Bert and Marjorie had lost their first child, a son, at birth and Marjorie decided to mark his grave in the airman's cemetery at Netheravon with a small headstone. She decided to move to be with her mother in Bournemouth and, alone save for the help of her sister Nancy, set to to pack up their house, "Tralee", Alexander Road in Andover. These must have been very difficult times to be apart, but the whole family pulled together and helped. Bert's mother and Joe visited them from South Africa.

Meanwhile Bert arrived at Alexandria racked by scarlet fever, which had developed on the ship. He was sent, along with several others, to the Anglo-Swiss Hospital in Alexandria. Here he recovered after a month of hospital treatment and, on being given the all clear from the RAF medical board, passed A1B, he was returned to his squadron at Mersa Matruh, about 150 miles west of Alexandria on the coast.

Squadron photo of 142Sq at Mersa Matruh while part of 'Truforce.' Bert in second row centre.

142Sq landing at Mersa Matruh in the usual dust.

Bert with his beloved Hawker Heart at Mersa Matruh.

The squadrons here were designated, collectively, as Truforce, assigned to counter any threat from Italy through Libya or even from the mainland of Italy. Tension was building in the area since the invasion of Abyssinia by Mussolini, and the League of Nations appeared impotent to take effective sanctions against the aggressor, Italy. In a letter home on December 2nd 1935, Bert says:

The 'Lido Hotel', officers Mess and Quarters at Mersa Matruh overlooking the sea.

Please God this business will not last long. We do not know much but there appears to be an increase in the political tension. If the balloon does go up I know that the Ito's will get something more than they bargained for. It takes a lot to rouse our tempers but if the show starts we will hit hard and continue to hit hard, asking for no quarter… We are staying in The Lido Hotel, accommodation is very limited, lads are double bunking in the rooms and I am sharing a room with the Padre, Cox… Our camp and aerodrome are some miles away, and here we eat and breathe dust and sand when the wind blows or the aeroplanes are running up their engines… Everyone is looking fit and as hard as nails.

Protected airplane pen at Mersa Matruh.

Having got their Hawker Harts assembled and in airworthy condition, they sought to establish landing grounds (LGs) out in the desert, prepared and equipped for possible future operations. Bert personally supplied the ground parties by air with water, rations and mail while also surveying new sites. This work was not without incident, the 22nd December 1935 was an event-filled day:

This bit looked very favourable and has the making of a good L.G. without much labour. On returning to the aircraft we had difficulty in starting the engines and it was a backbreaking job turning the handles before we got the engines running. I took off first and on circling the area I saw Taylor's machine on its back. I landed immediately and was very relieved to find Taylor and his air gunner Cpl Blake unhurt. Taylor on take-off hit a small cairn of stones ahead with his undercarriage and turned over; it was really carelessness on his part and he has learned a lesson which he should not easily forget. I came back with Sgt Peck, Walker's N.C.O., as my passenger so that he could lead the salvage party by road to the crash. On landing here I arranged for the salvage party to return as soon as possible… I flew back accompanied by Sgt James in another aircraft. We bought Taylor and Cpl Blake back, as I wanted the M.O. to see them in case they were suffering from shock. The M.O. saw them and said they were both O.K. The salvage party did a good job of work in dismantling the aircraft, this party with Walker's lot got in safely about 6 pm on Christmas Eve.

1. Bert and some of his 'lads' relaxing by the sea at Mersa Matruh.
2. Bert and Dick Grice at Bin Faud while building landing grounds (LG) and petrol dumps.
3. Bin Faud rest house.
4. One of the real hazards of desert flying, a sandstorm, at Mersa Matruh.
5. Sgt. Wolfinden working the portable radio at Bin Faud.
6. Another LG expedition on the road to Siwa. L-R Ellison, Baker, Grice, Thompson.
7. Bert and 142Sq saying fair well to his former boss, Grp. Cpt. McClaughry.
8. On the road to Siwa, surveying LG for Truforce.
9. Men of 142 Sq. having lunch after clearing and marking a new LG at Bin Faud.

Soon the LG's with their bomb dumps and fuel stores were in place. The expansion of the RAF led to many changes of trained officers and NCOs, resulting in a great need for training of new appointees to the squadron. After Christmas 1935 training was interspersed with three major exercises testing the readiness of the squadrons in Truforce and their co-operation with ground forces. Bert's logbook shows training flights with five aircraft to Palestine and Transjordan in February 1936, as well as intensive flying most days. In July 1936 S/L Gardiner was appointed as the new CO of 142(LB) Squadron and after handover he returned to England on leave. For the first time he was able to come home by Imperial Airways flying boat from Alexandria. The reinforcing squadrons were finally stood down in the late summer of 1936. No military action had been taken, or needed, but it had proved to be a valuable exercise in rapid reinforcement and put in place facilities and experience which were valuable for the coming war in the western desert.

After two months' leave in England Bert returned to assume command of 142 (LB) Squadron again, which by then had moved to Ismailia. In December the squadron returned to England, where it rearmed with Hawker Hind aircraft. The aircraft were manufactured at Hawkers' Brooklands works and collected by Bert from there in January 1937. The Hind was an updated version of the Hart, first bought into service in 1935.

In February 1937 Bert was promoted to Wing Commander and posted to Command RAF Hemswell in Lincolnshire, part of 5 Group, within the newly-formed Bomber Command. Part of the expansion and reorganisation of the RAF in 1936 was splitting it in to four commands: Fighter, Bomber, Coastal and Training. Bomber Command's role was strategic bombing and new medium and heavy bombers came into service.

Hemswell Station had been laid out on a much-expanded First World War airfield, with buildings, hangars and married quarters being built between 1935 and 1937, although concrete runways and dispersal areas were not laid until July 1943. On 9th February 1937 No.144 squadron arrived, equipped with Avro Anson and Hawker Audax aircraft, followed on 8th March by No. 61 Squadron Handley Page Hampdens. These became the first aircraft to bomb Germany, on 19th March 1940. As a matter of interest Hemswell was later used for the filming of the post-war film *The Dambusters*.

Bert's logbook shows he had now flown 2072.5 hours, but that as Station Commander, his flying was reduced to two or three hours per month, mostly communications with Group HQ. He used either the Anson or Audax but at times a Magister or even a Tiger Moth was made available for his use. Later, in early 1939, he flew the new Blenheim Bomber, which was being issued to equip No. 144 squadron in preparation for the start of hostilities. In May 1939 he flew on his own to AV Roe at Woodford, clearly in preparation for his next posting there.

To Bert and Marjorie's great joy they could now once again set up home in England together. They first rented Kettlethorpe Hall near Lincoln, then moved to Willingham House at Willingham-by-Stow near Gainsborough, within easy striking distance of Hemswell. On February 28th 1939 their daughter, Mary, was born at Devonshire Place in London, where specialist care was available. All was well, and mother and baby returned to Willingham; Mary was christened in Lincoln Cathedral later that year. The church magazine at Willingham recorded: 'We are very sorry that Wing-Commander Lewis-Roberts and family have removed to Wilmslow; it would be difficult to find more charming people. We wish them every possible blessing and good wish in their new home'.

Bert signed the handing over certificate to Group Captain E.A.B. Rice on 19th January 1939 and surrendered his command in preparation for his liaison duties with Civil Aircraft Works. Orders came from Headquarters, No. 1 R.A.F. Depot, Uxbridge on 8th March 1939:

Intimation has been received that you have been selected for posting with effect from 10th March, 1939, to Special Duty List whilst employed on liaison duties at a Civil Aircraft Works. You are to report to Group Captain Mansell, Room 6038, Berkeley Square House at 10.00 hours on that date.

As war loomed, this was to prove a most historic posting.

Chapter Nine

WORLD WAR II, 1939-45: A V ROE AND THE LANCASTER BOMBER

Great Britain declared war on Germany on 3rd September 1939 and so commenced the Second World War. On the 26th May 1940 the withdrawal of British and Allied forces from Dunkirk began, and by 3rd of June 345,000 troops had been evacuated, having lost vast quantities of armaments.

The Battle of Britain started in the skies over Southern and Eastern England later that summer. It became very clear that the defence of the UK was largely in the hands of the RAF and that without air supremacy invasion was a very real threat. Air losses in battle would require rapid replacement by a largely civilian manufacturing industry. Beyond this, any chance of taking the war to Germany would depend on a heavy bomber force which was still largely undeveloped. Replacing the losses incurred at Dunkirk and the needs of the RAF became a vital national priority in 1940.

Winston Churchill became Prime Minister of the coalition government on 10th May 1940 and on the 14th he set up the Ministry of Aircraft Production (MAP), with Lord Beaverbrook as the first Minister. Beaverbrook was well known as a dynamic businessman, maybe even a bully, but he got things done. Nearly all the wartime production and development of aircraft would come from the resources of privately-owned firms. Through the pre-war rearmament period sixteen aircraft producers and four engine firms formed the 'family' that enjoyed preferential treatment of orders from Government.

With the outbreak of war and the establishment of MAP, more intimate relations between the Ministry and the 'family' was needed to satisfy the demands of war. Resident Technical Officers were appointed to give general guidance on technical issues to both the main contractors and their suppliers. Many larger firms had an Overseer appointed to them by the Ministry. The Overseer was usually a senior RAF officer, and while he had a special responsibility to maintain close contact throughout the Commands, with service units and representing the RAF, he was the principal representative of MAP headquarters, the man to whom the firm could turn for advice and assistance in every way possible. The Ministry gave him plenipotentiary powers to act in an emergency. However the Resident Technical Officers did not have the same status.

Bert's early staff assessment was very creditable:

An intelligent and most capable officer with plenty of initiative. He is most conscientious and pays attention to detail. Though Wing Commander Lewis-Roberts has only had a few months' experience as an Overseer he has already gained the full confidence of the firm to which he is attached and has carried out his duties with marked ability and success.

It was as liaison officer and later Overseer that Bert was appointed to A V Roe, more often known as Avro, in March 1939. The firm was one of the sixteen preferred suppliers, with a long heritage of producing many proud marques, such as the 504 Trainer or the more recent Avro Anson, in March 1935. Bert's appointment coincided with a very interesting time with Avro and its relationship with the RAF. They had designed the Manchester in response to Air Ministry Specification P.13/36, a twin-engine medium bomber. Even before they received the order for the Manchester, they had been working on a four-engine version.

The Manchester was powered by two Rolls-Royce Vulture engines, a 24-cylinder X-block design which proved to be terribly unreliable in service. Although 209 of them were delivered, after an unreliable service history it had to be withdrawn in 1942. The four-engine version was designated the Manchester III. Powered by four Rolls-Royce Merlin engines, it exceeded expectations as a heavy bomber and, so as not to be tainted by the failing Manchester I and IIs, it was renamed the Lancaster I.

There was an intensive period of debate and discussion about this time to decide on the policy for future manufacture of bombers, and it is clear from Bert's log book that he was very involved. On the 18th July 1940, he, with Captain Brown, flew the first production Manchester to Northolt, where the plane was demonstrated to the Prime Minister and the Minister of Aircraft Production, Squadron Leader Collins and the acting CO of A&AEE, Wing Commander Gray. On the 19th they flew on to A&AEE at Boscombe Down, where they stopped over, leaving at dawn on the 21st to return to Ringway and back to A V Roe.

It is significant that in about August 1940, at a high level in Government, a decision was taken that the whole bomber force should be equipped with four-engine types. Very soon after this decision the Air Ministry was informed that as soon as the current order for 200 Manchesters was completed, the entire Avro manufacturing facility should be turned over to production of the four-engined Handley-Page Halifax. This suggestion could not have gone down well with Avro! They immediately countered by offering to produce the four-engine Manchester variant, and were able to show that they had been designing this aeroplane for two years and that 70% of Manchester parts were interchangeable, thereby allowing for a quicker change to the manufacture of the Lancaster than could be achieved if they had to switch to a new make. As Overseer at A V Roe Bert must have been intimately involved with these very important decisions. About November 1940 the Air Ministry instructed A V Roe to continue with development of the four engined variant of the Manchester to be renamed, eventually, the Lancaster.

Only six weeks later, on January 9th 1941, the first prototype took to the air. Bert notes in his flying logbook that on 16th August 1941, he, with Captain Brown, delivered the second prototype Lancaster (No. OG 595) to A&AEE Boscombe Down for proving trials. They flew at 2000ft and there were rain squalls! They returned to Woodford in an Avro Anson the following day. The Anson took them on with Avro staff to investigate the climbing speed of a Manchester at 47,500lbs all-up weight. Bert describes vibration and buffeting at climbing speeds up to 16,500ft. It was clearly serious, as members of the Royal Aircraft Establishment accompanied them and it was not long before the Manchester was taken out of service.

As Overseer Bert was involved in many issues as well as testing aircraft. He was involved in every way in expediting production of the Lancaster. Once he even recorded testing the camouflage of Woodford Aerodrome and Buildings, working with the Chairman of the Airborne Forces Committee of the Air Ministry, Sir Robert Renwick. Leasing with AOC No 5 Group

A horrific crash of an Avro Anson at Woodford, 5.04.1940. No one was seriously hurt. It is not clear whether it is the plane that Bert flew regularly, however he was not on board when it crashed!

at Grantham, no doubt the problems with the Manchester were uppermost in their discussions.

Early in 1940 Bert was promoted Group Captain and his superiors tried to move him on from being Overseer; this resulted in the most generous and supportive letter from the Chairman of A V Roe to the Air Ministry:

18th March 1940
From
A.V. Roe & Co. Limited,
Newton Heath,
Manchester, 10.
To
Air Marshal Sir Wilfred Freeman,
Air Ministry,
Department ZA
HARROGATE

Dear Sir Wilfred,

I was naturally very pleased to see our Overseer, Lewis-Roberts, get promoted to Group Captain but I did not realise at the time that it meant him being moved from here.

This worries me a lot. Lewis-Roberts is a very exceptional man and this is a very complex organisation and it takes a whole lot of understanding especially by anyone who is not a member of the firm.

It took even Lewis-Roberts a long time to get the hang of things. He has now got the organisation off at his finger tips and is easily the most useful man about the place.

To think of exchanging him for another alarms me greatly. He is doing a real man's job here, he really helps, and my staff look up to him in the most remarkable way.

There are few men who could have wormed their way into their hearts and commanded their respect as he has done.

When I told my leading executives that he may leave us they immediately suggested I should write to you and ask if there was any way of keeping him here as they will quite definitely feel the effect of his loss on the job generally.

Would you consider this matter please as I feel I am right in putting this up in the interests of production generally, not for our own benefit but more so that of the Air Ministry.

Yours sincerely,
R.H. Dobson. (Chairman A.V. Roe)

Picture of the Avro Lancaster from the specifications.

AV Roe presented Bert with this bound volume of the detailed specifications of the Lancaster.

Dual control cockpit.

The business end. Front guns, bomb aimer's position and cockpit.

Tail guns - four Brownings.

This charming reference was copied to Bert by the Air Ministry on 6th April with the following comments:

Dear Lewis-Roberts,
I have much pleasure in forwarding herewith, for your private information, a copy of a letter addressed to A.M.D.P. by Mr. Dobson. Apart from a personal appreciation of your ability, it reflects great credit on the Overseer scheme generally.

It is interesting to note, and it is on record, that Air Marshal Sir Wilfred Freeman was more responsible than any other single figure for the ordering of the Avro Lancaster bomber while running the Ministry for Aircraft Production.

The family moved again, this time to another rented house, "Moleside", at Wilmslow, near Manchester, from 16th July 1939 to 1st April 1942. Their second child, Margaret, was born in Manchester on 6th July 1941. Life for them as a family must have been a great improvement as Bert was not flying a great deal and could return home most evenings to be with his young family.

Bert stayed with MAP at A V Roe until Feb 1942, when he was posted as Deputy Director of Training for Combined Operations. His farewell from A V Roe was marked with a silver salver signed by all the directors and a bound copy of the specification of the Avro Lancaster, both given with great gratitude for his service as Overseer and still in our possession.

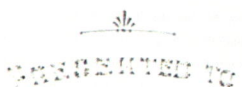

Salver presented to Bert by AV Roe, signed by its directors and senior staff.

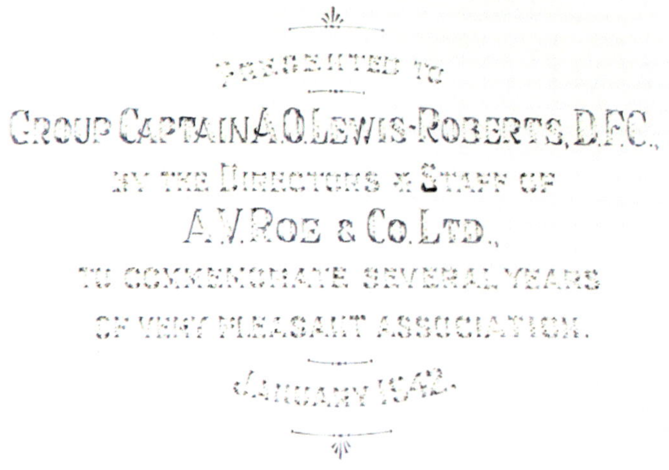

Main inscription on the salver.

Soon after his new appointment, based at the Air Ministry, Marjorie and the two girls moved south to Park House in Blandford, Dorset, happily near her mother and sister, Nancy.

Bert started a new and important job as Deputy Director of Operational Training, specifically responsible for the airborne part of Combined Operation Training. The Air Ministry Lists show he was appointed on 22nd February 1942.

There is an important context to this appointment; just before this date, on 27th October 1941, Louis Mountbatten had been appointed the new Commander of Combined Operations. It was an inspired nomination by Churchill, although it appears Mountbatten was less than happy with the appointment as he was keenly looking forward to commanding HMS *Illustrious*. His new job was broadly, firstly to develop a programme of raids on to the coast of mainland Europe, secondly to prepare for the re-invasion of Europe. His remit included:

- Coordinating inter-service training
- Running the UK Combined Operations Training Establishment
- Advising on tactical and technical research and development
- Devising the special craft needed "for all forms of combined Operations varying from small raids to a full scale invasion".

He found the Combined Operations HQ (COHQ) hardly fit for purpose. They had no planning staff, no signals staff, no training staff and no Chief of Staff. He immediately set about recruiting the staff he needed from both the Royal Navy, the Army, the Royal Marines and the Royal Air Force. The latter had been unfairly accused of having a rather nonchalant attitude to Combined Operations. Mountbatten requested from Air Chief Marshal Sir Charles Portal, CAS, the appointment of two officers of group captain rank, one to be Assistant Advisor on Combined Operations (Air) and the other, Bert, to be the Director of Operational Training (D of T).

From our records we can see that he threw himself wholeheartedly into the task. Much was new and he had a considerable battle with Bomber Command (Harris) to get enough aircraft for training purposes, although Fighter Command was more supportive of the policy and it was obvious that combined operations would have to be developed if ever the Allies were to get back into mainland Europe.

From his log book, on 21st June 1942 he flew himself, alone in a Leopard Moth (AX873), on a tour of training establishments. From Hendon he flew to Twinwood, about four miles north of Bedford, a satellite to Cranfield. From Twinwood to Croughton, satellite to Upper Heyford, to meet and lunch with Air Commodore Haines, CO of 92 OTU, and Group Captain Sheen. From Upper Heyford to Stanton Harcourt via Chipping Norton and Little Rissington. Finally from Stanton Harcourt via Kidlington, Weston-on-the-Green and Thame back to Hendon. From our available records of this time it would appear this whistle-stop tour was designed to familiarise Bert with training establishments and their staff prior to training for new airborne techniques such as gliders.

The next trip recorded in his logbook, on 11th July 1942, was from White Waltham to Netheravon to see a demonstration of glider-borne troops and paratroops. In August he flew to Brize Norton, in an Oxford aircraft, to try for himself the new Horsa heavy glider. He both flew as co-pilot in the Horsa and as second pilot in the Whitley tug aircraft with Wing Commander May as pilot.

The initial 695 Airspeed Horsas were built at their Christchurch factory in early 1942. Up to about 5000 were built in total during the war; largely made of wood, they were designed to be made by furniture manufacturers so as not to disrupt other weapons production. With pilot and co-pilot, they could carry up to 30 troops or a Jeep and a six pounder anti-tank gun. The gliders were first used operationally in the attack on the German Heavy Water Plant in Norway on night 19/20 November 1942.

Operation Jubilee, the disastrous raid on Dieppe, took

place on 18th August 1942 and a thorough reappraisal of the airborne part of this combined operation followed. What effect this had on the RAF's training programme I do not know, but Mountbatten claimed that the problems of Dieppe made a profound difference to the way Operation Overlord (the D-Day landings in June 1944) was handled. This included the addition of a large paratrooper and glider-borne element, which Bert was very much involved in training.

He again flew from Hendon to visit the Heavy Glider Conversion Unit at Brize Norton on 2nd September 1942, accompanied by Air Commodore Hardman (Director of Military Co-operation). This time, after another short period of instruction, he took over the controls and flew the Horsa himself. Very typically of Bert, he never demurred from flying anything, particularly as he could then discuss training on equal terms with first-hand knowledge!

military gliders as a way of delivering Allied armed forces into action, very much in Bert's sphere of responsibility. From there he flew to Snaith and then back to Hendon.

In January 1943 he again visited the Heavy Glider Conversion Unit (HGCU) at Brize Norton by air from Hendon. He noted in his airborne notebook some interesting comments: they had trained 950 first glider pilots from the HGCU excluding RAF pilots, each pilot having 12.5 hours daytime flying training and 2.5 hours at night. The output of second pilots was 160. Then a rather critical comment about American pilots: 'Five American pilots not yet trained, their group may appeal for help – F.T.C. can help if required. 42 O.T.U. crews are gaining experience satisfactorily at H.G.C.U.'

The war in North Africa was coming to an end in 1943 and planning was in hand for the airborne and seaborne landings in Sicily. Known as Operation Husky, the landings started on the night of 9-10th July 1943 and

Airspeed Horsa glider under tow, of the type Bert flew. Thanks to Wikimedia.

On the 15th September he flew to stay a night at the Parachute Training School at Ringway. The next day he went on to Sherburn-in-Elmet, near Leeds, to visit the Armed Forces Experimental Establishment. The AFEE was moved to Sherburn on 17th June 1942 from Ringway; it was charged with the development of

opened the way to landings on the mainland of Italy and the fall of Mussolini.

In preparation for this, on 17th May 1943, Bert made an entry in his flying log book recording a visit he made: 'From Hendon to Netheravon. Meeting with D.T.O., A.O.C. 38th Wing, G.O.C. 6th Airborne Div. Return to

Hendon land at Hartford Flat and drop Col. Bray'. They flew in a 'Stinson' aeroplane. The 38th Wing was a precursor of 38 Group; its role was troop carrying. GOC 6th Airborne was General Gale; Col Bray was a General Staff Officer of 6th Airborne. This date was two months before operation Husky and the AOC 38th Wing, Air Commodore Sir Nigel Norman, was about to leave for North Africa. Two days later he was, very sadly, killed when the Hudson bomber he was in crashed on take-off from Portreath in Cornwall. The gliders used in operation Husky were towed from England the 1500 miles to North Africa, an amazing feat in itself!

In the build-up to Operation Overlord, Bert was very busy, typically visiting the HQ of Flying Training Command and on to Brize Norton to visit HGCU. Here he again flew a glider in tow from a Whitley bomber. From his notes he was evaluating the single or double towing system and recommended the single tow as being more satisfactory. He interviewed Group Captain Horn, Station Commander of Brize Norton. Again he visited the HQ of 38 Group, which supplied many of the glider tugs, no doubt reviewing requirements for training for D-Day. His notebook is full of details of training both paratroops and glider crews, such as how should paratroops handle a kit bag in the air, or the best way of supply dropping on to a hill, etc. In April 1944 he spent a lot of time at the Parachute Training School, Ringway, clearly ironing out details of training for D-Day.

In September and October 1944 he had a further very intensive period of work in support of parachute training, eg:

27th October 1944. Dakota aircraft. Local from P.T.S. Ringway to Tatton Mere. Dead stick of five including S/L Onions, W/C Redding, Mr. Heeley, jumping with X type Parachutes landing in Lake. All paratroops wearing rubber suits and some with 'K' type dinghies. Drill good.

To my mind it is extraordinary that he went into so much detail to see that the training was appropriate, but very typical of the man!

Next, from his notebook, training for airborne operations in the Far East, after the end of the war in Europe. Some interesting notes of a briefing in preparation for air operations in Burma, repeated as written:

'Wingate's Own Air force'
Training very good – one force essential. Ellison second in command to Cochran. No interference up to D+5 when Spitfires arrived. Japs arrived on D+6. Radar equipment round landing strips. Gliders piling up on flare path.
V.H.F sets and any W/T sets disrupt Japs communications and call up bomber support.
Jungle or open warfare?
1. Can't use air over jungle
2. Fight Japs in the open
3. Need for heavy explosive power to defeat Japs in the open.
4. R.A.F. to provide the explosive power
Open area use 2 Para Brigades and 1 Air landing Brigade then make landing strips – Fighters – Transports with Divs.
One aircraft to land every half minute in 24hrs on strip
4 Divs. delivered in 5 days – 1000 aircraft transport. One div. wants 180 tons per day - 60 aircraft.
Choice of battle field.
Max range of 400 miles
Up to 500 for C47.
Types of aircraft. Light bombers B25, Fighter bombers, long range fighters, not dive bombers.
A need for long range A.O.P.
A need for Helicopters for putting in RADAR equipment.
Air support – V.H.F radio, control
Bombers – Targets indicated by smoke
No target for heavy bombers.
Airborne Divs.
Indian. Goes in first and consolidates the strips before regular divs. Carried in by Waco (gliders) and C47 (transports)
Endurance of transport crews on 400 mile radius.
3 sorties /day
1st and 2nd pilot first day then allow 6hours servicing.

I have repeated this as these are his last wartime notes, and I think of historic interest as a demonstration of serious intent had the war against Japan been prolonged. Indeed some of the techniques had already been used.

The war against Japan ended with VJ Day on 15th August 1945. Bert would never have to implement the airborne training in earnest for the war against Japan. In 1945 he was posted as Liaison Officer at Headquarters Control Commission, Norfolk House, London. With the end of the war many wartime commissions came to an end, as did many lifetime careers.

This was the end of his flying career. His flying log book shows that since his first flight on 6th August 1917 he had flown in total 2175 hours and 45 minutes and as observer 102 hours 55 minutes.

CHAPTER TEN

RETIREMENT

It would not be unreasonable to say Bert was addicted to flying and he had, in 1945 at the age of 50, been on active service for over 30 years. He had flown in war and peace well over a hundred types of aeroplanes, from the primitive Farman Longhorns of the First World War to the fast and sophisticated bombers and fighters of the Second World War. It had been an exciting time for a pilot who loved leading men and was brave and patriotic. So it was not surprising that he found the prospect of retirement at the end of hostilities to be very unattractive.

The family had now moved to Beech Lodge, Rowlands Hill, Wimborne in Dorset. They had all had endured many ordeals during and before the war, but Bert was still keen to continue in the RAF. Sadly for him this was not to be; on 7th November 1945 he was informed by the Air Ministry that they no longer needed his services. He was told it was the policy of the Air Council to gradually replace senior officers to maintain a sufficient flow of promotions through the higher ranks, and they regretted that it would be necessary to put him on the retired list. He was given 56 days terminal leave, making his retirement effective from 2nd January 1946, shortly before his 50th birthday. Sadly, again he had a medical problem. He required a throat operation, which took place on 27th November 1946 at Princess Mary's Royal Air Force Hospital, Halton, Buckinghamshire. The operation went well and he soon started to apply for jobs both in the RAF and the Control Commission for Germany. Old friends Air Marshal Sir Roderick Hill and Archdeacon Warner DSO were used as referees.

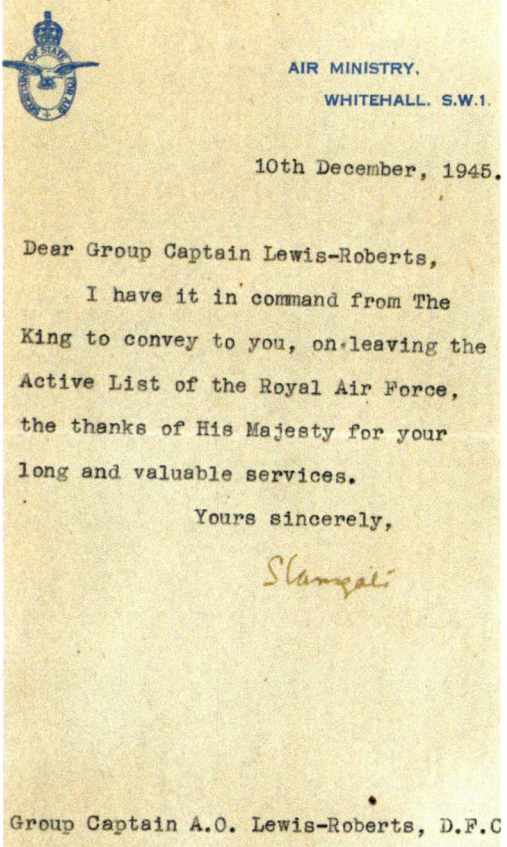

Letter from the King thanking Bert for many years' service on his retirement.

His application to the Control Commission for Germany (BE), Mechanical Engineering Branch, Economic Division, was successful and in the spring of 1946 he was again parted from his young family and moved to Berlin. The job in the Economic Division of the Control Commission involved appraising post-war German companies to determine whether or not they could be used for future warlike purposes. He joined the Mechanical Engineering Capacity Investigation Team at H.Q. 1 Corps District BAOR. Letters show he had a good time in Berlin and again took up squash playing, with, amongst others, Major G H Leggett, an intelligence officer in HQ Control Commission. The lack of squash balls seems to have been the main limiting factor, as they were almost unobtainable in post war Berlin!

On the 4th March 1947 he again received a letter making him redundant, as the department was to be drastically cut as a part of the post-war austerity measures. There were kind comments from his commanding officer:

I would like to take this opportunity of expressing my thanks to you for the service you have rendered, not only to the Branch but to the Commission as a whole, and trust that the experience you have gained whilst serving in Germany will prove of value to you in the future and thus compensate you for any disappointments you may have felt in having to leave the Service.

He returned by train from Berlin on 13th January 1947. The sleeper was on a special train from Bad Oeynhausen to Victoria. The rail warrant for the special train was quite elaborate:

Reason for travel (in detail). Returning to the UK on completion of 12 months service with the Control Commission…
I hereby certify that the movement of this passenger is necessary and essential on duties connected with the Military Government, reconstruction, rehabilitation or Post War development and that the mission of this passenger is of such urgency that transport by the special train is necessary.

This again shows that things we now take for granted, like freedom of movement by train, were then extremely coveted and in very short supply.

Bert arrived home at Beech Lodge in Wimborne, now fully retired at 51 years old. Pictures of him at the time portrayed him looking rather thin and drawn after his operation and the strictures of working in Berlin. His mother wrote: 'I just cried when I saw his photos, his brave smile but how terribly thin he had got and so much older. He must not grieve over being retired'.

Like many ex-servicemen, Bert found it very difficult to adapt to peacetime civilian life. However, with the help of his wonderful wife and family, he gradually adjusted and found a new life in Dorset, embracing voluntary service and even finding time to play cricket for Wimborne and tennis with his sister and brother-in-law at Charlton Marshall.

He was approached by Air Vice Marshall Sir Hazelton Nicholl, controller of the RAF Benevolent Fund, to ask whether he would be willing to help them by assessing cases for assistance in Dorset. This he agreed to do. The Air Training Corps also invited him in to help locally. He had a kind, if somewhat forbidding, way with young people and he enjoyed their company.

Civil Defence grew in national importance as the Cold War developed. Bert attended the Civil Defence Staff College and took No 44 (special) course in 1952. The course enabled him to take a leading part in the organisation in Dorset, indeed he had a warning siren based in his study! The British Legion was another way he kept in touch with kindred spirts.

Meanwhile, in the summer of 1948 he heard that his mother and Uncle Ted (AEG) were both ailing in South Africa, so he and Marjorie decided that he should pay a visit on his own. He booked a ticket to Johannesburg, flying by KLM. How it had changed in the fourteen years since they last flew to South Africa! In 1933 it took ten days, with no flying at night and some connections by rail; now the journey took a day and a half from London via Amsterdam, Tunis, Kano, and Leopoldville to Johannesburg. The aircraft, a DC6 MC2 called 'Prince

Bernhard', could carry just 56 passengers but had only 32 on board. It sported a men's lounge and a ladies' lounge! The ticket price was £221, return I assume, which seems reasonable. Departure from London was on 26th February 1949. Sadly his mother died on 30th November 1948, but he was in time to see his much-loved Uncle Ted, who subsequently passed away later in 1949. His mother is buried in the old Church of England graveyard in Dundee, Natal; laid to rest beside her now are her two daughters, Joe and Alice.

In July 1950 the Air Ministry was invited by the King and Queen to compile a list of retired and serving RAF officers to attend a garden party at Buckingham Palace. Bert and Marjorie were selected to attend; I could not help noticing that point three in the invitation notes: 'It is not essential that the persons recommended shall have been presented at Court, but they must be eligible to attend court in all other respects, i.e. they are not persons who have been guilty parties in a divorce case or have been adjudicated as bankrupt'. How times have changed!

Bert and Marjorie had owned Beech Lodge for eight years and in April 1952 they decided to sell and move out of Wimborne into the country. They purchased Chalbury Hill House, the lovely former Georgian rectory to Chalbury Church, some five miles north of Wimborne. This was their ninth and last move. With the house came a substantial garden, and best of all a gardener and his wife, Jim and Alice Poore, who lived in a cottage on the property and became stalwart, loyal supporters of the family.

Beyond the little churchyard lay the Old Church School, which in the early 1960s was converted into our family home. Bert and his family settled happily into their new home and he became known locally simply as 'the Group Captain.' He was highly respected and much appreciated for his voluntary work. For instance a letter from Air Commodore B C Yarde, CVO, CBE, the CO of No 62 (Southern) Group, to Bert in July 1954 stated:

My attention has been drawn to the valuable work that you have done during your period of voluntary service with the Air Training Corps. The efficiency and welfare of the Corps depend very much upon the enthusiasm and self-sacrifice of those who like yourself, have spent so much of their time in the service of the cadets.

It gives me great pleasure to express to you my special appreciation of your loyal support.

By now his elder daughter Mary was at Ancaster House School in Sussex, soon to be followed by her sister Margaret. Their next great adventure, this time as a family, was a trip round Africa, visiting relatives in Southern Africa on the way. It had long been Bert's dream to take the whole family to meet his family in Southern Africa. His brother Arthur in Bulawayo, his cousin Betty Price and family in Johannesburg and his two sisters in Dundee Natal were all long overdue a visit. The opportunity presented itself when both girls had left school in 1960.

Bert put a formidable amount of work into planning every detail of the trip. The plan was to go by sea in the *Kenya Castle* through the Mediterranean and down the East Coast to Beira, by train from Beira to Bulawayo, then on to Johannesburg, Dundee and Cape Town, then rejoin the ship and return to London, taking in all about five months. Their affairs were left in the capable hands of the family lawyer, with the redoubtable Mr and Mrs Jim Poore looking after the house.

On 23rd December 1960 the family sailed on the *Kenya Castle* from London, calling at Genoa, Port Said, Suez and Aden and arriving at Mombasa on 10th January 1961. After four days here, they moved on to Tanga, Zanzibar, Dar-es-Salaam and Beira. Here they left the ship to go by train to Umtali, where they met up with Bert's brother Arthur, who took them on by car to Bulawayo for a three-week stay in Rhodesia.

Sadly events intervened, as Margaret became very ill with Crohn's Disease and was hospitalised for emergency operations. It was decided that the family should stay together in Bulawayo until she was out of danger and they could move on. Extensive surgery was required, and it became clear that it would be better for Mary to fly down to Johannesburg to stay with the Price family for the Easter holidays. She returned, and when Margaret was fit to travel, Bert and Mary went south by train taking all the luggage, staying with Roger and Betty Price in Johannesburg, who very kindly entertained them. They moved on by train to Cape Town to stay with an old RAF friend in Constantia.

Having now missed the *Kenya Castle* for the return voyage they had to take the *Athlone Castle* instead, arriving back in England in May 1961. In the meantime Marjorie bought Margaret home by Comet jet airliner and delivered her to hospital in England, where she made a slow but good recovery. We all felt so sorry for the family who had planned such a momentous trip to meet their Southern African family only to be thwarted by poor Margaret's illness; the first thing we knew about it was when we said prayers for her in Chalbury Church.

Being neighbours, our two families became close friends. In the winter of 1961-2, by a strange quirk of fate, I was posted to South Africa (Basutoland) to undertake my Voluntary Service Overseas (VSO). This greatly pleased the 'Group Captain' and he went into overdrive to try and help me with introductions. I think he could see himself in me coming the other way in 1917 when he arrived in England armed with many written introductions. His introduction of me to his cousin Betty Price, on 17th February 1963, was as charming as it was old fashioned:

Dear Betty,

This is a note to introduce Mr Robert Lawton to you.

Robert is due to leave England shortly for South Africa, where he will join an Agricultural Mission in Basutoland under the aegis of the Overseas Voluntary Service. Sir George Schuster is giving Robert encouragement and support for the work that he is undertaking.

I hope that you will have received my Air Mail with advanced news that Robert was leaving for South Africa and may visit Johannesburg.

Please give Robert any help that he may need… Bert

Who could possibly go astray with such gracious introductions? My adventure in South Africa had started, but that is another story!

In 1963 the squadron that Bert served in in the First War, No. 83, was stationed at RAF Scampton. In preparation for presentation of the Squadron Standard by HM the Queen, he was asked to help write their early history. He recalled also helping in 1937/38 when the Squadron received its badge from Chester Herald; seemingly a long time after the occasion when he was one of the six DFC's awarded for one vital reconnaissance in 1918, commemorated by the six-point antler on the badge. This badge, flanked by eight battle honours, would now appear on the new No 83 Squadron Standard along with the motto, 'Strike to Defend'. The Standard is currently (2014) laid up in the RAF Chapel in Lincoln Cathedral, as the squadron has been disbanded.

The family, including Mary and Margaret, proudly went to the ceremony on 10th June 1963, when the Queen presented the Squadron Standard at Scampton.

About this time Bert's dear old Aunt Mabel passed away in Dawlish. She had been a great supporter of him all her life, from being with him in the siege of Kimberley to giving him a home when he came to England to fight in 1917. He was her executor, but he found travelling to Devon hard as his health was now failing. He had flown on active service in both world wars and, like many, had 'calmed his nerves' by smoking. Add to this many hours' flying in open-cockpit aircraft with engine fumes all too prevalent, and it was not surprising that doctors now diagnosed emphysema. He made frequent visits to the chest hospital in Southampton, but despite some respite, his breathing continued to deteriorate.

I returned from South Africa in May 1964 to take up a job working in the Agricultural Division of Imperial Chemical Industries (ICI). Mary and I began a very happy time leading to our wedding on 6th November 1965. Bert's health had deteriorated gravely, but he very bravely found strength to give Mary away at our wedding in the little ancient Church of All Saints Chalbury. After the wedding his health continued to deteriorate and he sadly died on 6th February 1966, just seventy years old.

Writing the story of Bert's life has been a journey I have enjoyed. It has taken me from the battlefields of the Anglo Boer War to the campaigns on horseback in German South West and German East Africa and to the fighting in the air over Flanders in primitive aeroplanes. Between the wars, in Egypt and Palestine, he helped to pioneer the great transcontinental air routes and police the Empire. He tested and developed many new and untried aircraft and the techniques needed to make them an effective force. The Second World War saw great responsibility for his part in helping to bring the Lancaster into service and the development of the training for vastly expanded and novel airborne forces. He was always a loyal and brave warrior on behalf of his country, only ever asking for the chance to serve. Bearing in mind the wonderful complimentary comments on his service record and his willing and varied experience, I am surprised he did not rise to a higher rank, as many of his contemporaries did.

Our wedding day 6.11.1965. The last picture of Bert; clearly very unwell, he carried out his duties bravely at the ceremony, but sadly died soon afterwards.

APPENDIX A

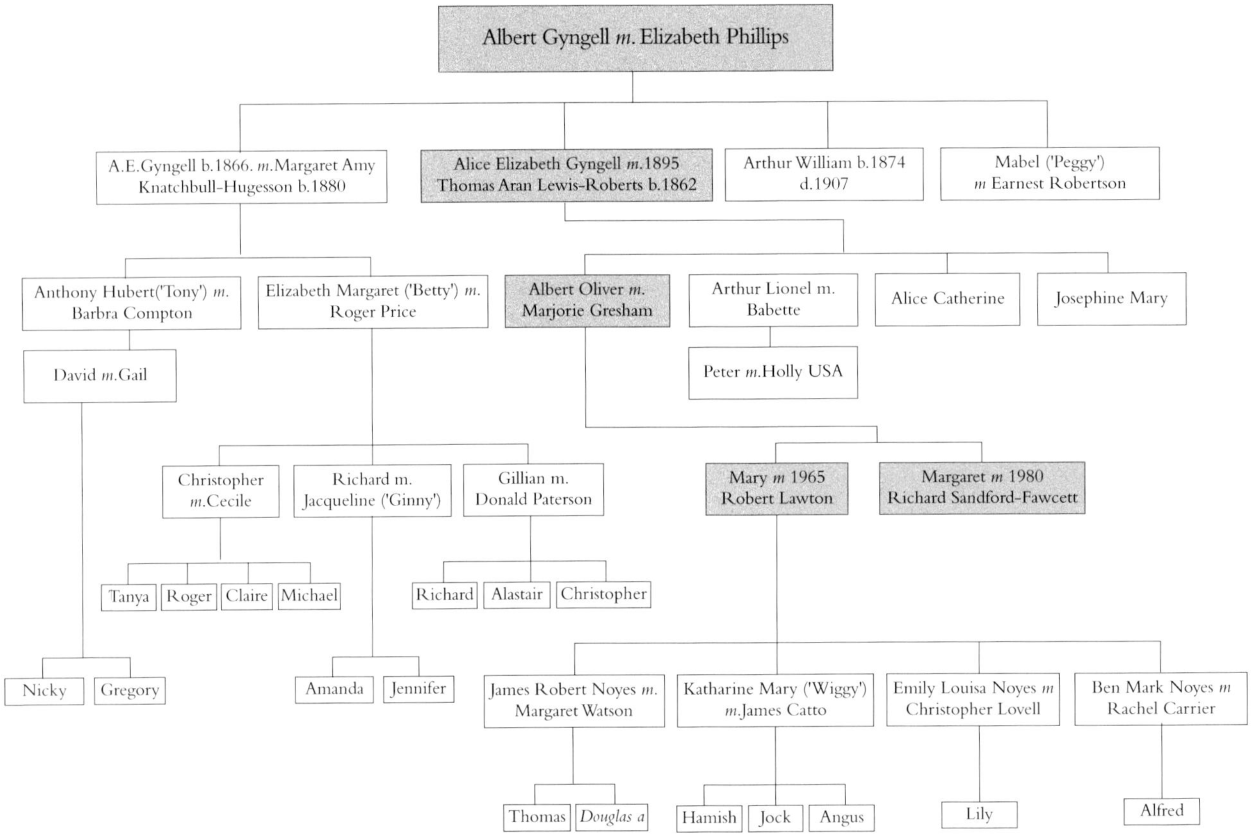

```
                    Albert Gyngell m. Elizabeth Phillips
         ┌──────────────────┬──────────────────┬──────────────────┐
   A.E.Gyngell b.1866.    Alice Elizabeth    Arthur William     Mabel ('Peggy')
   m. Margaret Amy        Gyngell m.1895     b.1874             m Earnest Robertson
   Knatchbull-Hugesson    Thomas Aran        d.1907
   b.1880                 Lewis-Roberts b.1862
```

- Children of A.E. Gyngell & Margaret: Anthony Hubert ('Tony') m. Barbra Compton; Elizabeth Margaret ('Betty') m. Roger Price
- Children of Alice & Thomas: Albert Oliver m. Marjorie Gresham; Arthur Lionel m. Babette; Alice Catherine; Josephine Mary

David m. Gail (child of Anthony)

Peter m. Holly USA (child of Arthur Lionel & Babette)

Christopher m. Cecile; Richard m. Jacqueline ('Ginny'); Gillian m. Donald Paterson

Mary m 1965 Robert Lawton; Margaret m 1980 Richard Sandford-Fawcett

Tanya, Roger, Claire, Michael (children of Richard & Jacqueline)

Richard, Alastair, Christopher (children of Gillian & Donald)

Nicky, Gregory (children of Christopher & Cecile)

Amanda, Jennifer

James Robert Noyes m. Margaret Watson; Katharine Mary ('Wiggy') m. James Catto; Emily Louisa Noyes m Christopher Lovell; Ben Mark Noyes m Rachel Carrier

Thomas, Douglas a (children of James & Margaret)

Hamish, Jock, Angus (children of Katharine & James)

Lily (child of Emily & Christopher)

Alfred (child of Ben & Rachel)

APPENDIX B

Timeline of A.O.Lewis-Roberts Career

Date From	Date To	
	01/02/1896	Born Kimberly, CP, South Africa. Siege 1899-1901
1909	1912	Educated Jeppes High School, Johannesburg. Matriculated
1913	1914	South African School of Mines and Technology, Now Witwatersrand University. Completed first year
13/11/1914	12/06/1915	Served in SW African Campaign as a Trooper in 2 Imperial Light Horse
08/12/1915	01/03/1917	Served in East and Central African Campaign as a Trooper in 4th South African Horse
	12/06/1917	Joined Royal Flying Corps as Cadet
	29/07/1917	Commissioned in RFC 2nd Lieutenant (Pilot)
04/12/191	12/01/1918	War Service Home defence Night Fighter
01/03/1918	11/11/1918	War Service France. Night Bombing and Reconnaissance
	12/06/1918	Promoted Acting Captain - RFC
	02/09/1918	Awarded the Distinguished Flying Cross
Nov-18	May-19	Flying Duties in France and Army of Occupation, Rhine, Germany
May-19	Jan-21	Flying Duties in Egypt and Sudan
	Aug-19	Granted Permanent Commission in RAF with Rank of Flying Officer
	Jan-21	Posted to Home Establishment
Mar-21	Oct-21	Posted to Central Flying School Upavon and RAF Farnborough for Engineering Course
Nov-21	1923	Posted to Cambridge University for Engineering Course
	1922	Promoted to Flight Lieutenant
	1924	Awarded BA Degree Cambridge University
1923	1927	Test Pilot and Flight Commander A&AEE Martlesham Heath. 15 and 22 Squadrons
1927	1928	Attended RAF Staff College
	1931	Marriage to Marjory Gresham - 17th January, Bournemouth
	1931	Promoted Squadron Leader
1929	1934	HQ RAF Middle East. Air Staff and Engineering Duties
1934	1937	Appointed Officer Commanding No.142 squadron Bomber Command
1935	1936	Posted with No.142sqn to TRUEFORCE, Western Desert Egypt.
	1937	Promoted Wing Commander
1937	1939	Appointed Officer Commanding RAF Station HEMSWELL. Bomber Command
1939	1942	Posted to Ministry of Aircraft Production for Aircraft engineering Duties as M.A.P. Overseer to Messers A.V.Roe & Co. Ltd. Manchester
	1940	Promoted Group Captain
1942	1945	Posted to Air Ministry as Deputy Director, Training Combined Operations Under the Director of Combined Operations Training
1945	1946	RAF Liaison Officer, Headquarters Control Commission, Norfolk House, London

APPENDIX C

E. African Campaign with 4th South African Horse.

Transcript of Bert's Diary 1916. Rather disjointed as written on active service.

Places Visited during Fighting in East Africa 1916–1917. (*Front page of notebook*).

Johannesburg	**Mombo** (*Rombo ?*)	Mission Place Umfiomi
Durban	**Moshi**	Camp 27 miles from latter place
Kilindini	*Moh Kover Camp on slopes of Lili Magari*	Wassi
Omboro		*Kon Meraiga*
Voi	Camp re 4th covered retreat of Infantry	Voi
Mashoti		Nairobi
Maktau	*Unterkali*	Elemantata
Bibi	Maschi	Nairobi
M'buyuni	Arrusha	Maktau
Serengeti	9 miles from Arrusha	Kilindini
Salaita	Lol Kisali	Mombasa
Taveta	Camp 45 miles from *letflase*	Dar es Salaam

1916

A small diary recording little events from Jan 27th

27th Jan. The regiment leaves Show Grounds. D Squadron leaves the last. Many kind friends with fruit and comforts to wish us the best. UT (*Uncle Ted*) saw me off, chattered a great deal, introduced his worthy to O'H. Met Mesdames Williams and Childe.

Last to board train find it extremely crowded. Have better accommodation later on.

T R in dumps wants to know what in blazes made him join; spends his time writing long tender letters. His misfortune and behaviour has given me timely warning. Not a bad fellow at heart.

We are all well treated down the line, hearty welcome re. the Natal folk.

Reach D (*Durban*) at 1pm. Embark on H.M.S. Laconia at 2pm. With all kit. Laconia, a fine, sturdy boat of 22,000 tonnage.

28th Jan. Mess no. 93 a distinct success. First days voyage, felt queer, fit as a fiddle after being sick. Start enjoying trip immensely. Good concerts at night!! Officer MT.C tells Archie his men are a superior type and not accustomed to do guards and fatigues, while others re SAH can perform these. Archie's hair up, gives him a good telling off. Hence "Taxis" "Honk, honk".

1st Feb. Celebrate a memorable B Day (*Bert's*), having a bad throat and thick head. Enjoyed boxing contest during the night. It appears many mainly "Jafies", have never been to a boxing match before, on account of behaviour and remarks passed. Nearly had a bust up through telling someone to keep mighty quiet.

Cannot understand behaviour of AN. I think his worthy is treated more as a joke than anything else. Shall make inquiries. I think FF is the cause.

2nd Feb. Have throat painted. Boat expected to reach Kilindini tomorrow morning. Heat very oppressing. His worthy, generally attired in open pyjama jacket, khaki slacks and barefooted, otherwise is found wandering like a lost sheep in nothing but a pair of slacks, enjoying the breeze. Better fed on board ship than our mess at Show Grounds.

Passed Mombasa and up river to Kilindini – estuary a wonderful sight.

Day of landing. Fall in for heavy fatigue carrying kit from the bottom of the hold to the deck, sweltering simply damnable.

Kilindini ladies very nice to hot and thirsty fellows, tea and lemon squash. Leave Kilindini that afternoon. Packed like sardines into native coaches, most uncomfortable, what with livestock heat and no rations. Reach Voi late that night and have a few hours rest. Instead of making for Nairobi, go on to Maktan. Kilimanjaro, visible in the distance. Camp hot and dusty poor rations. Horses miserable after the voyage but soon pick up.

Leave Maktan on 14th Feb and trek on to Mbyani. Enjoy trek immensely meet with all kinds of game, a veritable paradise.

"13th" Fight at railhead, bad management. Glad at hearing Melville and others safe.

Always kept busy, squadron each day going out to scout bush. Saturday night at 11-15 Regiment called to arms, saddled at 12pm and leave camp. Do heavy travelling through the bush. Trek on through night and morning. Horses kept saddled all the time. On right hand side of Kilimanjaro see signs of forts and habitation. Trek fully 70 miles finished Sunday night at 9.30. Reached camp have good food and flop down to sleep.

"Spilkins" (*Bert's horse*) goes splendidly, young horse and most uncomfortable to ride. Leave *Mbunyi* on the 8th, trek on to Serengeta. Next marching Selita bombarded by heavy guns.

9th Feb. Bombardment still continues; watch effect of high explosive shells. Same afternoon the Regiment go round Schita hill. Fully expect meeting askaris; our aim being to round them up. Heavy rain overtakes us everyone is soaked to the skin.

Selita impenetrable against rifle fire, one maze of trenches, hidden in thick undergrowth, barbed wire entanglements. After Selita Regiment goes as escort to guns and transport to *Teveta*. We get into *Teveta* on 10th early in the afternoon, plenty of water have most enjoyable wash for a long time. Next morning 13th the 4th (*SAH*) go out scouting the hills. B squadron come in touch with German and ascari machine guns. Ten horses lost, few men hit none killed. Big hill held by some men. Askaris come through donga (*gully*) but have to retire. C outflanked on the right flank.

Am on picket that night, heavy machine gun and rifle fire, am able to see flashes of guns. Hear afterwards that "Kortbrockies" get into Askaris with bayonets. Heavy fighting all that night. Next morning am still on picket, re-join troop later on in the day feeling very tired and empty. That afternoon, Regiment enters Mamba, get plenty of mealie meal, vermicelli, potatoes, and also green mealies. Other fellows find liquor and champagne. Beautiful river at Mamba, enjoy swim and wash immensely.

Next day at 2 pm D (*squadron*) act as escort to ammunition column. Reach Moshi at night at 8 pm very hungry. First camp on this side of the river. Just finish our meal when heavy tropical rain comes down; soon get soaked to the skin, but sleep well till morning when try to get warm and things dry.

D squadron re-join the regiment 15 miles further down, in the afternoon.

15th March. Spend afternoon writing up Diary, find it difficult to keep it up. Losing self, admire reflection in the river, very luxuriant and grand. Spent long afternoon after nights picket. Looks like rain again tonight.

16th March. Tommy has touch of dysentery. That night, camp alarmed, stand to arms from 12 to 2.30 a.m., continuous firing on our left front; but soon stops. One days rations for three days so have to go easily.

17th March. Kept busy building breast works in case of sudden attack.

18th-19th March. Observation Post, regiment leaves, leaving at *Mbunyi*

20th March. Found regiment late in the morning. Indian mountain battery at work. German guns kept us under cover. Am in heavy fighting this night 4th cover the retreat of the 12th infantry. One fool lets his rifle go brings enemy fire on to us. Big luck nobody hit, though shots very near, J. Dryer dragged bodily by mount.

21st March. Mail rations and horse feed, everybody very happy. Mac, one of the best fellows. Section works well. Tommy feeling better. Have Uncles letter re. Birth of Daughter (*Betty*) and re Maurice Military Cross.

Leave last scrapping place on the 20th at 3 p.m. for Mamba Bridge, but go on to Moshi, half way, an hour's halt. Reach Moshi at about 10.30 p.m. Leave Moshi, trek on all night till day break.

21st March Big guns at work. Some very narrow shaves. German K's guns (*Naval guns off the Battle ship Konigsberg*) keeping us very busy.

22nd March. C company evacuated place. Unterkali, naval guns found blown up. River full of crocks.

23rd. Thursday. Feel very sick. Above scrappy writing (*21st-22nd*) done on horse picket in the moonlight.

24th. Leave Unterkali late in the afternoon owing to footbridge collapsing. Reach a camp where Konigsberg gun blown up. Have 1.5 hrs. halt then trek on till 10.30 towards Mamba direction. Off saddle sleep until roused at 1.45, when have to resaddle, men and horses kept "saddled" close on 2 hrs. Waiting simply damnable, everybody cross and tired. Reach Mamba Bridge and trek on to Moschi, arrived at latter place fairly early in the morning, are camped a couple of miles out of the town in a badly situated place, a hollow and far from water; heat very tiring. Quite a number of men of the Regiment down with Malaria and Dysentery. Tony getting better but still rather peakish.

26th–30th. Are camped in house on slope of hill. We are very comfortable and well off at this place. Plenty of fruit, bananas and good rations atone for a lot. River close at hand. The scenery along the banks of unsurpassed beauty. Ferns, palms, huge monkey rope creepers and huge *fur* *tufted* trees, with the river rushing by in the valley below, a veritable garden of paradise. Being quite close to Kilimanjaro, we see both wonderful and beautiful sights i.e. early morning sun catching snow cap of Mt. Kilimanjaro, a wonderful sight.

29th. Tony sent to Hospital with fever, was not well for a long time; the best place for him.

Tsetse fly makes its appearance felt, several horses dying.

April 1st. All Fools Day. Regiment leaves Moschi early in the morning. Our stay at this place was a most enjoyable one. Plenty of grub, bananas. Our special stove a great success. Sleeping in house bit troublesome at night "Rats". While on first days trek have my haul of eggs. Each section gets 2 and half dozen with bacon for breakfast. Same amount for supper while on horse.

April 3rd. D Squadron push ahead leaving Regiment to look after our transport and get in to Arrusha on that day. This place a beauty spot. Leave Arrusha same morning at 10.30 and camp on hill with other SAH nine miles out. This camp covered in mud. While on previous trek rain and mud heavy going for horses. On night of 3rd sleep in tents, rain continuous on flanks of horses, camp next morning a quagmire.

4th. D push ahead with transport, veldt like a marsh. Am writing this after grub at 12.30 a.m. Van Deventer lot ahead. (*Maj Gen J. van Deventer commander 2nd East African Div.*)

5th. Country more open and very dry. On huge plain seen immense herds of game, Wildebeest, eland, quagga etc. Fellows on our left come in touch with troop of lions. As close as 10 to 15 yards. That afternoon camp 10 miles from Lol Kisali Mt. Picket that night Spilkins (*Bert's horse*) loses his front shoes and feet start becoming bad. Mac's eyes a good deal better.

6th. Leave last place in morning with transport. On the way in deep bushy donga come across lion and lioness quite close. Dead horses strew the way. Had word that force on Lol Kisali, 225 with 3 Maxims, surrender to van Deventers lot. Shortage of water, rations low. Quite True

6th, 7th, 8th. Horses' bad, water worse, rations low. Lot of Rumours flying round.

8th Leave Lol Kisali that night, the three horses in our section in poor condition owing to the total lack of water. Hardly expect them to pull through. Dead horses lying in the dozens, trek all night and next morning to a place where 2nd SAH and water are. Horses pick up wonderfully. Still no shoes for Spilikins.

11th. Leave this place next morning without rations.

14th. Left Mission Place Umfiomi. Previous day attacked by Malaria, really unfit for trekking, but think of section. Feel it bad that night in the rain and damp. Manage to hang out till morning do 25 miles. 1st, 2nd and 9th busy scrapping the days previously get into their camp and stop 2 days. Leave that camp on Sunday morning 16th worse with the fever and have terrible shivers, can barely hang on during the day am finished that night. On verge of collapse go to Medicals. Put in "Chrip House" a big Cement, clean place. Am told next morning I was delirious all night. Writing this on 18th. Fever gone, feel a little better, but damnably weak. That morning the others get into Cassearras; guns go at them too. Hope to get with section tomorrow afternoon, i.e. feeling better. Blosam looking after Sgt Roberts and self. Piet a real brick. Medicals bay left.

19th. Still the same. During the morning Van D… …. places self and four others under open arrest for utter piffle. News had reached him that we had driven Chief out of his house and had lit fires in his rooms. Natives round house continue to bring round milk. We get sweet potatoes, mealies and meat on small payments. Uncertain what will happen tomorrow.

20th Nothing farther happened, except during the night that 50 details including j D…… spend the night. Sugar flour etc. very low. Living on sweet potatoes and mealies. Still very weak.

21st. Good Friday Met Nick going forward with despatches. Jack Lamont and others come back for rations. Roads simply a quagmire no wagons can move. Rain every day. Hear Mac is bad

22nd. Nothing worth mentioning except plentiful supply of milk and managed to get 3 fowls and tomatoes. We have had no rations for days and we are now living on the land. Tomorrow Easter Sunday. Have decided that interest in A-H shall stop do nothing, the game has to be properly played.

23rd Easter Sunday. Wagons stuck all the way back, no rations at all everybody living on the land.

24th. Waiting for wagon or wagons to take us forward. Scouts pass this that tobacco supply has completely given out.

25th. No rain this morning. Managed to get a wheat supply. Regiment arrives at Wassi in a dilapidated condition. Grosse and Archie order whole heavy shoot to clean out of place.

27th. While waiting for wagons of 3rd SAH, stretcher with leaves arrives to take Sgt Roberts to *Kondoevaya*. And on the way Chief gives us five eggs. Reach Kondoevaya late that afternoon, see Hople and Ross and after much delay and waiting get fixed up in the hospital, which, by the way, is horribly overcrowded.

28th. Same state of affairs exists. See Major……… ……………..Had small cup full of fatty soup at 2p.m. Enjoyed it very much.

29th. See Dr Hofmeyer and leave hospital we leave at the same time for our camp.

30th. Sunday. Feel better but very weak in legs. Got Spilikin shod. Have some meat and sweet potato. Yesterday had letter from Alice and Granny. May. Regiment shift camp six miles out. Feel ride very much. Place of camp a bad position to hold, as hill to south dominates all the country around. Our tents come up and second line of transport……….

May

4th. Leave that afternoon on four day patrol, 18 miles among the hills. Sun does not shine.

8th. Returning to camp find it deserted. Camp attacked that morning 10.00a.m. So striking tent returned to safer place. That same day have another attack of fever. Pattle also feeling bad.

9th. Both sent to hospital. Night of 9th Germans and Askaris attack the town in force, 11th Inf. then attack, 11th lose Major. Lieut. and 2 men, 8 wounded.

10th. Still scrapping, Germans have big guns.

11th.4th SAH surprised to be in time. My fever temperature, 104.5,103,103,102,100.

Rest Camp …………………

18th. Germans have three big naval guns and bombard town every morning. Systematic shooting at the hospital seems to be their object. Hospital almost blotted out by shell striking and burying itself 5yards off the main wall.

Pattle and self on two occasions have had very close shaves.

19th. For a wonder no bombardment. Germans send word here that they intend blowing the place to smithereens, including hospital. Poor Liebenby and Wilde gone to rest. Wilde suffering from fits and ……………..on his way back to the

Union, shoots Fickenby while sleeping blots two donkeys out then blows his brains out………… ……………

Second troop A squadron ambushed and practically cut up. 6 wounded including Versfeld, 14 not rolled up yet. Rations insufficient to hold body and soul together, no money to buy grub from Somalis ….about it, no word yet.

24th. Gone to Hospital again. Told our Doctor… …………….

25th Throat very bad could only manage to take a spoon full of milk.

26th. Throat still bad can just about whisper. China Wahle gone to rest. Mosken, Forbes.

Doctor Heyns, decide on waiting for abscess to burst.

27th. Germans bombard both hospitals then plump 9 shells, 4.1 and naval 2 pounders, right in amongst tents. Poor old Cook killed by splinter. Two shells burst in infantry Hospital building. Biggest flook out nobody killed…….. …Brilliant orderlies and conductor lose the track, dysentery and malaria patients left in cold. Get back to place decided on at 10.0pm next morning.

2nd, 3rd June. Back to rest camp. Germans start their usual game. Sixteen big shells plopped in and around us.

5th. Sid Payne who is looking not fit. Ken Paget and Greathead.

8th. Aeroplanes up this day. Watch German shrapnel bursting in air round the machine.

9th. Pat and 98 others sent back to Nairobi

10th Major de Voss examined self. Went up to see Whilton I was fit for Detail Camp, says I must go back with the next batch to Nairobi. Monotonous lying at the rest camp gets on ones nerves. Burnel grandest fellow at Camp. The sight of daily burials worries one.

No letters or parcels for days, have given up hope of ever seeing them.

The writing in the little leather bound notebook gets weaker and weaker. Many men were dying round Bert and he was very weak and despondent. However, luckily for him, the Padre was a friend of the family and he had Bert transferred to a convalescent home in hills near Nairobi where he recovers and writes a letter home.

APPENDIX D

Flight Lieutenant A.O.Lewis-Roberts. RAF Staff College

6th Course.

December 1927

Service Experiences

In August 1914 I was a second year student at the South African School of Mines, Johannesburg. With the assistance of The Senate, I in the company of other students enlisted as a trooper in the Imperial Light Horse in October; this volunteer regiment had performed yeoman service in the Boer War. A number of us supplied our own horse, saddle and equipment.

German South West Africa

On the 7th August 1914 the Imperial Government through the Governor General invited the Union Government to seize such part of German SW Africa as would give it the command of Swakopmund, Luderitzbucht and the wireless station there or in the interior. The Union Government cordially agreed to carry out these proposals.

In the meantime the Union itself had been invaded, very shortly after the outbreak of war in Europe, a strong patrol of German Colonial Forces had advanced over the border and had entrenched itself in Union territory.

To add to this menace, the Rebellion broke out. Small but powerful factions of Dutch farmers and others who were really the irreconcilable element of the Anglo-Boer war, banded themselves into armed parties to assist the Germans in their invasion of the Union. As early as June 1913, negotiations had been carried on between these parties whereby the Germans had promised to recognise the independence of a South African Republic and had offered to assist the Boers with artillery and small arms. The Union Forces, regular, volunteer and commandos were hastily organised and a plan of campaign decided upon. Energetic manoeuvers were taken to round up the rebels, a task which was completed about the end of December with desolator fighting.

The plan of campaign was to attack German territory at three different points – Raman's Drift, Luderitzbucht and Swakopmund. To get to the two latter points required sea travel and required a considerable amount of shipping. Fortuneately the Union Government was able, without delay, to command sufficient sea transport and with the assistance of the Navy, Luderitzbucht was Occupied by the beginning of October, and Swakopmund by the end of December.

Country

The country between the Orange River and Walfish Bay, and stretching some 80 to 100 miles inland is a desolate waste of broken lava outcrops and miles of ever shifting horseshoe shaped dunes of fine sand varying in height from 50 to 150 feet, entirely waterless and devoid of the scantiest vegetation. Rainfall is on an average less than one inch per year. Farther inland the country rises to a plateau flanked by small mountain ranges. This plateau lying due North and South, contains grasslands in localities with widely separated waterholes and small springs, at which the towns of Windhoek, Gibeon and Keetmanshoop are situated.

Climate

Along the coastal belt the climate is fairly temperate and inland on the plateau it is exceedingly bracing with a wonderfully clear atmosphere. Visibility throughout the year is exceptionally good. As usual in dry climates the differences of temperature between day and night are considerable.

Narrative

On the occupation of Luderitzbucht, all water had to be sent up from Cape Town by ships until the big sea water condensing plant was able to produce sufficient supplies for the rapidly increasing numbers of troops.

In the meantime a railway was being rapidly pushed forward to Aus to cover the stretch of desert and to form reserve supplies of water.

The I.L.H., after taking part in the minor operations round Uppington on the Orange River, travelled over broken and unwatered country for 150 miles to Prieska and entrained for Cape Town. After a short delay, utilised to the full by replacing equipment and training squadrons up to strength in men and horses, the regiment embarked and arrived at Luderitzbucht in early December 1914. At the port there were no quays and all stores equipment and horses had to be landed on to lighters. The Regiment formed part of the Central Force commanded by Brig. Gen. Sir D. Mackenzie. This force now consisted of two mounted brigades and strong detachments of infantry.

When sufficient water was insured the Central Force left Luderitzbucht in jumps of 40 to 50 miles per day until Aus was reached in the beginning of April. These marches were exceedingly trying to men and animals as the going was extremely heavy. Limited supplies and sand storms added to this discomfort.

On arrival at Aus, all the water holes were found poisoned with arsenical cattle dip and dead carcases. From now onwards columns had to follow each other at intervals of a day owing to water troubles; they were not able to work together as one whole force until Berseba was reached 150 miles away. Water holes were few and far between and those that the Germans did not poison or blow up, they contaminated with carcases. When supplies had been pumped to the required degree of innocuousness the wells gave out as if in resentment to overworking them.

To add to our worries the Germans had laid mines with great cunning in buildings and promiscuously along stretches of road and in narrow defiles; these proved very troublesome to the transport waggons, a number of mule teams and waggons were blown sky high.

Up to now what fighting that had taken place had been an affair of patrols where our scouts had come in contact with the enemy who were retreating on Gibeon and Windhoek. But from Berseba, after a series of arduous marches over wild and broken country, the main German force was pinned and defeated at Gibeon on April 26th. Our journey from Aus, a distance of over 250 miles, had taken ten days. Travelling over this last stage of broken ground with very limited supplies of water and practically no rations had reduced men and animals to a stage of almost complete exhaustion.

The Northern Force under the command of Gen. Botha occupied Windhoek, the capital, on May 12th and took over the Wireless Station. This station at that period of the war contained the second largest wireless plant in the world and until the seizure had been in direct communication with Berlin.

As the result of well organised drives by the mounted Brigades of the Northern Force, the remaining columns of the German Colonial Force were rounded up near Otavi, 250 miles North of Windhoek, by July 1915.

Some Observations.
German Aircraft.

At the outbreak of hostilities there were three aeroplanes

in German S.W. Africa. It seems that at the beginning of 1913 the German Imperial Government conceived the idea of supplying their colonies with aircraft, the cost of which would be shared by these colonies.

In May 1914 the Germans received two aircraft, one a Roland biplane two seater, which was kept at Keetmanshoop, the second aircraft was and Aveatik also two seater biplane. Both aircraft were of a military type carrying essential military equipment; they were also equipped for ordinary use such as carrying mail matter and for carrying out medical services in outlying districts.

These aircraft were fitted with 100HP Mercedes engines and were built almost exclusively of steel tubing so that there would be no danger from warping also from white ants; they carried patent compasses, electric light heliographs and telescopic cameras.

The third aircraft was called Herzog but very little was known about its characteristics.

The Germans religiously refrained from flying after the cool of the early morning. This may have been due to the disturbed atmospheric conditions, the differences of temperature between day and night were very marked. The Germans on their early morning reconnaissance's carried out at a height of about 3000-4000ft were able to spot our dispositions with ease. Their bombing did very little damage although their initial attacks could surprise and a degree of consternation to the mounted regiments.

The Central Force never had aeroplanes of its own, although it ever lived in hope of being equipped with them. Aeroplanes could certainly have expedited matters considerably.

It was only when Windhoek was occupied that aircraft were available for the Norther Force, and by the time these could be properly used the campaign came to an end.

Union Defence Organisation and Training

Considering the very rudimentary stage of development which the Union Defence organisation had reached prior to the outbreak of war, the task of organising, equipping and training the volunteer regiments and commando forces was a very exacting one.

The period of training for the volunteer regiments was of necessity very intensive and short, and inculcation of discipline and morale under these conditions was not as difficult as one would first imagine. This success was mainly attributable to the number of enlisted regular officers and N.C.O. instructors who were on the permanent establishment of the Defence Force prior to the outbreak of war. Also very large numbers of officers and men had served in the Boer War campaign and this experience must have been invaluable.

Again the Union Forces were readily at home and excelled in this open and guerrilla warfare against the German Colonial Forces. Whereas conditions in Europe would have imposed a much longer and more arduous period of training before they could have taken the field.

Relative Numbers

In S.W. Africa the Germans were greatly outnumbered by the South African Forces. The in hospitability of the country and lack of communications put a limit on the number of troops which could be employed against them.

By poisoning available water supplies the Germans violated the articles of the Hague Convention and were able, for a short time, to delay and restrict the advances of the mounted troops. On one occasion after a long reconnaissance, the horses in our troop, were unable to be watered for 56hours, until a water hole had been cleared of carcases and arsenic dip. Even then the water was infected to such a degree that our animals never fully recovered from its effects.

East and Central Africa. 8/12/15– 1/3/17 Narrative.

Following the S.W. Africa campaign the South African

Forces were reorganised to provide contingents for France and East Africa.

The East African force came into existence in November 1915 and included the troops in East and Central Africa together with troops from South Africa and units from England. General Sir M Smith-Dorrien accepted the command but as a result of severe illness while on his way out to S. Africa the command then devolved on General Smuts.

I joined the 4th South African Horse (4SAH). This regiment was to have been attached to Gen. Smith-Darrien's staff but on the change of command it formed part of Maj. Gen. van Deventer's Mounted Brigade.

This brigade took part in the harsh fighting at Salita Hill, Taveta and in the country along the slopes of Kilimanjaro, and then advanced in rapid stages to Lolkissale and Kondoa Irangi in the rainy season eventually reaching the Dar-es-Salaam railway at Kilimatinde. At the latter place I went down with malignant malaria and dysentery and after many weeks was eventually evacuated to Nairobi. After several months convalescence I travelled to Dar-es-Salaam to re-join the regiment again. Malaria once more claimed me as a victim and a medical board evacuated me to the Union of South Africa.

Observations

Apart from the German troops the east African Force had great difficulty to contend with climate and the country. Under the most favourable circumstances campaigning in a tropical climate is unpleasant. The troops in the field had a very hard time. German East Africa includes within its boundaries tracts of country as bad as any to be found in other tropical parts of the world. The low lying parts of the country along the coast, in its river valleys and inland were intensely malarial. In these regions it was hot all the year round. Only inland above 4000ft was the air dry and the night temperature low, these regions are practically immune from malaria.

In the low lying country in addition to malaria there was the fever due to the infection by ticks, tsetse fly and other insects. Our horses were peculiarly sensitive to many forms of sickness as a result of infection by these insects and died off in great numbers.

Protection from infection by mosquitoes was extremely difficult. Although mosquito nets were provided and stringent orders were issued as to their inevitable use, these precautions could not prevent men from being bitten during the hours of dusk and early morning when on the move.

The tropical sun brought about exhaustion of vitality among the white troops, though to a lesser extent on the Indian and Native troops and made them less resistant to malaria and other diseases.

All together the wastage of men and animals from climatic causes was very great.

Country

The greater part of the area of East and Central Africa is covered with bush thick scrub and tall grass. To the Germans who were fighting defensively it would be hard to estimate the advantage they gained by fighting in this bush covered country. The main idea of the German commander von Lettow was to conduct the campaign in such a manner that we would be compelled to keep as large a force as possible for an indefinite time in East Africa and that the action most likely to bring this about was to fight delaying actions and to avoid risking the destruction of his forces in some general action; he realised that the ultimate fate of the German colony depended not on the result of the campaign in East Africa but on the result of the war as a whole.

We found that land marks were few and far between in the thick bush country which was imperfectly surveyed; the position of villages were doubtful; even the course of rivers were known only approximately; thus it was exceedingly difficult to bring about the concerted of small columns working at some distance from each other.

The Germans and their Askaris were adept at bush fighting and in camouflaging themselves and their machine gun positions; they avoided general actions and it was the bush that enabled them to exploit their success particularly in rear guard actions.

Artillery was of little use in the thick bush. The disturbed atmospheric conditions and the thickness of the bush precluded observations of German rear-guard patrols from the air. The aircraft of the R.F.C. must have operated in very trying conditions. On many occasions they were able to warn columns of impending ambushes where the Germans with machine guns lay hidden in bush and grass across the intended path of the columns. The work of the pilots carried out under these conditions in aircraft of poor performance and unreliable engines was meritorious. Their work would have been greatly facilitated with aircraft of increased performance and reliability.

Communications

With the exceptions of the main railways from Dar-es-Salaam to Kigoma on Lake Tanganyka and the short stretch from Moschi to Tanga the lines of communications from the many sea bases were very long, and in reality, merely tracks through the bush. From these lines the many small columns were fed, but they were never free from the menace of breakdown owing to the presence of black cotton soil which is very prevalent throughout the country. In dry weather the soil stood up fairly well to the action of wheeled traffic, but as soon as rain fell, even in moderate quantities, what would one day have been a fairly hard road was immediately turned in to a quagmire of sticky mud. Impassable to motor or even caterpillar traffic. The wet and dry season in E. Africa were fairly regular but there was always a danger of a heavy downpour at any time. The supply services could often not function without the wholesale employment of native porters for weeks at a time. Frequently columns were short of food for weeks on end.

Landing grounds in areas of this black cotton soil which we occasionally passed were similarly rendered useless after a deluge of rain.

The country and the climate, therefore, went a long way in neutralising any advantage the British force had in the matter of equipment.

R.F.C. and R.A.F.

I commenced my flying in August 1917 at Waddington on Maurice Farman Longhorns and Shorthorns, and after completeing the requisite number of solo hours flying was posted to a night flying squadron to be trained as a night pilot. I had previously applied to go to a day single seater squadron; approval had been given but at that particular period as the Home Defence Brigade was short of pilots, my position was countermanded and I joined a night flying F.E2B squadron.

I spent several months with 33 and 51 Home Defence squadrons on the single seater Rolls and Beardmore F.E2Bs and gained useful experience in the work of night patrols.

In Feb 1918 I went out to France with No83 squadron a new night flying squadron and remained with it until after the Armistice.

The main work of the squadron while it was based at Auchel, an aerodrome west of Bethune, before and during the German Spring offensive was confined to roads railways and dumps in the area between Courtrai and Cambrai, one flight concentrated on reconnaissance and pigeon dropping.

In the beginning of May the squadron was shelled out of Auchel and moved south to various aerodromes; all our work was confined to bombing and reconnaissance in the area opposite the 4th Army.

Observations.
Reconnaissance.

The 160 HP FE2b was an excellent aeroplane for night work although one wished its speed and rate of climb might have been a little greater. Pilot and observer could obtain a good view looking clearly downwards. This characteristic is most important in a night bombing aeroplane, not only because it facilitates the actual dropping of the bombs, but because it assists the crew to find their way and locate their objective.

Reconnaissance aircraft would carry from 6 to 8 Michelin flares and machine gun, no bombs were carried; flares would be dropped from 1500 to 2000ft and aircraft would circle round them as they dropped to the ground. The success of these flares depended largely on the strength of the wind, general visibility and the type of night. Generally to see anything aircraft were obliged to come down below a 1000ft. Better results would have been gained with flares of greater intensity such as we have today.

For the execution of an offensive the Germans concentrated reinforcements in materiel, guns and men opposite the sector to be attacked, nearly always during the hours of darkness. These reinforcements were bought forward in stages. At night motor transport and light railway activity would be observed in the forward areas, movements of small groups of horse artillery and of single tractors with heavy guns on the roads towards the front; and finally the movement of infantry and their transport from the back areas towards their concentration areas and the front line. The infantry were normally bought up in small columns not exceeding battalion strength along byroads so as to reach their jumping off point during the night preceding the attack.

Bombing

It was not always easy to find ones objective at night and great assistance was given to following pilots if an experienced pilot first found the target and then dropped a flare or a phosphorous bomb on it. The number of aircraft of any one squadron on a raid which would reach the objective was dependant on the weather prevailing at the time. Ordinarily there was no formation flying at night, though during the harvest moon period formations of three were tried with success. The results of a raid therefore depended on the skill and determination of the individual pilot and observer and not on the leadership of the flight commander.

The FE2b carried a very useful load of bombs. Aircraft in the squadron invariably carried 2x112lb bombs and 6to8x 25lb bombs and the ceiling of the average aircraft thus loaded was about 2000ft. It was not general practice to use flares when bombing targets excepting when these were aerodromes or small targets like bridges.

Photographs taken by the day squadrons were of great assistance to us when locating German aerodromes and other targets well behind the lines.

Night photography

Night photography was attempted on several occasions. Two or three Michelin flares were dropped simultaneously on the target and when these were burning the aeroplane would fly underneath them and plates would be exposed. Negative results were obtained on these occasions the aircraft proved to be excellent targets to machine guns on the ground.

Enemy AA Defences

AA fire and searchlights except over industrial centres and other places were generally ineffective. But owing to the very low altitude at which the night bombing aircraft flew they were excellent targets for well-placed machine guns. Casualties were caused more by forced landings due to engine failure and bad weather than by enemy action.

Enemy Morale

The night flying Camels (151sq) who were in the same wing as we were did extraordinarily well in shooting down so many German night bombers during the latter part of 1918. The effect of this success brought about a most marked decline in German bombing work. In the early stages this lack of efficiency and morale took the form of flying at greater hights and doing shorter raids and eventually developed in to raids where they merely dropped their bombs just on our side of the lines.

Night flying organisation

Lighthouses were of great assistance to navigation at night especially to our aircraft returning from raids in bad weather; these lighthouses were of the Morse flashing type placed at intervals behind the front lines.

Dummy aerodromes in the vicinity of our own aerodromes, to be effective, had to be manned with care. If found lights representing a flare path were left flaring brightly throughout the night, especially clear nights, they were immediately recognised as dummy flares.

We found that a good ground organisation was necessary at night to expedite aircraft taking off and landing with the minimum of risk of collision on the ground and in the air. With FE2b and Handley Page squadrons on the same aerodrome the officer in charge of the flare path could not be too careful.

The flare path consisted of three electric lights in the shape of a triangle, the apex of the triangle being placed in line with a red light representing obstacles or the perimeter of the airfield. Aircraft landed between the other lights forming the base of the triangle. This arrangement was changed some months afterwards in favour of the ordinary 'L' of shaded electric lights which were controlled by a switch. Only the minimum light was shown for landing aircraft; this practice gave pilots great confidence when compelled to carry out a force landings.

RAF Staff College. | December 1927

INDEX

14 Squadron, 103, 107
142 (LB) Squadron, 132, 135
142 Squadron, 131
144 Squadron, 135
15 Squadron, 92
200 Depot Squadron, 44, 46
206 Squadron, 67, 72-76, 81, 83
208 Squadron, 100
22 Squadron, 93
2ILH, 24, 27, 28, 29, 30, 35
2nd Imperial Light Horse – see 2ILH
30 Squadron, 81
33 Squadron, 46, 48, 67
45 Squadron, 98, 100, 105
47 Squadron, 79, 81, 83, 86, 87, 88, 106, 117
48 Training Squadron, 43
4SAH, 32, 35
4th Battalion SA Horse - see 4SAH
51 Training Squadron, 46
61 Squadron, 135
83 Squadron, 49, 50, 52-58, 60-62, 65-68, 148

A&AEE, 92, 137
Abu Hamed, 116
Abusueir, 100
Abyssinia, 130, 132, 133
AEG, Preface, 2, 3, 16, 17 18, 49, 123, 124, 131, 146
Air Training Corps, 146, 147
Airspeed Horsas, 141
Alexandria, 67, 75, 78, 86, 88, 109, 111, 127, 131, 132, 135
Alexandria Hospital, Cape Town, 36
Andrews, 36, 37, 39, 40
Anglo-Swiss Hospital, 132
Archie, 55, 57, 60, 61, 63
Aretitis, 29

Army of Occupation, 67, 69, 70-75, 77, 81
Arras, Battle of, 38, 39, 71
Ashe, Dr., 1, 5, 10, 19, 35
Asiut, also Assiut, Assuit, 84, 104, 105, 115, 127, 138
Askaris, 31
Assouan, 84
Aswan, 81, 104, 105, 106, 115, 127
Atbara, 116, 117
Athlone Castle, 148
Auchelle, 52
Aus 23, 25-28
Avros, 104,106

Baden-Powell, Robert, 4
Baghdad, 75, 81, 82
Bahr el Jebel, 120
Beaverbrook, Lord, 136
Beech Lodge, 145, 146, 147
Beira, 123, 147
Bennett, Miss, 37, 39, 49, 52, 57, 60, 74, 77
Benoni, 20,31,36,38
Berlin, 22, 146
Berseba, 29
Besondermaid, 29
Bethanie, 29
Bickendorf, 67, 73, 74
Bir-el-Abd, 112
Blenheim Bomber, 135
Board, Air Commodore, 100, 102, 103, 104, 105
Boer War, First (1880-1881), 1
Boers, 1 - 7, 12, 13
Bomber Command, 135, 141
Bor herd of elephants, 119
Botha, General Louis, 22, 23, 27, 28, 29, 32
Boxing, 37, 82, 85

Brand, Captain, 83, 84, 85
Broken Hill, 125
Brook-Popham, HRM, Air Commodore, 94
Brown, Capt., 137
Brown, surgeon, 37
Bulawayo, 85, 103, 124 147,
Burns, Dr., 14
Buxton, Lord, 27

Cairo, 75-87, 90-113, 127-130
Calcutta, Class, 118
Cambridge University, 88, 89
Camm, Sydney, 131
Cape Flight, 102, 104
Cape Police, 6, 8, 11
Cape Town, 1-39, 49, 83, 85, 113, 124, 147, 148
Carey, F/Lt., 175
Central Flying School, 89, 132
Chalbury Hill House, 147
Charleroi, 63
Chichester, Flt/Lt., 112
Christ's College, 89, 91
Churchill, Sir Winston, 68, 130, 136, 141
Civil Defence, 146
Coley Park, 41
Collins, Sq./Ldr., 137
Collishaw, Wing Commander, 100
Collyer, Brigadier General, 32
Cologne, 67, 72, 74, 74
Chamier, Colonel, 10, 16
Combined Operations, Commander of, 139, 141, 143
Cottle, Sq./Ldr. 114
Count Calabiano, 106
Cowies, 122
Cox, Captain, 14
Cox, Rev, 133
Cricket, 10, 54, 61, 88, 97, 130, 146
Cunningham W/c, 127

DFC, 50, 58, 59, 60, 147
Dar-es-Salaam, 44, 60, 61, 147
Davies, W F D, Col., 24
Dawlish, 40-53, 95, 104, 148

D-Day, 142, 143
De Beers, 7, 10, 12
Dead Sea, 100
DH66 Hercules, 124
DH9, 68, 73, 74, 85, 86
DH9a, 81, 86, 87, 92, 93, 94, 95
Dodoma, 125
Dronfield, 5
Du Toits Pan Road, 4
Dundee, 20, 77, 102, 103, 105, 113, 123, 147
Durban, 31, 32, 34, 35, 113, 122, 123

Ebani, 25, 49
Economic Division of the Control Commission, 146
Eldoret, 122
Elementeta Convalescent Home, 34
Eliott, Col., 32
Entebbe, 121
Estrée en Chaussée, 67

Fairey also Fairey 111F, 92-107, 117, 118, 127, 130
Fairweather, Lt. Col., 26
FE 2b, 46
Ficksburg, 20, 36, 38, 40
Fiedler, Lieutenant, 27
Fiervilles, 63
Fish River, 1, 29
Fisher, Captain, 9, 11
Fort Rhodes, 5, 9, 10
Fraser, Mr, 4, 9, 14
Freeman, Air Marshal Sir Wilfred, 138, 139
French, General, 13
Frontier Police, 108
Funviels, 67, 68

Gaika, 25
Gainsborough, 44, 46, 48, 135
Gardiner Sq./Ldr., 135
Garle, Major 10
Garub, 27, 28, 29
Gaza, 99, 100
GEA, 31, 33, 35
German East Africa, See GEA

German South West Africa, see GSW Africa
Gezira Club, 80, 82, 88, 112
Gibeon, 29, 30
Giles, 82, 85
Glencoe junction, 123
GOC Sir Peter Strickland, 105
GOC, 6th Airborne, 143
Gosport system, 39, 43
Gray, Wing Commander, 137, 81
Greathead, Bobby, 54, 62, 63, 69, 72
Green, Captain, 15
Gresham, Marjorie, 89-148
Grundorn, 29
GSW Africa, 22, 31

Handley-Page Halifax, 137
Harris Arthur, 46, 75, 103, 104, 109, 141
Hawker Hart, 133
Hawker Hind, 135
Heavy Glider Conversion Unit, 142, 143
Heliopolis, 75, 80-115
Helwan, 67, 75, 76, 77, 78, 80, 82, 84, 85, 105
Hemswell, RAF Station, 135
HGCU, See Heavy Glider Conversion Unit
Hilton, Sq./Ldr., 94, 101, 114
HMS Courageous, 94, 96, 98, 100
Homestead, 1, 3, 7, 19
Horn, Group Captain, 143
Howard Williams, also Howard-Williams, Sq/Ldr, 109, 117, 127
HQ Middle East, 80, 97, 130
HRH, 106

Ibis Hotel, 121
Imperial Airways, 75, 81, 82, 102, 105, 112-120, 124, 128
Ishandlewana, 1
Ismalia, 76, 77, 78

Jacobsdaal, 15
Jameson, Dr, 1
Je Vese, Lt., 14
Jean Don, Dr, 124
Jeppe School, also Jeppe, 17, 20, 35, 49, 124

Jerusalem, 84, 98, 99, 100, 107, 108, 109, 112
Jinja, 121
Jock of the Bushveld, 94
Josephine (Jo), 19, 20, 81
Juba, 106, 118, 119, 129, 127
Judaean Hills, 100

Kampala, 113, 120, 121, 122, 127
Kan Tara, 104
Kanus Poort, 28
Kekewich, Robert George, Col., 1, 5, 12, 14, 15
Kenya, 31, 34, 49, 78, 122,
Kettlethorpe Hall, 135
Khartoum, 14, 81, 102, 103, 104, 106, 109, 116, 117, 118, 127, 130
Kilwa, 49
Kimberley, 1, 3, 4, 6, 7, 8, 10-12, 14, 16, 19, 35, 88, 148
King Fuad, 104, 105
Kirton Lindsey, 46, 47, 48, 67
Kisumu, 126, 127
Kitchener, 14, 15
Kolundia, 100
Kondoa-Irangi, 32
Korosko, 84, 85
Kosti, 118

La Louvaine, 63
Labram, 10, 11, 12
Lahoussoye, 67
Lake Albert, 120
Lake Nabugabu, 121
Lake Victoria, 121, 127
Lancaster, 136, 137, 139, 149
League of Nations, 132, 133
Leggett, G.H. Major , 146
Lettow-Vorbeck, 31, 32
Leverson-Gower, Major, 52, 98
Lewis gun, 87, 131
Lewis-Roberts, Margaret, 28, 139, 147, 148
Lewis-Roberts, Mary, 27, 135, 147, 148
Lewis-Roberts, Thomas Aran, 19
Liaison Officer at Headquarters Control Commission, 144
Libya, 133

Lohmeyer, Lt., 50, 54, 55, 59, 61, 62
Lorenzo Marques, 123
Lotz, 60
Lubbock, R, 91
Lüderitzbucht, 22, 23, 24, 25, 26, 27, 28
Luxor, 80, 84
Lydd St Mary, 48, 67
Lympne, 52, 95

Maan, 107, 108
Macfarlane-Reid, Major, 73
Macgregor, Major, 7
MacNamara, 15
Macneille, Major, 38
Macrae, 51, 53
Magersfontein, 9
Majuba, 1
Malakal, 106, 118, 119, 127
Mallet, Captain, 4
Manchester, 89, 103, 137, 138, 139
Mansell, Grp. /Cap., 135
MAP, 136, 139
Marseilles, 75
Martlesham, 92, 93, 94, 95, 96, 100, 103, 114
Mattishall, 46, 47, 67
Maurice Farman, 43, 145
Mbeya, 125
McCrae Major, 64
McGregor, 84, 95, 96, 117, 127
McKenzie, Brigadier General Sir Duncan, 25
Mechanical Engineering Capacity Investigation Team, 146
Mersa Matruh, 132, 133, 134
Methuen, 14, 15, 16
Middle East Command, 98, 99, 102, 109, 112, 130
Mildenhall, 131, 132
Miller, Captain, also Miller, A.M. Major, 35, 36, 37, 38
Milner, 15
Ministry of Aircraft Production, See MAP
Modder River, 16
Mongalla, 106
Mountbatten, Lord Louis, 141, 142
Mozambique, 123

Mpika, 125
Mr Fraser, 4, 9, 14
Mussolini, 130, 132, 133, 142
Muthaiga, 34

Nairobi, 33, 50, 60, 102, 103, 105, 106, 113, 121, 122, 123, 126, 127
Nakob, 22
Narborough, 50, 51, 52, 67
Natal Light Horse, 29, 30
Netheravon, 100, 131, 132, 141, 142
New Maschi, 33
Niven, 25, 35, 36, 40, 44, 49, 60, 61
Norman, Air Commodore Sir Nigel, 142

O'okiep, See Okiep
Okiep, 3, 16, 17, 18
Operation Husky, 142, 143
Operational Training, Deputy Director of, 141
Orange River, 4, 22, 24
Ortlepp, Dr, 11
Oudtshoorn, 19, 20, 78
Overseer, 136, 137, 138, 139
Oxland, 80

Palestine, 88, 98, 99, 100, 102, 106, 130, 135, 149
Parachute, 92, 93, 103, 142
Payne, Mr, 49
Peirse, Group Captain, 98, 104, 107
Penderell, Sq./Ldr. 112
Permanent Commission, 67, 68, 69, 72, 77, 88
Petra, 107
Playfor, Group Captain, 100
Port Nolloth, 17
Porton Down, 132
Potchefstroom, 7, 24
Prendergast, 118, 119, 127
Price family, 148
Price, Betty, 124, 147, 148
Prieska, 24
Pritchard, Mr, 9
Pyramids, 76, 82

RAF Benevolent Fund, 146
RAF Club, 98
RAF Staff College, 92, 94, 95, 96, 97
Ramlah, 106, 107
Ranby Hall, 46
Redvers Buller, Sir, 7
Refugee Quarters, 3, 7
Reid, Sq./Ldr. 84, 87
Reitz, Col. Deneys, 32
Retford, 46, 67
RFC, 35, 36, 38, 39, 40, 41, 42, 48, 52, 92
Rhodes, Cecil, 1, 6, 19
Ricardo, Colonel, 14, 15
Rice E.A.B., Grp/Capt., 135
Richardson, Mr and Mrs, 127
Roe, A V, 135, 136, 137, 138, 139
Rolls-Royce, 131, 137
Rorke's Drift, 1
Rorkuppe, 27
Rose Bank, 123
Royal Aircraft Establishment, 89, 137
Royal Flying Corps, See RFC
Royal Navy, 22, 141
Rugger, 51, 55, 62
Rule, A.W.F/O, 130
Russell, John, Wing Commander, 107
Rutter, 60, 62, 64, 70, 71, 72, 75, 77, 89, 95, 98, 104

Salmond, General, 59, 75
Sancroft Baker, Major, 88
Saunders, Mr, 14
Scampton, 46, 148
School of Mines, 17, 19, 20, 24, 30, 31, 54, 65, 88
Schuckmannsburg, 23
Scott-Turner, Lieutenant-Colonel, 8
Serny, 67
Shellal, 104
Sholto, Douglas, 98, 102
Shute, Captain, 16
Silver Queen, 83, 84, 85
Smith-Barry, R.R., Major, 39
Smuts, 17, 23, 30, 31, 32, 34
Sollum, 86
Spring Offensive, 50

Spytfontein, 12
SS Cameronia, 132
SS Khandalla, 123
SS Narkunda, 104
SS Nestor, 36, 37
St. Ambrose's Church, 109
St. Omer, 50, 52, 55, 56, 66, 67
Station Six, 116
Stockdale Street, 4
Sudan, 81, 98, 104, 106, 116, 118, 124, 126
Sudd, 106, 118, 119, 127
Suez Canal, 78
Swakopmund, 22, 23

Talana Hill, 124
Tarltons, 122
Taylor Captain, 127, 134
Ted Uncle, See AEG
Tel-el-Kebir, 104
The British Legion, 146
Thompson, Katie, 16
Tighe, MJ, Major General, 32
Tororo, 121
Town Guard, 1, 5, 6, 9, 17, 18
Transjordan, 98, 100, 106, 107, 108, 135
Trenchard, Hugh, 38, 68, 92
Truforce 132, 133, 134, 135
Tschaukaib, 26, 27, 28

Ufiomi, 33
Uganda, 31, 112, 120, 121
Umtali, 147
Umvoti Mounted Rifles, 29
Union, 22, 23, 26, 29, 30, 31, 35, 85
Upington, 22, 23, 24, 25

VAD, 55, 60
Van Deventer, J L, Brig. General, 29, 32, 33
Van Ryneveldt, Col., 83, 101, 112
Vereeniging, 17
Vickers Victoria, 98, 112
Vickers, 87, 92, 94, 131
Vincent, Sq./Ldr. 105
Von Scheele, Lieutenant Alexander, 27

Waddington, 42, 44, 67

Wadi Halfa, 81, 84, 104-106, 114-116

Walvis Bay, 22, 23

Wessels, Boer Commandant, 6

West Africa, 22, 109, 110, 112

White Nile, 118, 119

White, Captain, 11

Willingham House, 135

Wimborne, 95, 145, 146, 147

Windhoek, 22, 29

Woodford, 135, 137, 138

Xhosa wars, 1

Yates, 38, 43, 44, 46, 48, 57, 62, 69, 72

Yombio, 106

Zambezi, 19, 125

Zanzibar, 123, 147

Zepps, 48

Note: several individuals and places which are mentioned frequently throughout the book have not been included in the index for the sake of practicality.